James D
Kessingla
3d. Oct., 2000
(Our Tri-Colour Shelvé,
Dylan's 11th. birthday,
God love him!)

C000076403

COMING OUT OF THE KITCHEN

Women Beyond the Home

UNA A. ROBERTSON

SUTTON PUBLISHING

First published in 2000 by
Sutton Publishing Limited · Phoenix Mill
Thrupp · Stroud · Gloucestershire · GL5 2BU

British Library Cataloguing in Publication Data
A catalogue record for this book is available from the British Library

ISBN 0 7509 1993 0

Typeset in 10/12 pt New Baskerville.
Typesetting and origination by
Sutton Publishing Limited.
Printed and bound in England by
J.H. Haynes & Co. Ltd, Sparkford.

Contents

Preface

Women have always worked but they have not always worked for
wages.[1]

Nowadays, the phrase 'the working woman' carries a very narrow
definition and it is generally taken to mean a woman who is in paid
employment outside the home. The woman who does not 'go out to
work' but is fully occupied with caring for her home and tending her
children is not considered to be a working woman, even though she is
kept at full stretch throughout the day. It is true that housework today is
very different from previous centuries. The benefits of electricity, for
example, are incalculable and have obviated the need for much of the
hard physical labour previously required to maintain a dwelling and its
occupants. Alongside the benefits of electricity can be set those of piped
water. Keeping a home, though, still requires a degree of organisation
and forethought: cleaning, laundry work, provisioning, child care and so
on must be done in some sort of order or the results are negated.

That the modern woman is unique in 'working' is a myth frequently
repeated. Women have always worked, and worked hard for extremely
long hours, and the housewife of yesteryear was proficient in a wide-
ranging array of domestic arts. However, over the years, while gathering
material relating to the housewife it rapidly became apparent that for
every woman in the past who was immersed in her household duties
there were as many women who were not. The 1851 census suggested that
50 per cent of women of working age were in paid employment and many
and varied were the activities they engaged in. Some were in paid labour
away from home, some were involved in a cottage-based industry, some
were able to create and market a particular product or expertise – all
were, therefore, contributing to the household income through their
labours. Others were not 'employed' *per se* but were involved in amelior-
ating the suffering of those less fortunate than themselves, while a
further group directed their energies into campaigning to end such
abuses and change the existing system to one fairer to all.

In no way did these women conform to the generally accepted
stereotype of the woman who stayed at home in a state of idleness and
dependence, which was, in any case, limited to the middle- and upper-
class family. Whichever way one turns, in whichever period, further

examples surface of women who were active 'beyond the home'. In fact, the nineteenth century witnessed legislation to stop women doing certain work, whether on account of harmful conditions or of substances injurious to their health.

The career woman, therefore, was not invented in the 1970s, nor did she emerge in the 1870s. Yet these earlier women carried on their enterprises despite considerable restrictions on their legal, financial, spiritual and moral existence; few received anything other than a basic education and they were barred thereafter from most forms of further training. Also to be taken into account was the dead weight of social convention, which decreed what was or was not acceptable behaviour in a woman (which was not the same as for a man) and which bore most heavily on the middle and upper classes. The qualifications, therefore, for the majority of women's ventures outside the home were precisely those skills honed in the course of carrying out the myriad of duties involved in running a household, caring for a family and managing servants or those abilities considered 'natural' in a woman.

This book considers those women who were active in the wider world. To bring a semblance of order into the amorphous mass of material on which the work has been based each chapter has been designed around one of the housewife's normal duties: the chapters start by discussing, quite briefly, how a particular activity was practised within the home and then moves on to look at some of the women who made use of their proficiency in the world beyond. This form of division might seem irrelevant to the rural labourer's wife in a two-room cottage or the city dweller in a back-to-back, but these women would be carrying out domestic chores similar to those being done in more spacious surroundings.

The chapters fall naturally into related groups. Chapters Two to Five have a domestic orientation and relate to the general perception of a housewife's concerns – cookery, the supply of food, the management of servants and the provision of clothing and domestic linen. The next three relate to the housewife's personal accomplishments in the fields of entertainment, art and learning, while Chapter Nine examines women who were themselves – women with personality plus who followed their own path through life. This is followed by three chapters on women as carers – of babies, of children and of gardens and animals – while the final chapters mix together the carers, the professionals and the women of independent ideals.

There is some overlapping of subject matter and so the dividing lines have sometimes been drawn arbitrarily. Does 'hospitality' as a topic come under cookery or entertainment? Should 'education' belong with children or be listed as a campaign? The women themselves are equally difficult to pigeonhole accurately as some are multi-faceted: with regard to Aphra Behn, for example, there were her travels, her time as a spy and a prisoner, her celebrated novel drawing attention to slavery, as well as her status as a prolific playwright and an early feminist. Again, take Nell Gwyn, Charles II's 'pretty, witty Nell', but where to place this seller of oranges, comedienne, actress, royal mistress and mother and, by tradition, the prime mover behind the setting up of the Royal Chelsea Hospital for veteran soldiers? A worse problem occurs with the many governesses employed abroad: generally single women and despised for being unmarried, should they be classified according to their spinsterhood, their role as servants, their travels, their ideals of education or their literary output – a number wrote books either of an educational nature for children to use or about their own lives and experiences? And so it goes on. The methods vary: some women slot into just one place, while others are scattered across several chapters as their interests or lifestyles are revealed.

Another particular problem with women is the way their names change from time to time. Which one to use? That pertaining to the time of the action being commented on, the highest ranking on the social scale or the latest in time? The Duchess of Lauderdale is a complex example. Born Elizabeth Murray, she married Sir Lionel Tollemache in 1647 but three years later inherited the title of Countess of Dysart on her father's death and then, in 1672, married her long-time lover, John Maitland, Earl and then Duke of Lauderdale. Sarah Jennings married plain John Churchill in 1678 but over the years he was elevated in the peerage, first becoming a (Scottish) Baron in 1682 and achieving a Dukedom twenty years later. She is generally called Sarah, Duchess of Marlborough, which is only accurate, strictly speaking, after December 1702. At a much later date, who would recognise in Mrs Montagu Porch or Mrs George Cornwallis-West the celebrated hostess Lady Randolph Churchill, née Jennie Jerome? The method chosen to deal with such vagaries is, again, necessarily inconsistent and adopts the surname most commonly used.

If the topics for discussion and the women themselves are difficult to define, there is also the tendency, especially after the mid-nineteenth century, for the women to be personally involved in or to give support to more than one line of action. Increasingly, they derived support from family relationships, marriage networks, close friendships and inter-connecting societies and institutions. Similarly, an awareness of what was happening elsewhere in the world influenced their actions. The French Revolution with its clarion call for 'Liberty, Equality and Fraternity' provoked a parallel demand for the rights of women but its instigator, Olympe de Gouges, stirred up such hostility that she died on the guillotine in 1793. Mary Wollstonecraft took up the theme, writing

A *Vindication of the Rights of Women*, which examined the tenets upon which society with its male dominance was based.

Women in the USA became an example to others while their campaigns for the abolition of slavery caused women elsewhere, especially married women, to query their own non-existence in the eyes of the law. American women, frustrated by their lack of progress in the anti-slavery campaign, often turned to the feminist movement, arguing that unless they had the right to vote and some means of bringing about change they could achieve little. Alternatively, they campaigned for greater protection for prostitutes or for access to better education and further training or for the temperance movement – all of which were causes working to improve the lot of women.

The number of women worthy of consideration has caused a problem in itself and so difficult choices have had to be made. There emerges a marked preference for individuals, for women who can be named, as against so many who formed part of a crowd and as such are nameless. Those sufficiently famous – the Jane Austens, Sarah Siddons or Nell Gwyns – can be found in the *Dictionary of National Biography* (*DNB*) or other compendiums and therefore have not necessarily been given the space or attention proportionate to their fame. With this in mind it is instructive to query the number of women omitted from the earlier editions of the *DNB* despite their contemporary celebrity, but who have been reinstated in the 1993 volume entitled *Missing Persons*. Gertrude Jekyll, for instance, the garden designer, writer, artist and craftswoman; Winifred Holtby, novelist, feminist and social reformer; Elizabeth Jesser Reid, founder of Bedford College; Ada Byron, mathematician; and Dorothy Ripley, missionary in Ethiopia. To be added are names of the stature of the Countess Markievicz, Isabella Beeton, Celia Fiennes, Frances Hodgson Burnett, Marion Phillips, Emily Davison, Frances Mary Buss and Margaret Llewelyn Davies . . . Where to stop?

Hopefully, any bias towards middle- or upper-class women has been avoided but the risk remains in so far as these women tend to leave behind more in the way of written records. Larger houses, with greater numbers of servants and belongings, led to a consequent need for inventories and accounts; their châtelaines were more likely to be literate and, more importantly, to have the time in which to maintain their journals, their correspondence or their household books and to have money to spend on paper and ink. Any writing intended for publication might well have been considered more marketable and therefore more readily taken up by a publisher; alternatively, they could afford to pay for the printing of it themselves.

Since so many women have had to be omitted those that have been included should be seen as being representatives of a genre. Few were truly unique in their actions: there were generally others in the background and a successful conclusion in any one field tends to obscure these earlier efforts.

In 1650, at the start of this investigation, Britain was enduring a period of civil war. Three-hundred years later when the story is brought to a close the country had just experienced a similar period of horror and destruction, the Second World War. In both instances old loyalties were fractured, traditional habits were broken and the effects, filtering right down to kitchen, parlour and nursery, meant that earlier lifestyles and tenets were no longer viable: in the second half of the twentieth century women have increasingly claimed the right to leave their homes for the freedoms of the workplace. That they can not only do so but can also personally enjoy the fruits of their labours is due entirely to those who have gone before. Not all wished to be 'independent' in today's terms but they could see no logical reason why they should be denied the same opportunities and privileges accorded their fathers, husbands, brothers and sons.

CHAPTER ONE

The Writing on the Wall

Ask any group for some names of women who lived in past times, the famous or the not so famous, and it is a fairly predictable selection that is recalled. Royalty, of course, quickly springs to mind – Queen Victoria, Queen Anne, Mary, Queen of Scots and so on. Another name generally mentioned is that of Florence Nightingale, followed by one of the early woman doctors, Elizabeth Garrett Anderson perhaps. The Suffragettes headed by the Pankhursts also tend to be included, while the literary field proves a fruitful source once called to mind – of novelists, poets or even a playwright. Then maybe a missionary or an intrepid woman traveller who has left an account of her travels and possibly a doer of good works, such as Elizabeth Fry who did so much to reform prisons. After that inspiration runs dry but, with prompting, generally elicits the response 'of course'.

That women of such significance did exist is attested, in many instances, by memorials to those who were celebrated either for one particular action or for a lifetime of achievement recognised as being worthy of commemoration and as an inspiration for generations to come. Their memorials can be found in varied guises: the familiar plaques attached to buildings, statues or other forms of monument in public places; institutions carrying a woman's name; and gravestones carrying a record for all time. However, in the light of the general perception of woman's role in the world it has to be asked how many people actually take notice of these monuments to female achievement, or to male achievement either? The plaque on the wall might invite the inquisitive to read it once, the statue on its plinth in the public garden forms a seat for the footsore shopper or lunchtime perch for the office worker; in a busy street or at an intersection the monument with its paved surround is either disregarded, considered a nuisance by traffic or acts as a transitory resting place for harassed pedestrians crossing the road.

Public recognition can also come in a different format altogether – in the shape of inclusion in that august record of achievement, celebrity or notoriety *The Dictionary of National Biography* which had the stated aim 'To supply full, accurate, and concise biographies of all noteworthy inhabitants of the British Islands and the Colonies (exclusive of living persons) from the earliest historical period to the present day.'[1] The *DNB* does include a number of women in its pages but, although there are far fewer listings than for men and the entries are often shorter, women and their achievements are, nevertheless, on record. A search of the columns in Volume 3 reveals that approximately 80 women are listed out of an estimated 1,560 entries in the volume. These biographies describe an eclectic mix of activities, the most prominent being the categories of 'literature' (novelist, poet, diarist and so on), 'entertainment' (music, singing, acting) and 'artistic' (engraver, miniaturist, flower painter). Women were also involved in religious activities, in scholarship and patronage, travel, midwifery, philanthropy and cookery and the list includes a couple of malefactors and a (royal) mistress.

The imbalance between the sexes has been partially addressed in recent years with the publication of the *Missing Persons* volume in which the proportion of female entrants is about 12 per cent, whereas in the earlier volumes as a whole it was just 3 per cent.[2]

It is not only modern historians who see fit to rescue numerous women from oblivion. Midway through the eighteenth century the antiquarian scholar George Ballard (1706–55) compiled his *Memoirs of Several Ladies of Great Britain,* an enormous undertaking comprising 470 pages and some 60 biographies. He wrote: 'Yet I know not how it hath happened, that very many ingenious women of this nation . . . are not only unknown to the public in general, but have been passed by in silence by our greatest biographers.'[3] Fifty years later Mary Hays (1760–1843) took up a similar theme on behalf of the sisterhood and wrote no less than six volumes of *Female Biography, or Memoirs of Illustrious and Celebrated Women of All Ages and Countries. Alphabetically Arranged.* At the end of the century Georgiana Hill took up the story once more with a two-volume work entitled *The Women of England,* and many have since followed in her footsteps. Some of the women so recorded acted alone, exercising their particular talents and prompting little in the way of emulation; some acted as the catalyst that made things happen, generating such energy that a section of public opinion was roused to take action; others were part of a more generalised movement in favour of or against a particular course of action. Women in the past have lived a life beyond their homes; women have done much and achieved much – their lives have been noted and their memorials are there for all to see. Yet, the general perception still implies otherwise and is convinced that, until quite recently, women were frail, incapable and had no life other than within the domestic environment.

It is difficult to say why, despite so much evidence to the contrary, these notable women have more or less become invisible. Is it a question of brainwashing? That if it was said often enough that women had no place in the wider world so this came to be accepted as the truth? Is it due to women's natural modesty? That for generations they learned to take second place and so came to be content to let their menfolk take the limelight while they themselves quietly followed their own interests? Is it that for the most part men wrote the history books and emphasised the areas of greater interest to men than to women – warfare and diplomacy, politics, legislation, finance and ecclesiastical affairs – and the men who were engaged in these matters. Since women were excluded from participating in these fields, so they involved themselves either in what they were trained to do (i.e., marriage and motherhood) or where they thought they might influence events, which in turn led the men writing the history books into thinking of women's activities as being of little interest to their readers and of less worth. This male bias makes it easier to understand how the few women who did merit a mention were considered as isolated examples, exceptional in one way or another, marked out for fame by birth or bravery, action or accomplishment, but they were not considered representative of woman's experience in general. Yet it is illogical to suppose that these high-profile individuals could spring from nowhere, from the half of humanity that supposedly sat quietly at home waiting for something to happen, for such is the general perception.

It is often considered that a woman's life in earlier generations was certainly circumscribed, if not deprived. Married off when still a child, once immersed in the affairs of her home a woman could expect to suffer ill-health and constant child-bearing, leading to an early death. Meanwhile, she had no legal identity, being considered a minor at law; she received little in the way of education because her future was to marry and produce children; she had no economic independence since on marriage any property she owned at the time and any money that came to her thereafter was transferred to her husband; she had no role in public affairs and no means of expressing her opinions through the ballot box. A husband also had rights over his wife's body and any children of the marriage were regarded as his property. His adultery was not considered grounds for divorce but hers would lead to a legal separation. The best scenario was to become the widow of a reasonably wealthy man, as at that level one might hope that his money would not be tied up to such an extent that his widow could get little benefit from it. Those without property or money were much freer in this respect and were more likely to please themselves in the matter of a marriage partner.

The concept of women's position in the seventeenth century derived partly from biblical precept and partly from the concept of chivalry. Since Adam was created first he took precedence over Eve, and Eve's part in falling into temptation and being the ultimate cause of their expulsion from the Garden of Eden led to women being considered weaker than man and therefore inferior and thus, necessarily, subordinate to men. The Renaissance added examples from the days of ancient Greece and

Rome to the general theme but they merely reinforced the message – women were of lower status than their husbands. The power of the Church was immense and the argument was generally accepted, though women could well put up the case that Adam was the weaker in succumbing to Eve's temptation. By the nineteenth century the claim of male precedence on account of prior creation received short shrift from Annie Besant, who declared that, by that reasoning, the fishes and beasts were created before man ever walked the earth.

When man adopted the moral high ground it implied a measure of physical protection for the weaker sex, along with economic support; the other side of the bargain was that the woman became the mother of his children and the keeper of his home. Increasingly, therefore, marriage was seen as the only option available to a girl, whatever misgivings she might have about a future mapped out for her and over which she could exercise little influence.

If a woman was to be a housewife, then a woman had to be married and increasingly their education was designed to please their theoretical spouse and to prepare them to be good wives and mothers. Mothers with social ambitions had to ensure their daughters would attract the attention of a husband. Greater observance was therefore paid to skills that could be exercised in public, such as dancing, music-making or singing, alongside a knowledge of etiquette, a good deportment and fashionable clothing, rather than to a grounding in the housewife's arts. The Puritan/Non-conformist attitude, on the other hand, was to decry the frivolity and hollowness of social accomplishments and to educate their daughters at home, where piety and the domestic arts could be assimilated at the same time. The weight they gave to personal salvation, where every woman was independently responsible before God, logically led to the conclusion that women needed education in order to lead their households in the correct direction and that a woman was therefore the companion, helpmeet and equal of the man.

Marriage was the ideal. The alternative was to stay unmarried which was accounted a disaster both socially, since it implied the girl had failed to attract a husband, and economically, since she would be dependent on her own menfolk, be it father, brother or nephew, for the rest of her days. Her training in acceptable accomplishments rather than in a modicum of scholarship meant that if a marriage failed to materialise then the girl was untrained for any alternative. It is interesting that women from Hannah Woolley (or Wolley) and Bathsua Makin onwards were calling for women to be given the wherewithal that could enable them to earn their living, should the need arise. Throughout the period women recognised that their lack of education was one of the principle reasons why they were at such a disadvantage.

For the majority of women therefore, marriage was the sole, approved option and following marriage came housekeeping and potential motherhood. Until the early years of the seventeenth century it had been taken for granted that a housewife, apart from the very wealthiest, would exercise personal control over her household, directing her maidservants and often working alongside them. She would bring up her daughters in the same expectations, largely teaching them herself and certainly seeing that they were able to carry out the multi-faceted responsibilities laid upon their shoulders. It was said about one such housewife, Lady Cholmely in 1600, that, 'having ordered the day's duties in the morning and instructed her numerous daughters in a variety of arts, elegant and domestic, she would go round the whole of her domain "from hop garth to hen yard, from linen closet to lardour", prying, tasting and admonishing until the family and the servants were summoned to dine "at xi of ye clocke"'.[4]

Any housewife worthy of the name was assumed to be knowledgeable in the wide range of domestic skills necessary when households were predominantly self-supporting and ready at a moment's notice to cope with the unexpected illness or arrival of guests. Over and above the housewife's proficiency Gervase Markham enumerated the essential qualities of her character: 'Our English Hous-wife', he observed, 'must be of chaste thought, stout courage, patient, untyred, watchfull, diligent, witty, pleasant, constant in friendship, full of good Neighbour-hood, wise in discourse, but not frequent therein, sharpe and quicke of speech, but not bitter nor talkative, secret in affaires, comfortable in her counsels, and generally skilfull in the worthy knowledge that doe belong to her Vocation.'[5] The housewife had yet one further role to play: in being the 'mother and mistris of the family [i.e., household] . . . where from the generall example of her vertues, and the most approved skill of her knowledges, those of her family may both learne to serve God, and sustaine man, in that godly and profitable sort which is required of every true Christian'.[6] These sentiments echo across the years when, two and a half centuries later, Mrs Beeton likens the mistress of a house to the commander of an army: 'Her spirit will be seen through the whole establishment; and just in proportion as she performs her duties intelligently and thoroughly, so will her domestics follow in her path.'[7]

Although these and similar sentiments continued to be expressed, attitudes were changing and by the mid-eighteenth century there had been such a reversal of opinion that domestic talents were coming to be regarded as old-fashioned, leading in turn to the increasing importance of the housekeeper's role. Many specimens of the old-style housewife could still be found, like the one encountered in 1788 by the authoress Miss Hutton, who was travelling round the country with her invalid mother. 'The progress of the arts,' she wrote to a friend while in Blackpool, 'even the art of cookery, is from south to north. We have here the wife of the rector of Rochdale, a gentlewoman of the old school, in person and manner resembling a good fat housekeeper, who, I dare say, never heard of a curry in her life, yet is excellently skilled in pickling shrimps, potting herrings, raising goose pies and flourishing in pastry.'[8] A contemporary was Susanna Whatman, whose husband was a wealthy paper manufacturer, although this did not prevent Susanna worrying about domestic matters while away from home and writing to her housekeeper about such tribulations as the sunlight fading the furniture or the way she wished the floorboards to be scrubbed. On one occasion she sent home a sample of fabric that she thought the maids might like for their dresses: 'It is a finer one than I should have given them, but it is *so pretty* that if they *fell in love* with it as I did, I should be tempted to take it.'[9]

By the early nineteenth century and in the aftermath of the French Revolution and widespread fears regarding the stability of society innumerable domestic manuals were telling the housewife, in virtually identical phraseology, that it was her Christian duty if not her lifetime's profession to run the household, care for the servants, nurture her children and to make it 'home, sweet home' for those living under her roof. Her prime obligation was to make an attractive home for her husband, 'fatigued by intercourse with a jarring world' and to make herself 'his enlightened companion and the chosen friend of his heart'.[10] As the years passed, though, there was no pretence that the housewife should do the work herself, as had happened in earlier days. Many of her duties were no longer necessary since, as a result of the Industrial Revolution, goods previously produced in the home were now factory made, while developments in agriculture and transport obviated the previous preoccupation with the supply and preservation of food. At a certain social level to do household work herself would be demeaning to her husband's status and denying employment to someone else. Instead, with servants around her to do the actual cleaning, cooking, child care and marketing, there were all those empty hours to fill and the manuals instructed the housewife how to while away the time with schemes for self-improvement and pastimes such as reading, fancy stitchery, painting, practising a musical instrument, collecting botanical specimens and similar worthwhile pursuits. She was also encouraged to undertake charitable work but this she had always done.

Once domestic occupations were being left to the servants, they came even more to be perceived as being of lowly status and therefore unsuited to anyone with a modicum of education or social position. Servants, therefore, left the housewife filling the empty hours with endless pastimes that gave her little sense of direction and it was at about this point that she began to think working outside the home might lead to a more meaningful existence. However, social convention restrained her ambitions. In 1799 Hannah More asserted: 'The profession of ladies, to which the bent of their instruction should be turned, is that of daughters, wives, mothers and mistresses of families.'[11] For many years the convention was that no 'lady' could work for payment without losing her genteel status – hence the numerous female authors who hid their identity under the title of 'A Lady' or similar designation – while the lack of an adequate training led many to experience real hardship. This situation applied in the main to middle- and upper-class families, although even here numerous examples are to be found outside the home whether out of necessity earning a living or engaged upon some other enterprise. Otherwise, ladies or no, they were in paid employment. From the 1851 census returns it was said that 'three millions out of six of adult Englishwomen work for subsistence' and that they were employed in most of the jobs enumerated in the returns.[12] The same authority declared: 'The total number of women who are earning their bread, exclusive of the many wives who help their husbands in their various callings, numbered at the last census [1891] over four and a half millions.'[13] Of these women, it was variously estimated that about half needed to be self-supporting whereas the remainder were contributing to the family income.

Other factors were in the background. What was going on in France and the USA influenced thinking elsewhere, as already noted; aspirations to the middle-class lifestyle and a large family were difficult to support on the average middle-class salary, unless augmented from other sources, and it was certainly stretched to its utmost to include widowed mothers and unmarried daughters. The other principal catalyst to emerge concerned the census reports which revealed a shift in the balance of the population amounting to 1 million or more of what were termed 'surplus women' who would have little or no chance of marrying, however many accomplishments they might acquire while they waited. What was to happen to these women? Were they to be kept in virtuous idleness all their days – and, more importantly, at whose expense? Without education, without professional training, without a legal identity even, and lacking in self-esteem, there was little the great majority could do to help themselves. Some, though, thought otherwise.

Since time immemorial the housewife had expected to care for those less well-off than herself and innumerable women had been vigorous in this sphere, not only coping with the day-to-day problems of the poor at the gate but building schools, churches and almshouses, healing the sick and providing funds for widows, orphans, wounded soldiers and so on. Others took even stronger action, confronting the authorities and demanding changes. Elizabeth Fry's exertions on behalf of women prisoners is generally well known, as is Florence Nightingale's work in the Crimea, while Caroline Norton focussed attention on children in factories and Josephine Butler campaigned on behalf of the prostitute. Numerous women were engaged in similar activities and by so doing stirred up fearful antagonism, if not hatred, while they sought to improve the lot of others but they carried on heroically, upheld by their Christian beliefs.

Women were prepared to challenge the authorities in other areas, too. It is interesting to find that, throughout the period, women were aware of the problems caused by their lack of education and endeavoured to remedy the situation. Bathsua Makin, a woman of considerable learning, Mary Astell and ultimately, two-hundred years later, Emily Davies, who opened up university education to women, were all calling for girls to be given a similar level of education as their brothers. Instead, while boys' schools were gradually improving and the range of subjects taught was widening, girls' mental faculties were being neglected. As a result, since educational qualifications were seen as the means of entry to professional organisations, women were denied access to such careers.

Not every woman wanted a career but many but could see no logical reason why they should not enjoy their own income. Instead, any money they earned or inherited went by law to the husband, even if the marriage had failed and a legal separation had taken place, as actress Susanna Cibber, campaigner Caroline Norton and authors Anna Jameson and Mrs Gaskell discovered to their cost. Caroline Norton's case in particular also provoked an outcry over a married woman's total lack of any rights over her own children and she campaigned tirelessly on both points until there were changes in the law. At the same time women could see no reason why they should be denied access to the ballot box. The right to vote was extended to greater numbers of the male population; but, while the illiterate labourer was given the vote, the educated woman of means was still excluded. The Suffragettes took matters into their own hands and initiated a policy that aroused much opposition, not only from the generality of the men but from many women too, who believed in the virtue of patience (or in male superiority). The struggle to win the vote resulted in much bitterness. Ultimately, it was the First World War and women's exemplary behaviour in tackling the jobs vacated by their menfolk as well as the bravery of the medical staff at the front line that led to a change of opinion and enabled a limited franchise to be introduced.

But, until such time, change came slowly into women's lives and often at great personal cost. Considerable opposition was expressed to their demands. In the broadest of terms, men feared losing their general supremacy, whether in terms of politics, economics, religion, education or in the wider sphere of the employment market. Husbands saw nothing wrong with the existing arrangement whereby they had complete control of the family finances and wives acted as housekeepers to ensure their comfort. From a position of superiority it was so much easier to disregard demands for change. But not all men acted in this way, and some were supportive of their womenfolk and encouraged them in their chosen paths. A few daughters were given the same education as the sons, in the way that Florence Nightingale and Barbara Bodichon were; some inherited money or a business from a father or husband, as did Miss Harvey of Knightsbridge or Hester Bateman, widow of a silversmith; Josephine Butler's husband gave her moral support and whenever he could he would meet her at the railway station on her return from some speaking engagement on behalf of prostitutes; a few Cambridge academics supported Emily Davies when she opened the doors of the first college for women at Hitchin, some 25 miles away, by travelling there and back by train to lecture to the girls. Without a minimum amount of encouragement, some small toehold of opportunity, the struggle by women to improve their own personal situations and the lives of innumerable other women as well would have taken even longer.

CHAPTER TWO

The Kitchen Professionals

*As with the commander of an army, or the leader of any enterprise,
so it is with the mistress of a house.*

It was with these words that Mrs Beeton opened her celebrated publication *The Book of Household Management*, which might well lay claim to being the best-known cookbook in the English language. It first appeared in book form in 1861 and although it deals with household management in general, with lengthy passages on the duties of domestic servants, cleaning methods and so on, it is as a cookery book that it is mostly remembered. However, '*Mrs Beeton*' as it is affectionately known was far from being the earliest published work on cookery written by a woman. Over a hundred years earlier, Hannah Glasse's cookbook supposedly contained a recipe that opened: 'First catch your hare'. The words were never actually written but are thought to have been a twisted rendition of 'First case your hare', where 'case' means to skin the animal.[1] It is then necessary to go back almost another hundred years to find the book of recipes generally accepted as being the first published by an Englishwoman, Hannah Woolley (or Wolley).[2] At that time it was nothing new for a woman to be jotting down scraps of information on a wide range of domestic topics acquired from family and friends, whether it be for a new method of cooking pigeons, a whitewash for the byre, a remedy for a child with a colic or a better way to preserve apples for winter use. These domestic bits and pieces were never intended for anything other than personal use, although by its very nature many household hints were passed on to others, but Mrs Woolley wrote her books with publication in mind.

For many years now it has been taken for granted that women should write cookery books, just as it was assumed that their natural place was in the kitchen. Even half a century before Mrs Woolley's book was published a proficiency in cookery was included in the list of attributes necessary for the competent housewife: 'as her skill in Physick, Surgery, Cookery, Extraction of oils, Banquetting stuffe, ordering of great Feasts, Preserving of all sorts of Wines, . . . knowledge of Dayries . . . of Brewing, Baking . . . and all other things belonging to an Houshold'.[3] Cookery was indeed a woman's pastime in the majority of households, whether it was the housewife herself who was engaged in it or a female employed on her behalf. But it should be borne in mind that innumerable women up and down the country had no choice but to do their own cooking; others had little choice over how or what they cooked, lacking either the fuel or the foodstuffs, or both.

At the wealthier levels of society things were different. In the sixteenth and earlier seventeenth century, men acted as cooks, scullions and household servants in general. Few women were employed, apart from the occasional nurse, the companions or waiting women of the lady of the house and those working in the laundry or dairy. The kitchen fireplace in such an establishment was designed to burn vast logs and was capable of roasting whole beasts, for the number of people to be fed was considerable. The cooks needed to be weightlifters, while the heat from the fire was so intense that those working in the kitchens were only half dressed. Any women employed in the kitchens were of lowly status and engaged in menial tasks. At about the time of the Civil War, women began replacing men as domestic servants and one of the first places in which they could be found was the kitchen.

In those parts of the country where supplies of timber and peat were running low and coal was used as a substitute the actual fireplace decreased in size seeing that considerably less fuel was required to produce the same amount of heat. Smaller fires were better suited to the more modest houses being built in towns and were also easier to manage. Simultaneously, and for other extraneous reasons, women began to be engaged not only in the kitchen but throughout the house. In the course of time, male servants acquired a prestige denied to their female counterparts and thus attracted higher wages which in turn meant that fewer households could afford to employ them. By the 1820s it was estimated that there were 400 male cooks, at most, employed in the whole country,[4] which meant that innumerable households were fed through the agency of a female cook, whether working in her own kitchen or employed in someone else's.

Whether it was men staffing the kitchens or whether it was women was immaterial to the work involved. The actual methods were similar to today's, though the technology was a little different. For much of the period cooking was carried out over an open fire; only in the better-off households would there have been what was always called a bread oven, although it was used for many things other than baking bread. Over an open fire it is possible to roast, boil, stew, poach, fry and grill and, with the aid of an iron girdle, produce certain baked items. A lidded pot pushed into the hot ashes forms a makeshift oven, as does a bake-stone. This is a stone with a flat surface heated before the fire; items can then be set on it, covered over with an upturned pot and either pushed into the embers or surrounded with hot peats. An oven, requiring separate firing to heat it, was beyond the reach of many households. Fuel was expensive or hard to come by and poorer folk had barely enough food to cook to warrant such an extravagance. Generally, the village baker would 'oblige' by cooking items that they had prepared, a custom that continued until the 1940s in certain areas.

During the eighteenth century the kitchen 'range' was developed, so called because it provided a range of cooking methods within the one unit. To begin with the open fire was given an iron box or 'hob' on each side, which provided a flat surface for slow cooking. The next step combined the open fire with, on one side, an oven for baking and, on the other, a tank for heating water. A further development kept the central fire open in front, for roasting, but put a flat surface across the top. These two, with variations, continued to be used throughout the nineteenth century and well into the twentieth.

At much the same time people were experimenting with gas as the cooking medium but the concept was slow to catch on, despite its many advantages. Not until the 1870s or '80s did the idea become acceptable and this was largely due to the demands made on the market for gas lighting by alternatives such as paraffin and electricity. Gas companies, in looking for new markets for their product, promoted it for heating and for cooking and improved their appliances. By contrast, electricity for cooking was promoted much more quickly, although its relatively high cost and distribution problems delayed its general availablity until the 1920s. It was at this point that the Aga came on to the market. Developed in Sweden by the blind physicist and Nobel prize winner, Nils Gustaf Dalén, the Aga burned solid fuels such as coke or anthracite and was advertised as needing attention just once a day.

The pots and pans used would depend on the type of fuel being burnt and the economic standing of the household. Earthernware would be likely in areas where peat was common as, although peat burns well, the heat given off is less than for wood and that, in turn, is less than that of coal. Where coal was the fuel such pots would be stood in a water bath to prevent them succumbing to the intense heat. Otherwise, iron skillets took their place and resembled a modern saucepan on three short legs and with a long handle. The legs balanced the pan on an uneven surface and the long handle was significant in view of the open fire; generally speaking the longer the handle, the larger the fire. In more modest households an iron cauldron was an all-purpose vessel, with three stubby legs on the base, to enable it to stand among the embers, as well as a handle for hanging it over the fire. Broth, stews, porridge and many other things were cooked in it and it was also used for other domestic purposes such as heating water for laundrywork, bathing the baby or making up dyes for home-spun wool. Copperware became fashionable in the kitchens of the wealthy as it was lighter and conducted the heat more evenly, and its use became more widespread after the discovery in 1763 of the Parys Copper Mine in Anglesea (known locally as 'Parry's Mountain') with its huge deposits.

The *batterie de cuisine* was extensive and comprised many items found in today's kitchens, albeit made in different materials and on a larger scale than contemporary housewives might appreciate: knives, mixing bowls, beaters, whisks, skimmers and strainers, sugar sifters, moulds for jellies and similar delicacies, shapes in which to bake pies and puddings and many other items.

The format for fashionable dinners required many dishes to be prepared simultaneously and even at a modest level a choice of dishes would be offered. A busy housewife would be grateful for help in the kitchen. Households tended to be larger in those days, with children and servants to feed and, frequently, the farmer's labourers or the husband's apprentices to care for as well. Earlier in the period, provisions were mostly home produced or bought from the local market; in times of plenty food would be preserved against future shortages; goods would be stored for winter use; guests would need to be entertained and benighted travellers, along with their servants, taken in and cared for until they could continue their journey.

Few housewives were without some help. Until the eighteenth century most would work alongside their maids, teaching them what to do and supervising their work but, later on, a division came between mistress and maid. Catering and its associated workload was often the first job to be delegated, thus giving rise to 'Cook', that autocrat of the Victorian kitchen. Untold numbers of households employed a female cook, who might well demand the services of a kitchen maid to do the more menial parts of the work and this youngster would expect to pick up the elements of cooking meanwhile.

Once a woman had grown into a competent cook, what then? What could she do with her talents? How might she advance her career? There would always be a demand for her services in someone else's kitchen, though few women could command the wages paid to a male cook or the prestige, and a good cook could choose her employer. That they frequently took advantage of their position to do so becomes apparent when reading about the scarcity of good, plain cooks during the latter part of the period. In the words of Saki: 'She was a good cook as cooks go; and as good cooks go, she went.'[5]

It was a habit of long standing. Lady Grisell Baillie of Mellerstain, near Kelso, when setting up her household in London early in the eighteenth century was no luckier with her cooks than with her domestics generally. Over the years covered by her *Household Book* it is difficult to keep track of the many servants that flit in and out of the accounts. In 1715, for example, no less than eight cooks were employed: one lasted a day, one a night and another, after two months, 'was taken away by the constables'. The situation was marginally better in 1717: only four cooks were mentioned, with one staying a night and one a fortnight.[6] Neither was it any easier during the nineteenth century. Between 1829 and 1832 Hopetoun House, South Queensferry, witnessed four different cooks, two male, two female, and a comparison was made of the amount of meat that passed through the kitchens during the same five-month period of each one's employment.

It was always possible that someone who had been cooking for a number of years might not wish to be at an employer's beck and call all her life but might think of branching out into other avenues: what was available to her?

Some became freelance cooks, taking over a kitchen and its staff for a special function or for a limited period when, for example, the family went to its country estate and entertained during the local race meeting or for a shooting party. Similarly, if the family stayed in the capital for 'The Season' a high-class cook might be employed for that period. Many male cooks operated in this way but so did some women. Towards the end of the nineteenth century there was a celebrated example in Rosa Lewis, nicknamed 'The Duchess of Jermyn Street', who died in 1952. She was born Rosa Ovenden, was one of nine children and received four years' schooling. At the age of twelve she went into service as a kitchen maid in the household of the Comte de Paris, then at Sheen House, Mortlake, and was lent out to other members of that family. Before she was twenty she was in charge of the kitchens of the Comte's father, the Duc d'Orleans, at Sandhurst. She also undertook freelance work for a few select households. In about 1889 she met the future King Edward VII – the stories vary as to how that happened and what happened thereafter – but in 1893 she married Excelsior Lewis, a butler. Together they took over a lodging house in London's Eaton Square but her husband proved jealous of her increasing success, took to drinking and gradually faded from her life.

In 1902, Rosa Lewis added the acquisition of the Cavendish Hotel to her other activities. During the later Victorian period the first London establishments of the calibre of the Buckingham Palace Hotel, the Grosvenor, the Westminster Palace and the railway hotels had been opened so that dining in a hotel restaurant was still something of a novelty. At the Cavendish some favoured guests had their own suites, permanently reserved for them. Rosa's accounting methods were simple: those who could pay contributed to those who were less able to pay or, as one authority said: 'Rosa embarked on the Robin Hood tactics of robbing the rich to pay for the poor.'[7]

Rosa Lewis fitted in well into the society of the period, both as an innovative cook and 'the world's first lady caterer'.[8] When she took over a kitchen there tended to be trouble with the resident staff so she always introduced her own helpers, who were drilled like soldiers. Not only did she take all the kitchen staff she needed but also all the washers-up, the carvers, the tools and utensils, the gilt chairs and anything else that might be required. She claimed that she earned as much from hiring out her chairs and tables as she did from her pots and pans. Among those helping for the evening might be other people's cooks, who came to her to learn her methods at three guineas for six lessons (£3.15p).

Teaching other people to cook had always been a means of earning a living and women could be found setting up schools of cookery or running classes in conjunction with other subjects. In eighteenth-century Edinburgh, for example, there were a number of such teachers. Lady Grisell Baillie soon after her marriage in 1691 attended cookery classes run by a Mrs Addison, which cost her almost as much as her footman's cash wage for the half year. By the mid-eighteenth century Mrs Wilkie was advertising herself as the keeper of a pastry school, while Mrs Cleland, her contemporary, was also teaching cookery in the city. In the same decade Mrs Johnstone started as a teacher of cookery but then opened a boarding school for girls; conversely, at the end of the century Mrs Anderson was in charge of a boarding school and was maybe the same person running a pastry school close by. Other girls' schools, such as Mrs Ainslie's, sometimes specified that cookery classes were on offer. Mrs Maciver and Mrs Frazer were fixtures on the Scottish cookery scene for many years but Mrs Maciver presuambly died while in harness as Mrs Frazer then took over and described herself as 'late colleague and now successor to Mrs M'Iver [*sic*], deceased'. Their syllabus was wide-ranging, offering 'cookery, pastry, pickling and preserving'.[9] These examples are limited to eighteenth-century Edinburgh but similar schools and classes proliferated throughout the country.

Despite the many opportunities it seems the demand for 'good, plain cooks' always outstripped supply. Increasingly, the middle-class housewife employed others to do the work she had previously done herself with the help of her maids. Not long after the publication of Mrs Beeton's great work complaints were being voiced about the lack of 'good cooks' and 'plain cooks', by which was meant a cook who knew her craft and could run her kitchen economically. Strenuous efforts were being made at this time to get 'domestic economy' added to the curriculum for the board schools, the reason being that girls were no longer being taught such things by their mothers since so many women went out to work.[10] Dedicated women like Mrs Catherine Buckton in Leeds campaigned tirelessly to this end. She prepared a systematic course of instruction based on elementary science and, after school hours, talked to large mixed-ability classes on topics such as food, infant care, good and bad air and so on. She recorded that: 'After preparing the information, my own cook gave four demonstration lessons on cookery.' The School Board adopted her plan soon afterwards and also her syllabus on the laws of health, for which they employed a 'lady sanitary teacher' who went from school to school taking the apparatus she needed on a handcart. Mrs Buckton published her ideas in book form, too, spelling out the principles of both domestic economy and health in the house, which concluded: 'I trust that women of every class will soon possess a sufficient amount of knowledge about the construction of a dwelling, to spread terror among unscrupulous landlords, tenants, speculative builders, and working men, and also create a demand for well-built houses.'[11]

Mrs Buckton was not alone in her efforts. Similar moves were afoot in Birmingham and elsewhere; there was concern, though, over the supply of suitably qualified teachers. It was suggested that private enterprise might fund cookery schools nationwide, some static and some peripatetic, and the example of 'those canny Scotch ladies' who had set up and made a success of the Edinburgh School of Cookery was cited: 'The indefatigable Secretary, if permitted, would instruct older boys, too, in School Board classes and wishes to be ready to instruct soldiers, sailors and intending colonists in food preparation, cooking apparatus . . . supplies . . .'[12] However, the Edinburgh ladies were fearful that the demand for their classes could lead to half-trained persons being sent out, thereby bringing the movement into disrepute.

To some extent this problem had been foreseen when the National Training School of Cookery opened in 1873 in London's South Kensington. It was intended to work in alliance with the school boards and training schools on a national scale, rather than on a merely local level and there was general agreement over the need to teach the children rather than 'the present generation'. Its objective was to pioneer a national effort for the recognition and teaching of cookery and hygiene as being vital to the interests and well-being of the country. To do this 'The National', as it was always called, would train women to become teachers of cookery so that they would be qualified to give instruction in a variety of institutions; it would also instruct anyone wishful of knowing more about the principles of cookery; and it would send out lecturers, with the appropriate equipment, to wherever there might be a demand, as long as the school or institution was willing to pay the expenses incurred.

At the end of its first year, 3 students gained their teaching diplomas, while 2 years later a further 34 diplomas were awarded, with 37 students in training. Altogether, in its first 15 years over 40,000 students attended classes and 327 of them qualified as teachers.[13] A wide variety of courses were offered for non-teachers such as married women, who attended with their cooks, or for intending scullery maids. One whose career started at 'The National' was Maud Ward, who was denied the opportunity of attending university as her brothers did and so accepted the only opening offered to her, a two-year cookery course. She cooked at country houses and institutions, became an itinerant teacher of cookery, and having made a study of the Health Insurance Act of 1911 was trained as a lecturer by the Ministry of Health to travel round the country addressing conferences for those affected by the Act. She was appointed the Chief Woman Inspector in the new Health Insurance Service and retired in 1930 to gardening and local affairs. However, that was all in the future when, in December 1883, HRH The Prince of Wales (the future Edward VII) became patron of the school and took a keen interest in its work. Soon afterwards, the school moved into spacious premises in Buckingham Palace Road where it remained until it closed because of lack of funds in 1962.

Although the Executive Committee in 'The National's' early years was almost entirely male, many of the teaching staff were female, while two gifted and capable women were in charge of its day-to-day running. After forty-five years as Principal Mrs Edith Clarke was succeeded by her eldest daughter, Miss Gladys Clarke. Both were very aware of the changing needs of their students and of developments in contemporary educational practices with the result that the syllabus was revised on several occasions, classes re-organised and a wider range of subjects introduced with greater academic content. The school had certainly introduced the innovatory gas cookers by 1892, in order to give students the opportunity of learning how to use them, and by 1912 were installing an electric cooking stove and three boiling rings for sweet-making.

'The National' generated favourable publicity by lecturing and catering at the 1883 Fisheries Exhibition and producing a book of fish recipes; there was further involvement at subsequent international exhibitions. The school had links with the Army and the Navy, resulting in an improved diet for their personnel, and when the Boer War broke out Mrs Clarke campaigned for better feeding of the war-wounded. She was also consulted by the Prisons Commission with regard to the kitchens at Wormwood Scrubs. The Local Government Board approached her for advice on feeding workhouse inmates across the country, and this work resulted in the compilation of a *Manual of Workhouse Cookery*, which cost 4*d* (under 2p today). Many other guides to cookery and domestic practices were also produced by the school, forming a mere handful in a genre with long-established roots.

The publication of a cookery book, whether connected to a cookery school or issued independently, was teaching in a different format. Almost as soon as women took over the cooking they began to collect recipes, though many were intended solely for the writer's own use. The housewife who could read and write was able to jot down odds and ends of information, whether she had them from a newly acquired book or from a kindly neighbour, and several have now been published. Elinor Fettiplace lived in Oxfordshire and her manuscript collection is dated 1604. It contains a miscellaneous assortment of culinary recipes alongside those for home-made drinks, pickling or preserving and medical or cosmetic matters – the dividing line is a fine one – with cures for the bubonic plague, including one grandly called 'a medicine of King Henry the eighth for the plague or pestilence'. Lady Fettiplace had friends who supplied her with information, including Sir Walter Raleigh and Shakespeare's son-in-law, Dr Hall.[14]

Lady Castlehill was of a later generation. The headings of some of her recipes, or 'receipts' as they were called, evoke the image of a group of ladies comparing notes in front of a cheerful fire. 'To make the Countess of Norwich her Almond Butter', 'Mistress N's Cheese Cakes' and 'To make Caraway Bunns. Ldy Atkins' are among those that figure, with the said 'Ldy Atkins' also providing 'A Recept to make very Good Pancakes'. Others imparting recipes to the collection included 'Lady Cartret', 'Mrs Honywood' and 'Capt Godfrey'.[15] Rebecca Price (1660–1740) was a contemporary of Lady Castlehill's and lived in Buckinghamshire. She bequeathed to her daughter not one but 'two receipt Books in folio written by myself one of which said Books being for Surgery and physick and the other for Cookery and Preserves'.[16] Many of her recipes are accorded their provenance: 'An Almond Pudding baked. Mrs Whiteheads' Receipt', 'My first Cousen Clerkes receipt' – for a French barley pudding, 'my Lord Gray's receipt' – for the best sort of French bread, or 'To preserve red Rose Leaves: my Mother's Receipt' – all the more poignant seeing Rebecca had been left motherless when a child of ten.

When it comes to collections that were written with publication in mind Hannah Woolley is generally regarded as being the first of a long line, although a case could be made out on behalf of rival claimants. The books of Elizabeth Grey, Countess of Kent, were published some years earlier; however, one deals with medical matters while the other, although on the subject of cookery, confectionery and preserving, is of questionable authorship, as are others of that era. Hannah Woolley was the author of several books on domestic practice and the conduct of ladies and wrote from her own experiences. She was orphaned at fifteen and kept a little school; she became governess to a noble lady's daughter, learnt cookery and preserving and was promoted to be her employer's 'woman', then house steward, scribe and secretary. At the age of twenty-four she married a schoolmaster, looked after the boarders at his school and, in due course, their four sons. They moved to Hackney where they opened a larger school but her husband died and it is thought she began writing at that time, presumably to earn some money. In 1666 she married again, to a widower of her own age, and she continued her writing.

In the eighteenth century Mary Kettilby was the major contributor to a collection of over three-hundred recipes encompassing both cookery and medical matters, which went through seven editions between 1714 and 1759. Eliza Smith's compendium comprised over five-hundred recipes and was so well received that at least eighteen editions appeared between 1727 and 1773. Despite such popularity both were overshadowed by Hannah Glasse, famous on account of those four words she never used! She was clearly both an early feminist and in favour of 'good English cooking'. She complained bitterly about the extravagance of male cooks in general and French cooks in particular, and poured scorn on those who employed such staff when a woman could produce good wholesome dishes at a fraction of the cost. The identity of the author has long been questioned and Mrs Glasse now stands accused of plagiarism, though Dr Johnson thought the book so good that it could only have been written by a man. 'Women can spin very well;' he declared, 'but they cannot make a good book of Cookery.'[17]

In 1760 two more of Mrs Glasse's books were published, one on the duties of female domestic servants and their working routines and the other on confectionery and preserving, which were considered to be completely separate skills from cookery. Whereas the kitchen produced the staples for the dinner table, the dessert course, which followed in the wealthier echelons of society, was either the housewife's own handiwork or came from her store-cupboard, a duty later delegated to the housekeeper. Mrs Glasse was not the first woman to write of such matters: Mrs Eales was Confectioner to both King William and to Queen Anne and had already published her collection of receipts in 1718.

Although the majority of cookbooks were published in London, the north of the country was also active. In 1741 Mrs Elizabeth Moxon of Pontefract produced her *English Houswifry* [sic], *exemplified in above four hundred receits* [sic], a book, she claimed, 'necessary for Mistresses of families, higher and lower Women Servants, and confined to Things USEFUL, SUBSTANTIAL AND SPLENDID, and calculated for the Preservation of HEALTH, and upon the Measures of FRUGALITY, being the Result of thirty Years practice and Experience'. It is interesting to note both that emphasis on women in the kitchen and on the connection between health and food; and how she also stresses the practicality of her recipes, predating Mrs Glasse's views by some years. Also published in Leeds but some twenty-five years later and echoing the views of her compatriot was Ann Peckham who claimed her recipes to be: 'the most genteel yet least expensive receipts . . . in every branch of cookery and good housewifery'. Doncaster was the venue for Sarah Martin's 'entire new collection of original receipts . . . in every branch of cookery, confectionery etc.', published under the title of *The New Experienced English Housekeeper.*

Several works were published in Newcastle upon Tyne, possibly due to the activities of the Kellet ladies, Susanna, Mary and Elizabeth, who had run a cookery school in the town for over fifty years before their own *Complete collection of cookery receipts* was published in 1780. Meanwhile, the first edition of Ann Cook's work appeared there in 1754, of Mary Smith's in 1772 and of Elizabeth Marshall's in 1777. However, it was from Manchester that the first edition of Elizabeth Raffald's book *The Experienced English Housekeeper* was sent out into the world in 1769, although subsequent editions were mostly published in London. Mrs Raffald (1733–81) was an energetic character. For fifteen years she was housekeeper to Lady Elizabeth Warburton of Arley Hall, Cheshire. She married the gardener there in 1763 and, despite giving birth to fifteen daughters in eighteen years, she became a confectioner in Manchester, opened a cookery school, wrote her book, ran a couple of inns and found time for a variety of other activities too.

For some eighty years, Scotland proved a fruitful source of culinary works. From Glasgow in 1736 there came Mrs McLintock's slim volume of recipes, many of which relate to pickling, preserving and confectionery and thereby pre-dating Hannah Glasse by a number of years. Elizabeth Cleland's book was 'chiefly intended for the benefit of the Young LADIES who attend Her SCHOOL'.[18] Another teacher was Hannah Robertson who claimed to be a granddaughter of Charles II; her life had taken some extraordinary twists and turns and she was now writing because she had fallen on hard times and needed to make some money for her old age. Mrs Maciver modestly assures her readers that she only wrote her cookbook because she had succumbed to the earnest solicitations of her scholars and in the hope it would further her business; later editions were produced by Mrs Frazer. In the next century Mrs Hudson and Mrs Donat, former housekeepers and cooks to a large establishment in East Lothian published a cookery book. Then, in the 1820s 'Meg Dods', pseudonym of Mrs C.I. Johnstone, novelist and journalist, produced her cookbook and such was its popularity that it totally eclipsed the businesslike and practical work by Mrs Dalgairns which appeared shortly after.

The nineteenth century witnessed a plethora of cookbooks compiled by women who wrote on every possible aspect of the kitchen. Mrs Rundell was one of the more famous, of whom more later. There was Eliza Acton who had already published one book of verses, somewhat gloomily concentrating on death, solitude, abandoned love and similar matters, and reputedly offered her publisher a second volume of 'further fugitive verses'. He told her to go away and write a cookery book, which she did. Her recipes are short, to the point, clear to follow and, a novelty at the time, each one ends with a summary of the ingredients needed. The work proved popular and was followed by her *Book on Bread* a decade later.

However, just as Mrs Dalgairns had been overshadowed by 'Meg Dods', so Eliza Acton's book was overtaken by Isabella Beeton's *Book of Household Management*. Originally printed in twenty-four instalments as a supplement in one of her husband's magazines, it embellished Eliza Acton's idea of a summary of ingredients by adding details as to the cost of the dish, the cooking time, the number of people it was designed for and, where appropriate, the season of availability. The success was such that, as soon as the supplements were all out, they were published in book form in October 1861. The idea had probably been Mrs Beeton's as she had virtually taken over the editorship of the *Englishwoman's Domestic Magazine* from her husband. Soon after their marriage in 1856 she was proofreading, clarifying the layout, contributing articles, coping with foreign correspondence (she spoke fluent German and French) and devising ways to increase the circulation: the supplements were an innovation to this end, preceded by dress patterns of her own design.

Mrs Beeton was just one of a number of women who put their knowledge to good use by writing for the many magazines that were springing up to cater for the rapidly expanding middle-class market. One contemporary was Mrs Isa Knox, contributor to periodicals such as *Fraser, Good Words* and the *Quiver*, while she also edited the *Argosy* for a short time. Mrs Loftie contributed pertinent weekly essays to the *Saturday Review*, which were subsequently collected together in book form. In an earlier period Esther Hewlett described herself as being editor of the *Christian Gleaner, or Domestic Magazine* and said she had long wished to improve the daily lives of 'the labouring classes of society'.[19] Mrs Johnstone ('Meg Dods') wrote on a variety of topics for assorted publications.

Running parallel to the articles on cookery and household matters there were innumerable publications focussing on one particular aspect of the kitchen or for the needs of different groups of people, whether it be bread, ice-cream, game, home-made drinks, entrées, herbs, fruit, invalids, the working classes, children, vegetarians or a comprehensive guide to *Electric Cooking, Heating, Cleaning &c., being a Manual of Electricity in the Home* by A Housewife (E.M. Lancaster): any and every subject was catered for.

There was also a feeling that old days and old ways were vanishing and that a record should be kept of them while they were still fresh in people's minds. Lady Llanover's work was the first collection of Welsh recipes to be published in English (1867) and although many emanated from her own kitchen a number seem to belong to an earlier age altogether and are thus a valuable commentary. In addition, Lady Llanover and her husband Benjamin Hall (the Ben of 'Big Ben') made their home a centre of Welsh culture and she campaigned tirelessly in the cause of Welshness. 'Meg Dods' had already included a chapter devoted to 'National Dishes embracing Scottish, Irish, Welsh, German, Spanish and Oriental',[20] while a hundred years later her compatriot F.M. McNeill took the matter further. Her object, she said was 'to preserve the recipes of our old national dishes, many of which, in this age of standardization, are in danger of falling into an undeserved oblivion'. She sketched in the background to the foods themselves, the methods of cookery and the plenishing of the kitchen and accompanied it with a comprehensive selection of recipes from every part of the country and 'from Old Holyrood to island sheiling'.[21]

Cooking, collecting recipes, writing a cookery book or teaching students were not the only callings for a trained cook, despite being the occupations frequently engaged in. Many, on leaving domestic service and particularly after marriage with a fellow servant, took to dispensing hospitality professionally – as lodging-house keepers, innkeepers and so on. At the highest level of society there were the likes of Rosa Lewis, who catered for private parties, special weekends and ran a hotel. A century earlier Mrs Cornelys, nicknamed 'the Sultana of Soho', was a professional hostess at Carlisle House in London's Soho. Viennese in origin and a courtesan by occupation, she ran her assembly rooms there from 1760 onwards and introduced the concept of fancy dress balls. Society flocked to the card parties, dances, musical events and masquerades staged there, paying handsomely for the privilege. Fanny Burney visited the place in 1770: 'The magnificence of the rooms, splendour of the illuminations and embellishments, and the brilliant appearance of the company exceeded anything I ever before saw. The apartments were so crowded we had scarce room to move, which was quite disagreable, nevertheless, the flight of apartments both upstairs, and on the ground floor seemed endless . . .'[22] Despite its sensational success, or maybe because of it, other equally fashionable venues were established soon after such as Almacks and The Pantheon. Mrs Cornelys took up the challenge by making her rooms even more splendid and her entertainments more exotic than ever but in so doing fell into debt and was declared bankrupt. For some years thereafter the rooms remained open but the class of clientele slipped somewhat. On weekdays, concerts and other events were staged and on Sundays a milder form of entertainment was provided, involving a stroll through the rooms while refreshments comprised tea, coffee or chocolate as well as some modest alcoholic beverages.

Until the latter part of the nineteenth century there were few opportunities for ladies to eat in a restaurant or hotel; entertaining was done in the home. They might buy refreshments from a high-class establishment such as Gunters in Berkley Square but it was the custom to eat whatever they purchased in the privacy of their carriages, drawn up by the side of the Square. Tea and coffee were available at public gardens such as Vauxhall and Ranelagh, while a herd of cows was kept in Hyde Park with a milkmaid in attendance so that fresh milk was on offer to those who wished to imbibe. The first ABC tea shop opened in London in 1880 and proved popular as women could meet there without being escorted by a husband or brother, and the company opened other shops thereafter. Lyons Corner Houses began business in 1894. However, by this time two women had already taken matters into their own hands. Mrs Fuller, an American lady, so deplored London's lack of decent places where women could meet their friends or the professional woman could eat alone that she opened her own tea shops where the surroundings were gracious and the food above the ordinary. In Glasgow Mrs Catherine Cranston was working to create similar establishments.

Kate Cranston was the daughter of a tea merchant and hotelier. From 1884 onwards she opened a chain of tea shops in the city which were highly successful and celebrated for their original, 'artistic' decor. Charles Rennie Mackintosh was commissioned to design the furniture and fittings for the Argyle Street Rooms, the decorative schemes of the Ingram Street branch and, perhaps the most famous of all, the Willow Tea Rooms in Sauchiehall St.* She also organised and ran the tea rooms for the international exhibitions held in Glasgow in 1901 and 1911, which was reminiscent of 'The National's' efforts in the 1880s. After her husband's death in 1917 she began selling off the rooms and retired a couple of years afterwards. Despite her eccentric appearance she was a highly respected business woman; not only did she provide the women of Glasgow with pleasant meeting places for social occasions but she was also instrumental in drawing attention to, and popularising, the high quality of the art and design emanating from Glasgow.

Hospitality could take other forms too. The short-lived attempt of Rosa Lewis and her husband to keep a lodging-house has already been noted but the street directories of most towns reveal a proliferation of women renting out rooms or apartments and catering for their tenants; included

---

*   A play on words: 'sauchie' in Scots means the willow.

under this heading would be the stock comedy figure of the seaside landlady. Similarly, the directories reveal the numbers keeping a wide variety of hostelries. An early example was the widowed Mrs Davys (1674–1732) who moved to Cambridge where she started to write and established a coffee house. Her near contemporary Christian Davies (1677–1739), who joined the Army in search of her husband, ran a public house thereafter and, as a former soldier, spent her final days in the Royal Hospital, Chelsea. Somewhat later at Nando's, a London coffee house much frequented by the legal profession, it was said: 'There was no-one who could supply coffee or punch better than Mrs Humphries; and her fair daughter was admired at the Bar and by the Bar.'[23] The pseudonym of the writer Mrs Johnstone, 'Meg Dods', related to a fictitious innkeeper who cooked with great flair but the character was modelled on Miss Marion Ritchie of the Cross Keys Inn at Innerleithen. In this same locality was Tibbie Shiels who kept the inn at St Mary's Loch and counted Sir Walter Scott among her clientele. Further examples relating to taverns and so forth kept by former servants will be found in Chapter Four.

Edinburgh had a coterie of female landlords. There was Mrs Rutherford's Tavern near the Mercat Cross and Mrs Flockhart's tiny room where three bottles, containing brandy, whisky and rum, were set out in the window for the men to help themselves, accompanied by a plate of her 'parlies' or 'parliament cakes', a type of gingerbread. 'Lucky' Middlemass ran an oyster cellar where young folk gathered for lively oyster parties. 'Pudding Lizzie's Tavern' sold rum under the name of 'Popish Whisky' to avoid the tax and was famous for its mealie puddings. Mrs Douglas, 'a large fat woman, in a towering head-dress and large-flowered silk gown,'[24] ruled over her husband's tavern – and her husband.

The brewing of beer had long been in the hands of women and this became all the more so after the Dissolution of the Monasteries, but even before this 'ale-wives' or 'brewsters' were producing drinks for sale. Early in the sixteenth century Eleanour Rummynge of Leatherhead was a brewster and landlord who sold her beer on credit (with due interest) and ran a pawnshop: she is considered to be the model for Shakespeare's ale-wife in *The Taming of the Shrew*. A later example from the 1670s was the so-called 'Mother Louse', supposedly the last woman in England to wear a ruff, and her tavern, Louse Hall, was at Hedington Hill, Oxfordshire.

Early in the seventeenth century Markham numbered 'preserving of all sorts of Wines, Conceited Secrets, Distilations [*sic*], Perfumes . . .'[25] among the housewife's talents and for the next two-hundred years or more such activities were a part of the domestic scene. The practice flourished in times of war when foreign wines were hard to acquire or when import tariffs rose sharply, but many housewives took a pride in their skill. Welsh housewives were noted for their excellent meads and metheglins, while those in the West Country made full use of the local apples and pears for their cider and perry.

Cookery books, such as those by Mrs Eales, Mrs Cleland, Mrs Rundell and 'Meg Dods', included instructions for various ales and beers, ciders and wines based on fruit and vegetables, and many medicinal cordials and healing liquors. There were also instructions for distilling not only alcoholic beverages but also perfumed waters and other compounds, thereby confirming Markham's tenet that such were matters for the housewife's attention. Later authors tended to separate the subjects and it is interesting to note that whereas Mrs Beeton includes many home-made beverages, by 1861 the brewing of beers at home had become a thing of the past. The advent of the railways were the final blow in a process that had been developing for some time, in that capital and machinery enabled production to be carried out on a large scale in centralised factories.

CHAPTER THREE

Producers and Purveyors

Food has been a preoccupation for the majority of women throughout the ages and it was a question that surfaced again during the Second World War and its aftermath when so many foods were scarce or 'on ration'. How to get hold of it, how much might or might not be available, what its quality might be, how to store it until needed, how best to serve it – all these questions and many more have exercised the minds of those responsible for feeding a household. Information on how to recognise fresh goods and avoid the stale or inferior was sometimes included in the cookbooks. Alongside the innumerable women who were professionally concerned with cookery and hospitality, many others dealt with producing, transporting or trading foodstuffs.

From the farmer's wife of the seventeenth century to the 'Land Girls' of the Second World War women have been involved in the production of foodstuffs. When towns were smaller the countryside was correspondingly closer and, therefore, far more people produced their own food, or a proportion of it, and would sell the surplus. Others needed to sell as much as they could for cash with which to pay their rent or buy necessities. Some households were almost self-sufficent: Welsh farmers in easy circumstances ate the produce of their own land, as did the same class in England, 'waste not, spare not' being their watchword.[1] However, by the 1890s such self-sufficiency was considered worthy of comment when met with in Wales. On the other hand, accounts from the larger landowners' households would suggest that they were rarely as self-sufficient as imagined, though it might well be that it was precisely because money was readily available that non-essential purchases could be made. The mansion would have its spacious walled garden with a series of hot houses and a team or two of gardeners; the more modest property would still have its kitchen garden and a man to work it. Poorer country folk, if they were fortunate, would have a piece of land attached to their dwelling in which they could raise some basic vegetables for the cooking pot.

Flora Thompson's reminiscences of her childhood in an Oxfordshire hamlet later in the nineteenth century would be typical of many other households. Each year a piglet was bought to be kept in a lean-to shed beside the cottage and fattened on whatever scraps could be made available. The children would bring home armfuls of vegetation from the hedgerows and buckets of snails to feed it on and if money was scarce a bargain would be struck with the miller: a supply of grain to feed the pig against part of the meat when it was killed. Bacon was the mainstay of the cottagers' diet for much of the year. Fresh meat was too expensive, except for a few pence-worth for a Sunday treat, and most of that was given to the man of the household. 'Then, in addition to the bacon, all vegetables, including potatoes, were home-grown and grown in abundance . . . Fat green peas, broad beans as big as a halfpenny, cauliflowers a child could make an armchair of, runner beans and cabbage and kale, all in their seasons went into the pot . . . with the bacon'. The family ate plenty of lettuce, radishes and young onions with slices of home-made bread and rosemary flavoured lard from the pig. A farmer might allow his labourers' wives and children to glean in the fields once the crop had been harvested and children scoured hedgerows and woods for wild fruits, mushrooms and nuts.[2]

In Lark Rise it was the men who looked after the family pig and dug the garden after their long hours at work but, just as frequently, the women did what they could, over and above all their other domestic chores. Had not William Lawson many years before written a book designed to help the womenfolk get the most from their gardens? *The Countrie Housewife's Garden* first appeared in 1617 and the following year this Yorkshire parson published a similar book for their husbands. Advice to the women included laying out the area, fencing it and the need to separate the flowers from the vegetables – seeing that the latter suffer 'deformity' when items are harvested – alongside planting requirements and some 'general rules in gardening'. Even if he did not expect every housewife to dig her own vegetable plot, he nevertheless presumed they would supervise the work and he concluded: 'withal I advise the Mistresse, either to be present her selfe, or to teach her maides to know hearbs from weeds'.[3]

In his final chapter Lawson counselled: 'There remaineth one necessary thing to be prescribed, which in mine opinion makes as much for ornament, as either Flowers, or forme, or cleanlinesse . . . which is Bees, well ordered. And,' he continued sternly, 'I will not account her any of my good House-wives, that wanteth either Bees, or skilfulnesse about them'.[4] Bees were a necessary adjunct as the honey was the prime form of sweetening before the large-scale import of sugar. Honey was (and still is) a potent preservative and the basis of many home-made drinks such as mead, metheglin and hydromel, in which the Welsh wife was said to excel. Beeswax made very superior candles which burned with a delicate scent of honey and, prior to the Reformation, had been in great demand for church use. The careful housewife set aside beeswax to make into furniture polish and assorted cosmetics, creams and healing ointments.

One of Flora Thompson's elderly neighbours, 'Old Sally', had a garden larger than the others with apple trees, a flower garden and a row of beehives. Another villager 'Queenie' also kept bees and would sit, whenever the weather was fine, beside the hive, making lace and 'watching the bees' in case a swarm emerged. When straw skeps were common, as opposed to the wooden hives with movable frames developed from the 1850s onwards, it was difficult to prevent the bees from swarming so that if a swarm emerged from a hive it was better to catch it then and there before it had time to abscond. There are many beliefs about bees, including the theory that they must be told the family news. After 'Queenie's' husband had died she was seen tapping on the roof of each hive in turn and saying: 'Bees, bees, your master's dead, an' now you must work for your missus.'[5] She believed the bees would have died if she had not told them. In corroboration of this story there is a similar case in quite another part of the country. In her youth Miss Stirling Graham had translated a book on beekeeping by a Swiss pastor and at an advanced age she became patroness of the newly formed East of Scotland Beekeepers' Association. She died in 1876 at the age of ninety-six and some weeks later 'her beloved bees . . . were found in an impoverished state', but the story ended happily as they were promptly removed to a new home where they would be kindly treated 'for her sake'.[6]

Curiously, poultry keeping did not feature widely in the story of *Lark Rise* yet the activity was widespread. Poultry provided not only eggs and meat but feathers for stuffing pillows and mattresses; their bones and feet boiled up provided a strong stock for setting jellies; and the fat served several purposes, especially goose fat which was considered particularly beneficial in certain medical conditions. Until the enclosures of the eighteenth century, when much common land was taken into agricultural use, many poorer households such as 'Old Sally's' had been able to graze a cow or a donkey, some pigs or geese on the local common or in the woodlands; after the enclosures it was beyond their means to buy in the necessary fodder. In certain places the custom continued of allowing agricultural labourers the grazing for a cow as part of their wages. Livestock or poultry were not only kept for the cottagers' own consumption but took on a monetary value, seeing that many rural rents in the early days were payable to the landowner in kind, rather than exclusively in cash. The locality would dictate the commodity: in a dairying area a specified amount of butter or cheese would be handed over, whereas elsewhere payment might be made in poultry or eggs. On farms, as opposed to labourers' cottagers, the surplus was destined for sale in the local market. The making of butter, cheese and cream along with the preparation of poultry and eggs was carried out by the farmer's wife or under her supervision; by tradition, the money from the eggs was hers to keep.

How could women put such ordinary, everyday knowledge to good use in the world outside the home? As with other kitchen matters women were able to pass on their knowledge via the written word. Mrs Dalgairns was just one author who included instructions on the keeping of bees, poultry and cows,[7] while others such as Mrs Rundell and Mrs Beeton omitted the bees.

Despite Lawson's assumption that all women would keep bees, given their importance in the domestic economy, references to women beekeepers are scarce – and there is even less evidence of women writing about bees. When women practised cookery they wrote cookery books in considerable numbers; when they practised medicine they wrote their manuals; yet, in beekeeping they left little trace of their involvement. One of the few to do so was Margaret Clifton, of Timberland Thorpe, Sleaford, who addressed an essay on her method of apiary management to the Society of Arts in 1791 in order to claim the premium offered to beekeepers with over thirty stocks. Her award was 7 guineas (£7.35p), whereas two men applying were awarded 10 guineas each (£10.50p). The resurgence of beekeeping later in the nineteenth century led many women to become qualified beekeepers while they also became lecturers, honey show judges and researchers: it was the sharp eyes of a laboratory assistant, Elsie Harvey, who first observed the parasitic mite causing untold damage to bees and beekeeping early in the twentieth century. Her contemporary, Annie D. Betts, started keeping bees in 1900, frequently contributed to beekeeping journals and wrote one book on the anatomy of bees and another on bee diseases prior to taking up the editorship of the influential journal *Bee World*. She was also involved in the formation of the (International) Bee Research Association. The book for beginners written by the felicitously named Dr A.B. Flower went through numerous editions from 1925 onwards. The author was described in the Foreword as an experienced and practical beekeeper of many years standing whose services were greatly in demand around her own locality: 'her motor-cycle enables her to travel many, many miles in the exercise of these duties'.[8]

In view of the increasing number of women who became beekeepers at the turn of the century it is interesting to find a novel written at this time devoted to the theme of beekeeping as a career for women.[9] Set against the background of rural Australia and the excitements of the gold fields, the story is about a young woman, unmarried, bored with the emptiness of her life and looking for a measure of independence. Although her mother considers beekeeping an 'unladylike' pursuit, it is through keeping both bees and poultry that the heroine gains self-respect, financial independence and, eventually, the man she had always loved. The author Mary Gaunt, 'Mrs H. Lindsay Millar', though born in Australia was based in England for many years.

If women working with, or writing about, bees were limited in number until latterly, the keepers of poultry knew no such restrictions since the custom was so widespread. There were also more specialised books available, such as *Poultry: An Original and Practical Guide* of 1867 by Elizabeth Watts, which was dedicated 'To young amateurs and beginners in poultry-keeping' and covered 'breeding, rearing, feeding and exhibiting'. She described herself as being for 'many years editor of the poultry department in *The Field* and editor of *Poultry Yard* and *The Poultry Chronicle*'. She was also the author of *Modern Practical Gardening*, which demonstrates the close connection between the subjects, while the Hon. Rose Hubbard, under the pseudonym of 'Henwife', was the author of *Table Poultry &c.*, as well as a book on *Ornamental Water Fowl*.

Working in the dairy, preparing items both for immediate use and long-term storage was traditionally a woman's duty, though in some places foreigners were scandalised to see cows being milked by the menfolk. However, it was generally a dairymaid who did the job, although 'cowmen' cared for the animals and cleaned out the byres. Early in the nineteenth century Glasgow witnessed a pioneering enterprise to supply pure fresh milk to its citizens. The Willowbank Dairy operated on a huge scale and with the highest standards of hygiene, so much so that 'the cows were kept as cavalry horses'; there was an efficient milk house, a punctilious delivery service with smartly dressed male and female operators and a viewing balcony built on to one of the cow houses for the many visitors who came to see this novel establishment. Byremen cared for the cows but the milkers were women. Each took charge of between twelve and fifteen cows and would milk them twice a day, at the rate of about eight an hour, although some managed more. The owner himself wrote: 'The milkers were generally women, their wages being only half that of men, and they were found to milk as well'; he also expected them to sing while they worked.[10] The principal dairymaid had complete charge of the milk house and the churn house and was directly responsible to the management for all sales of new milk, skim milk, cream and buttermilk. It was a well-thought out operation run with military precision that was to be copied in many other towns, including London where the East Acton Dairy, with up to 200 cows milked on the premises, was one of several run on similar lines. It was said to be 'far superior to most' and the whole was 'projected, completed, and continues to be conducted by a lady'.[11]

Some fifty years later, a husband-and-wife partnership established a small dairy in London's Drury Lane, with tiled walls and marble-topped counters. He had a head for business but it was her butter that was reputedly the best in London. Within a few years they had a second shop in Kentish Town and another in Croyden and had added bacon and hams of their own smoking, cooked meats and other delicacies to their stock. Their six sons all entered the business and by 1939 there were 250 shops and the Sainsbury's empire was developing.

Presumably, their early shops stocked a traditional English cheese with an international reputation. Called after the village where it was sold, the first real evidence for this blue cheese dates back to the early eighteenth century and a housekeeper named Elizabeth Scarbrow, although it is just possibly a descendent of an earlier cheese made from goats' or ewes' milk. In 1720 Elizabeth Scarbrow became Mrs Oxton, a farmer's wife, and continued to make her cheese. In due course one daughter married the landlord of the Bell Inn and another married a local farmer; both were supplying cheese to the inn, where it became increasingly popular with the travellers who stopped there and it took on the name of the locality – Stilton. Another world-famous cheese, although this time from France, also owes its success to a woman who pefected the method of making it at some point during the eighteenth century, although the dates quoted vary widely. Mme Marie Harel is commemorated by a plaque erected by the farmers of Normandy but the cheese does not carry her name as it is known to the world as Camembert.

Women's names were frequently used to name almost any type of flowering plant, whether to preserve the memory of a birth or a marriage, a celebrity or a cherished child. Some famous women are now better known for being a variety of rose or a sweet pea than for being the name's original owner. 'Mrs Sinkins' is a much-loved white dianthus that is incorporated in the coat of arms of the Borough of Slough and it was named after her by her husband, Master of the Workhouse there. 'Annie Elizabeth' is a cooking apple introduced in 1868 in memory of the raiser's baby daughter who died in infancy. It is less common to find vegetables so designated, though some fruit varieties – apples, pears, peaches and so on – carry women's names. Not a variety of peach as such but a recipe called 'Pêches Melba' incorporating peaches, ice-cream and a purée of raspberries was devised by Escoffier to honour the Australian prima donna Dame Nellie Melba. Similar commemorative recipes are often found, especially in connection with dishes incorporating fruit – 'Pavlova', 'Apple Charlotte' and 'Crepes Suzette' to name but a few.

Seemingly, few women actively participated in the raising of new garden varieties, though it might well be worth bearing in mind that behind many a successful gardener would be a wife. It is the exception, though, that proves the rule and in this instance gave rise to a popular cooking apple. In 1809 the Brailsford family moved into a cottage in Southwell, Nottingham, but four years later their young daughter Mary Ann married and moved away. Meantime, an apple pip she had planted eventually grew into a fruit-bearing tree, nurtured by her widowed mother who continued to live at the cottage. Some two decades later, after cuttings of the original tree had been handed out to friends and neighbours, the son of a nearby head gardener happened to meet someone in the street carrying a basket of the apples. He was told they came from the garden of Mr Bramley, a local butcher. He asked permission to take material for propagating purposes and called the resulting variety 'Bramley's Seedling', today one of Britain's foremost cooking varieties. The area was apparently favourable to new apple varieties. Another one raised at much the same time in a cottage garden not far from Burghley was Betty Geeson's 'Barnack Beauty'; a decade or so later in nearby Stamford a Mrs Peasgood, who might have been the wife of a hairdresser, germinated the future 'Peasgood's Nonsuch'; while further south the original 'Lady Sudeley' was growing in a garden near Petworth, Sussex. On the other side of the world the first 'Granny Smith' was raised from a chance seed thrown out by Maria Ann Smith in New South Wales.

Surplus produce could be sold easily in the local market as the buying and selling of fresh goods remained at a relatively local level until Queen Victoria's reign. Transporting fresh goods from any distance was a problem when everything had to be carried, pushed or pulled by a person or an animal, be it donkey, pony or horse. The potential of the railways was realised at an early stage and their coming revolutionised the feeding of large conglomerations of people. A journey such as that from Aberdeen to London, which even by sea with favourable conditions would take several days (and just how often might they have been favourable?), could now be accomplished overnight; trainloads of beef and fish could leave Aberdeen one day and be on sale in London the next. Milk for cities like Manchester or London came in from 60 or 70 miles away and after refrigeration was introduced from even further afield, whereas 25 miles had previously been the absolute limit for a fast-trotting pony. Canals had started the process but although they were efficient at moving heavy goods in bulk – potatoes, for example, or cheese or pottery – the boats themselves were not particularly speedy and thus were unsuitable for foodstuffs that spoiled easily.

Until transport had speeded up, the purchase of basic necessities was done in the market-place. Villages would have their market on a specified day of the week, larger towns might have two or three each week, whereas the markets in London and other cities would operate on most days. Markets were strictly regulated by the town's authorities as to trading hours, places where stalls could be set up, the weights and measures to be used, prices that could be charged and so on and while this type of 'marketing' continued shops dealing in fresh foods were discouraged 'as interfering with the collection of the dues'.[12]

A description of just such a market day in South Wales was painted by Mrs Hall and her husband who visited the area before 1860. The day started early as people thronged the roads, the majority on foot, all chattering and exchanging the news as they made their way to the market. There 'they form picturesque groups, vending in the market-places the produce of their gardens, their farms, their dairies, or the looms which so many continue to ply at home, producing the flannel and woollen stuffs for which Wales has long been famous.'[13]

Not all market scenes were as convivial. Memoirs written in the 1850s recalled Edinburgh's market, although perhaps its condition was affected by its undesirable location along the spine of a hill. 'Our only fish market was in Fish Market Close, a steep, narrow, stinking ravine. The fish were generally thrown out on the street at the head of the close, from whence they were dragged down by dirty boys or dirtier women; and then sold unwashed – for there was not a drop of water in the place – from old rickety, scaly, wooden tables, exposed to all the rain, dust and filth.' The writer continued: 'Our vegetables had to pass through as bad a process. They were entirely in the hands of a college of old gin-drinking women who congregated with stools and tables around the Tron Church.* A few of the aristocracy of the ladies . . . marked their dignity by an awning of old canvas or tattered carpet; and every table had its tallow candle and paper lantern at night. There was no water here either, except what flowed down the gutter, which however was plentifully used. Fruit had a place on the table, but kitchen vegetables lay bruised on the ground.'[14]

Two centuries earlier one of the city's 'green wives' had played a leading role in a notable incident. In 1637 a new episcopal service book was introduced to the congregation in St Giles Cathedral and Jenny Geddes led the opposition to it by hurling her folding stool at the Dean. There was rioting inside the Cathdral and pandemonium outside. Tradition says that Jenny continued selling her goods for the next twenty years and to celebrate the Restoration she and her fellow green wives made a great bonfire of their folding stools.

It seems as if the selling of fruit and vegetables was deemed a woman's occupation, seeing that they also predominated as stallholders at Covent Garden. In nearby Drury Lane Nell Gwyn's early career saw her selling oranges in the Theatre Royal before she took to the stage, while tradition says that an apple woman with a pitch at what is now Hyde Park Corner blocked the building of Apsley House, 'Number 1 London', until bought out for a considerable sum. Elizabeth Neale kept a fruit shop for many

---

* The church was so called on account of the 'tron' in front of it, one of two public weighing places in the city.

years in fashionable St James's Street and was accorded an obituary in the *Gentleman's Magazine*.

Markets dealt in local produce. For goods from outside the area or for major, but occasional, purchases of a wide range of items it was the annual fair that filled the gap. The fair was a big event in the local calendar and servants in the vicinity would often be given leave to attend. While the daily market lasted only a few hours, the fair stretched over a week, or even two weeks, and was often centred on a local saint's day or a Church festival. Just as the market was regulated by the town's corporation, so the owner of a fair – be it town, church or landowner – laid down the regulations for trading. There were even temporary law courts to sort out disputes that might arise among a floating population coming from far and wide. They were known as 'Pie Powder Courts' from *pieds poudrés*, meaning the dusty feet of the travellers.

Everyone went to the fair, not only the local folk for the serious business of stocking up on goods unavailable at other times of the year, but also merchants from far and wide, who came to buy locally produced items in bulk for redistribution elsewhere in the country. Some fairs specialised in certain commodities: for example, Yarmouth for fresh or salted fish, Winchester for wine and spices, Exeter for serges. Alongside the serious business other folk were selling their wares or plying their trades. The barber, the puller of teeth and the quack doctor shouted for custom; domestic servants and farm workers waited to be hired for the following year; itinerant traders hawked gingerbread, pears and other comestibles; jugglers, musicians, ballad singers and actors entertained the crowds, which gave rise to the expression 'all the fun of the fair'. So much was this so that in due course the serious purpose of the fair was gradually overtaken by the entertainment element and it became the 'fun fair' of more recent times.

While women were involved in producing wares to sell in the market and were actively involved on the selling side, they were also engaged in the transport of goods. The market gardeners who supplied Londoners with their fruit and vegetables employed innumerable women, mostly from North Wales, on a seasonal basis not only for the menial jobs around the gardens but to walk into the city carrying the more tender produce, as it would suffer less damage than in a cart. One commentator marvelled at their energy: 'The fruit women will labour several hours in the garden, and go to and from the London markets twice a day, though at from four to seven miles distance.'[15] The Edinburgh markets were also serviced by women who left their children in the care of their tradesmen-husbands and walked in from East Lothian villages with baskets or creels of fruit or vegetables or salt on their backs; loads of sand for scrubbing floors could weigh up to 200 pounds. Having sold their goods, they returned home laden again, either with items for their neighbours or with huge bundles of dirty clothes for laundering in the purer waters of the countryside.[16]

A group of women who might from time to time have used that very same Prestonpans salt as they worked their way along the coast were the numerous 'fisher girls' who followed the shoals of herring and gutted, salted and packed the fish into barrels. The gutters worked at incredible speeds, dealing with between thirty and fifty fish in a minute and because the catch had to be processed swiftly the women would often work a twelve-hour day, standing out in the open. In 1913 it was estimated that some 12,000 Scots women were involved in the work and almost half of them followed the herring south through the English ports.

A less specialised but a more numerous group involved those women who were itinerant vendors. The streets of many towns were noisy with innumerable traders, of both sexes, all drawing attention to themselves by 'crying' their wares. Virtually any item that could be laid on a tray, tied in a bundle or carried in a basket could be sold in this way. Household necessities such as brooms or pots; personal items such as combs, ribbons, pens and inks; fresh foods to take home, others to eat on the spot; cooked foods, both hot and cold; a wide assortment of drinks, some of which might be sold hot from a handcart with heating apparatus; and luxuries like song sheets or ices. James Kendrew described the activities of the street sellers in early nineteenth-century York, Henry Mayhew left a lengthy description for mid-Victorian London and a similar account exists for Edinburgh.

Some towns had particular specialities and the Scottish capital was no exception: 'Scottish people have for centuries been great consumers of butter-milk . . . and towards the end of the eighteenth century . . . one might have witnessed daily the picturesque sight of milkmaids on horseback riding into town with soor-dook [buttermilk] barrels strapped across the saddles behind them'. The nursery rhyme about 'Little Miss Muffet, Who sat on her tuffet, Eating her curds and whey' brings to mind another favourite summer dish that was also 'cried' and in 1910 one writer recalled: 'The last of the race of such criers was Kirsty, . . . and not a few remember her, trudging along the High Street'.[17]

The city was also celebrated for its fish, shellfish in particular: oysters, cockles and mussels were all gathered locally and carried into the city by women from the fishing villages several miles distant; when at home, the women baited the fishing lines for their menfolk ready for the next fishing trip. Rumour asserted that the fishwives simultaneously engaged in a different occupation altogether and that other more desirable items, such as highly taxed tea and tobacco, were smuggled into the city hidden under the fish in their creels. The fish itself was either sold from a market stall, hawked through the streets or sold at the door. Sometimes a favourite oysterwoman would be invited into the house to open her wares for immediate consumption by the dinner guests; sometimes a party would go to one of the city's oyster cellars for an impromptu feast and dance, an entertainment that, for women, carried risqué overtones.

Local fishwives carried their fish from door to door, a practice that lasted into the 1960s. They came either from Leith, Edinburgh's port, or from the smaller fishing village of Newhaven to the west. When a suburban railway from this district to the city centre was put in, they were given a separate window in the booking office and an open carriage at the rear of the train so that passengers would not be inconvenienced by the lingering smell of fish.

Not all domestic commodities were traded at a market stall; some shops and smaller booths existed for non-food items and for provisions that were not fresh, although increasingly during the nineteenth century as markets were losing their importance, so shops were proliferating. Grocers' shops sold assorted dried or preserved goods: herbs, roots, spices, oils and ointments, syrups, medical ingredients, dried fruits, confectionery and household items such as turpentine. Although these dealers tended to overlap both with the apothecary at one end of the scale and the chandler at the other, generally speaking a grocer dealt in dried goods, a provision merchant or victualler handled fresh foods – butter, cheese, eggs and so on – while the sellers of imported foods ('far-fetched' originally meant just that) were Italian warehousemen, who sold olive oil, Parmesan cheese or French mustards.

'For centuries,' said one authority in 1949, 'the English were known as great mustard eaters – the greatest in the world. An Englishman may almost be identified by his liberal use of it in normal times', a reference to the post-war food shortages of the 1940s.[18] For long enough preparing mustard was a tedious process. The housewife had to steep the seeds in water overnight, then rub the seeds dry before beating them in a mortar with some additional wine vinegar, strain the mixture through a cloth and keep it covered until required. 'Or grinde it in a mustard quern, or a bowl with a cannon bullet.'[19] For Dijon or French mustard the initial steeping was done in vinegar and after the seeds were thoroughly dried they were to be pounded as before with extra vinegar, honey and cinnamon until the right consistency was reached. The housewife was saved from this labour when Mrs Clements of Durham, in about 1720, devised a method of grinding the mustard seed in a mill and turning it into a flour to which only water need be added to make it into a paste. Although she was then aged seventy-five, she kept the secret of its manufacture to herself for some years. She travelled to London and other principal towns twice a year for orders and from this arose the name and fame of 'Durham mustard'.

The grocery business generally seems to have been popular with women. After her husband's death 'the Widow Bourne' in London's St James's Street sold dried goods and suchlike to the local gentry. The shop itself was built on the site of Henry VIII's tennis court and the widow was its first occupant in 1698. She would surely be amazed and gratified to know that her business had passed through various hands over the intervening years, reaching its tercentenary and that it currently trades as a wine merchants.

A former household name started in a similar way but a generation later. It was in York that Mary Tuke took over a grocery business after the death of her parents, although both she and her husband suffered harassment as she had not followed the traditionally regulated route into the business. Her husband then died and Mary turned to dealing in tea, at that time a highly fashionable commodity. A nephew joined her and inherited the business in 1752, which had fluctuating fortunes thereafter. In 1784 the duty on tea which had been 100 per cent was reduced to 17 per cent with a consequent leap in consumption. 'Tukes Teas' were on sale throughout the north of England, Scotland and the West Country and they also sold chocolate from Churchman's, a Bristol firm established in 1728. The business expanded when the next generation joined the company: up to 12 tons of coffee were roasted a year, which were sold throughout the north alongside commodities such as chicory and salt. Philanthropy accompanied their trading interests but the decision was then made to concentrate on tea, so the chocolate trade was sold off to Fry's of Bristol – itself a firm managed for a while by a widow and her son – while the chicory business went to a young Rowntree, a newcomer to the grocery trade in York.

At about this time Mary Craven, née Hick, was left a widow with three young children to support. Her father was a partner in a business dealing with wholesale and retail confectionery and coffee roasting but left to start up on his own. After both her father and her husband died, Mary was unable to sell the business so she ran it herself. In 1888 it became 'Mary Craven & Son' and was soon employing 120 people and producing a great range of sweets, bakery products and specialities such as wedding cakes; a French recipe acquired for sugared almonds added to their fame. Further expansion saw the business employing 250 people and running 4 shops. Mary Craven was renowned for her energy and enterprise and the way in which she cared for her workforce, making provision for the sick, arranging works outings and so on. She died in 1902, much mourned, and her son died soon afterwards. Thereafter the firm went into decline, was taken over by another family connection and in due course became a subsidiary of Cadburys.

The activities of Mrs Raffald, Mrs Glasse, Mrs Eales and others in this line of business have already been noted in the previous chapter. Confectionery was an obvious commodity for women to deal in, given that it was akin to cookery and thus deemed a 'suitable' occupation. Even in fiction it maintained this role. In Mrs Gaskell's *Cranford* Miss Matty's friends agreed that, after she had lost most of her income due to the failure of a local bank, she would demean neither herself nor the family's memory by opening a little sweet shop and selling a few select teas, whereas that most genteel of societies had been none too happy when one of their number had married a Mr Hoggins – such a coarse name, they thought.[20]

Confectionery of another type also engaged the attentions of the womenfolk. That popular preserve marmalade has a long and honourable history, with origins in a Portuguese dessert of puréed quinces (called 'marmelada', from 'maramelo' meaning quince) brought into the country by the Moslem invaders. A confection of oranges preserved in sugar was a popular component of the dessert course at one time and although Scotland likes to claim that Mary Queen of Scots introduced marmalade into the country,* the evidence just does not support the premise! What is not in doubt is that the Scots can be credited with taking the idea one step further, by spreading this preserve on bread or toast and eating it at breakfast rather than as a sweetmeat at dinner. Meanwhile, it was a Scotswoman who developed the method of using Seville-type oranges to make it. Whether the stormbound ship with the cargo of bitter oranges arrived off-shore at the end of the seventeenth or the eighteenth century is open to debate but whichever Janet Keiller it was, her husband, a grocer, bought the oranges cheaply as no one else wanted them. His wife used the shop's stock of sugar to preserve them and the result proved popular with their customers. The product was made in the back of the shop until 1797 when a marmalade-making factory was built and in 1876 'Keiller's Dundee Orange Marmalade' became one of the first trade marks to be entered on the register after it had been set up. The firm went from strength to strength, especially after jams and jellies were added to its stock, all made with the excellent soft fruits grown in the area.

Further north a similar story concerns a small grocery shop opened in 1868 by a former gardener George Baxter and his wife Margaret, who

---

* Mary was seasick while crossing from France and is reputed to have said 'Marmelada pour Marie malade' when offered sweetened orange juice to drink.

made jams and jellies from the locally grown fruit. Their son William cycled all over Scotland collecting orders and when demand began to outstrip supply it was William's wife Ethel who supervised not only the building of their factory on the banks of the Spey but also the research and development of new lines, all based on the area's produce. During the Second World War the factory merely ticked over and afterwards the next generation had to rebuild the business. Again, a Baxter wife rose to the challenge, experimenting in her own kitchen and evolving new recipes; only after meticulous research does a new line go into production.

While some women traded in a range of products, others specialised. Visitors to Bath were regaled with quality local foodstuffs, one of which was a rich yeast bun called a 'Sally Lunn', supposedly named after the girl who 'cried' them through the streets. Some claim the girl was a Huguenot called Solange Luyon, while others say the name derives from her cry of 'Solet Lune' in reference to the yellow and white colouring of the bun.[21] No documentary evidence exists to support either theory but a fifteenth-century house is pointed out as the place where the girl worked. It was in the 1850s that Sarah Nelson started making her Grasmere Gingerbread for visitors to the Lake District and the business has continued ever since. This type of gingerbread is thinner, harder and grittier than the normal product. In nearby Kendal and at much the same time, Barbara Gray's shop was selling both gingerbread and the local mint cake. From somewhat further south come Chorley cakes, resembling Eccles cakes, which were sold in the 1880s by the Misses Corbitt from their confectionery shop. Banbury cakes have a long history and a shop in the town of that name, known to be selling them from before 1833 until the late 1960s, was supposedly started by one Betty White back in 1638.[22]

Women were often concerned with confectionery, some of whom have been noted earlier, while others were concerned with its making. A special form of her own 'gundy', an old-fashioned sweetmeat resembling a hard toffee, was sold by Mrs Flockhart, who kept a diminutive 'hotel' in Edinburgh known generally as 'Lucky Fykie's'.[23] In the Borders town of Hawick were two notable sweetmakers Jessie McVitie and Agnes Lamb who made the local speciality of 'Hawick Balls', while marmalade-maker Janet Keiller started cooking her mixture in the pans she normally used for sweetie making.[24]

CHAPTER FOUR

Out of the Servants' Hall

The supreme Lord of the Universe has, in his Wisdom, rendered the
various conditions of mankind necessary to our individual
happiness: – some are rich, others poor – some are masters, and
others servants. – Subordination, indeed, attaches to your rank in
life, but not DISGRACE. All men are servants in different degrees.[1]

These are the words of Mr and Mrs S. Adams in 1825 on the relationship
between employers and servants, an opinion echoed by many other
writers during the century. Generally, the advice was coming from the
employers and being directed to the employed: what was unusual about
the Adams was that theirs was the viewpoint of the domestic servant, since
they had both been 'in service' all their working days.

Domestic service, even as it existed in the Victorian era, was a
throwback to feudal society of medieval times when a Very Important
Personage would attract lesser personages into his household as his
'servants', whereby prestige, power and a measure of security was
conferred on both sides from the attachment. In turn, those lesser
mortals would be attended by their own 'servants' and somewhere
sufficiently low in the hierarchy would come servants who would actually
be dealing with the domestic work.

As an example of this even the beautiful and high-spirited Duchess of
Marlborough, wife of the national hero of the day and builder of
Marlborough House, London, was a 'servant' to Queen Anne. Duchess
Sarah was not only for a number of years the Queen's friend and
confidante (in private they referred to each other as Mrs Freeman and
Mrs Morley to banish the differences in rank between them) but she also
served as Mistress of the Robes. That the Duchess had her own ladies to
attend her, as well as lesser servants to do the actual work, including
Abigail Masham who came to play such an influential role in her life, was
immaterial; the Duchess was a servant of the Queen.

Prior to the period under review a number of far-reaching changes had
taken place, in architecture, in domestic habits, in diminishing levels of
ceremonial and so forth, which, when coupled to severe price inflation
and the burdens of the Civil War, had forced many households to
economise. One of the first effects was the way in which women began to
replace men as domestic servants, primarily because their wages were

about half those of the men's and they were also considered to be more amenable to supervision. The trend accelerated through the next century. To employ men servants, therefore, carried an aura of prestige and all the more so after 1777 when a tax of 1 guinea per head (£1.05) was introduced on male staff; by 1808 the level of tax stood at £7 per year and so, as fewer households could afford to employ them, the element of prestige increased. The duties of the more expensive men servants such as the butler, footmen and coachmen kept them in the public eye both in the house and outside it, whereas the lower-paid women servants beavered away out of sight.

The nineteenth century saw a further period of transition when agriculture and cottage enterprises declined and manufacturing, commercial and service industries expanded. The division introduced between workplace and home profoundly affected the status of women and their role in society. Although women would ultimately benefit from the new opportunities, it did not happen immediately and so for many there was little choice but to start their working lives as domestic servants for which there was a never-ending demand.

The names of the great majority – the innumerable Nellys and Hannahs, the Bettys, Anns and Janets – can only be conjured up by reading through domestic records, whether account books, dinner books, lists of wages or other material of that nature. Few stayed in domestic service all their life, to become what might be termed the career servant; most left it behind them and some became celebrated later in life on account of talents unrelated to their previous situations. Mary Wollstonecraft acted as companion to an old lady in Bath and as governess in Ireland but she is remembered today as an author, feminist and educationalist. Gladys Aylward laboured for years as a maid-of-all-work in order to save her fares to China so that she could take up the missionary work for which she became renowned – and all the more so after the making of the film *The Inn of the Sixth Happiness* which was based on her own dramatic story. Sarah Siddons was one of the foremost actresses of her day but she spent time as a lady's maid and entertained her fellow servants by declaiming Milton and Shakespeare in the servants' hall and was sometimes summoned to entertain the company 'upstairs' as well. In the meantime, her contemporary Frances Barton was a domestic servant, cook, maid, flower seller and street singer before she became acclaimed as an actress. Elizabeth Raffald is known today for her cookery book and other activities, rather than for the many years she spent as housekeeper, and many more names could be added to the list.

The peak years for domestic service were between 1851 and 1871; after that the rate of increase was slowing down even though actual numbers continued to rise. Until 1914, it was the largest single branch of employment for women and the second largest of all forms of employment in the whole country. The 1881 census revealed that 44 per cent of all employed women were in domestic service and in 1901 the figure was still 40 per cent but by then the world was changing and new avenues of employment were opening up.[2]

Domestic service came as an opportunity for a youngster to earn a little money, which could either go to help her family or be set aside as future capital, and to be trained in a skill such as laundrywork or confectionery making. The wages for her year's service seem derisory in today's terms. However, servants were given their lodging, their food, a daily ration of beer and, later on, an allowance of tea and sugar. Some had their 'washing found' which meant their clothes were washed with the household's laundry. Some jobs had 'perks' attached, which were a further source of income, while others were in addition given a stated amount of oatmeal or similar goods. Many were taught their skills as they went along. The men were supplied with their livery, while the women might be given clothing appropriate for their work.

The number of servants employed tended to reflect the income and status of the householder. In the wealthiest establishments the servants' departments and hierarchies were clearly defined and the servants' work increasingly specialised. The men servants would be headed by the House Steward or, latterly, the Butler; under him came the Under-butler, the footmen, the porter at the door and other male workers such as the coal men. The kitchen department was headed by a Clerk to the Kitchen or, later, by the Cook who would be in charge of a staff increasingly made up of women. In the stables, the Coachman oversaw the grooms, stable boys, postilions and other workers. As to the women, the Housekeeper controlled the chambermaids, subsequently called housemaids, who swept and scrubbed and polished; the laundrymaids who spent their days washing, boiling, starching and ironing; and she supervised the work of the dairy where cream, butter and cheeses were prepared. She also had her own duties to carry out, especially those connected with the still-room where the jams and jellies, pickles and preserves, pastries, cakes and medicaments were made up. Over and above these domestic servants were those who were termed 'personal' servants, which included the lady's maid and the valet, the children's nurse and the governess.

More modest households might employ two or three female domestics and a man servant, usually a footman; while in the smaller households again any servant was likely to be a general-purpose helper and an extra pair of hands. It was this type of household that was most commonly found, according to the census returns between 1851 and 1871: of households with servants 34 per cent had only one servant and a further 25 per cent had two.[3]

The earlier servants had generally been far less specialised in their work. According to Lady Grisell Baillie's 'Derections', written in the 1740s, her housekeeper was to see 'the dairy maid, house maid and the kitchin maid' sit and spin of an evening or at other times 'when they are not otherways necessarily imployd which they will often pretend to be if they are not diligently lookt after and keep to it'.[4] The wide-ranging services anticipated by her contemporary, Mrs Purefroy, who lived in a comfortable style in Buckinghamshire and was seeking a new maid – yet again – were outlined in a letter:

> Edward Reefe tells mee that one Betty Hows of Torcester has a desire to serve me as a Cookmaid – if you [i.e., Betty] can roast & boyll & help clean an House, & make up Butter, & Milk 2 or 3 cows, but you go into the cowhouse to milk, which is near the house, and yᵉ Boy fetches up the Cows. Wee wash once a month, one day soap & another day yᵉ Buck [steeping in lye] & you help iron & get up yᵉ Cloaths. If you can do these things wee will endeavour to teach you yᵉ rest of the Cookery.
>
> Your freind [*sic*] to serve you E.P.[5]

The editor of the *Letters* added a footnote explaining that the girl duly entered the household on the 8th, took up her duties on the 10th, was mentioned for a couple of days and then vanished without trace.

This style of servant, able and willing to turn her hand to different categories of work, was common for much of the seventeenth century and well into the eighteenth. It was also the practice for the mistress of the household, apart from the grandest, to work alongside her maids, supervising them and teaching them at the same time. She kept an eye on their morals, taught them their Catechism, treated them as part of the family and was proud when they married well and set up house for themselves. Even in the 1790s Susanna Whatman was following this pattern as she obviously worried about domestic matters when away from home and corresponded in detail with her housekeeper about the servants and their work.

Increasingly, though, there was a separation between mistress and maids. As the years passed changing economic and social conditions led to an expansion of middle-class households and, as many of the proprietors had only recently achieved their status, servants were a means of reinforcing it. To ensure that the somewhat narrow divide between them was never breached the housewife held aloof from domestic life and harsher restrictions were imposed on her staff. It was at this point that the housekeeper came into her own. Originally someone who cared for an invalid or a widower, she gradually assumed the role of substitute housewife and became the top-ranking servant in the female hierarchy, dignified by the title of 'Mrs' whether married or not. At this level, she had generally been in service for some time and had worked her way up through the ranks, often becoming the trusted confidante and friend of her mistress.

The housekeeper is a figure to be met with in literature. Who could forget in Daphne du Maurier's *Rebecca* the fearsome Mrs Danvers of Manderley, whose allegiance to the hero's first wife is pivotal to the story? There was loyalty from servants, too. The story of *Lark Rise* has a portrait of Zilla, the devoted maid to Miss Lane, post mistress at Candleford Green and owner of the blacksmith's business. *Cranford*, too, recounts how Martha, to mitigate the disaster that had fallen upon Miss Matty on the failure of the local bank, baked a special pudding 'made in the most wonderful representation of a lion *couchant* that ever was moulded',[6] and, furthermore, persuaded her bashful 'follower' to marry her so that she could take Miss Matty into their home and look after her.

However, there is little need to look to literature when so many real-life examples are extant. Across the years the diaries of a Samuel Pepys, a Parson Woodforde or a Francis Kilvert include many references to domestic matters and from the domestic memoranda of the Verneys or the Yorkes, from a Lady Grisell Baillie or an Elizabeth Grant of Rothiemurchus much can be gleaned about servants and their activities.

From the records of the Yorke family at Erddig, near Wrexham, a picture emerges of servants such as Harriet Rogers who spent her life in their service. Her father was employed on the estate in various capacities – pig-boy, thatcher's assistant and slater – before going into the joiner's workshop and by the time he died aged ninety-four he had served the family for an amazing seventy-three years. His daughter Harriet devoted her life to the family, caring for them in one capacity or another. She followed her sister Eliza as nurse to the children, then for twelve years was personal maid to Mrs Yorke, cook-housekeeper for twenty and ultimately took on the less onerous duties of ladies' maid to the owner's unmarried sisters. Harriet spent some years in retirement near Wrexham and died in 1914.

A further example of a lifetime of domestic labour is that of Hannah Cullwick who was just eight years old when it began. She was generally employed in a humble capacity: to scrub front steps and kitchen passages, to carry coal and blacklead grates, to sweep and to polish. The records she later kept of her day-to-day activities were not intended for publication but were written to please the man she married in 1873 after a secret courtship lasting eighteen years, Arthur Munby, poet, solicitor and civil servant. Few people knew of the marriage and it was only after Munby himself died that the story became a *cause célèbre*. Because he so admired her as a housemaid and enjoyed watching her work, she flatly refused to become 'a lady' and take her place at his side, although in the early days of their courtship Munby himself acknowledged that she could easily have done so. A few years later, however, he said it was too late for such a change: she had grown incredibly strong through her working life (not a ladylike attribute) and her hands had coarsened irrevocably (equally unladylike). After they married Hannah acted as housekeeper in her husband's establishment, including in her care those renting their premises from him. When visitors came to see her husband she would slip away discreetly to her own rooms in the basement.

For whatever reasons, the marriage came adrift and Hannah left London for Shropshire and other localities; when Munby retired he left London for the delights of rural Surrey. After some years there was a reconciliation of sorts and he would travel to Shropshire from time to time, staying with Hannah in her cottage in Shifnal for short periods: she, though, never travelled to Surrey. She died in the summer of 1909 and his death occured a few months afterwards.

Such unconventional marriages had happened before and would happen again. In 1763 Thomas Coutts, later the sole partner of Coutts Bank, married his brother's maidservant and in due course their three daughters all 'married well'. As a widower he remarried, this time to Harriet Mellon, an actress, and after five years of widowhood Harriet remarried, thereby becoming Duchess of St Albans. On her death in 1837 she bequeathed the property and shares in the bank inherited from her first husband to a granddaughter of his first marriage, who added the name Coutts to her own name of Angela Burdett and became a celebrated philanthropist, peeress in her own right and the first woman to be a Freeman of the City of London.

Not all these marriages proved acceptable, though. Mrs Smith of Baltiboys, née Elizabeth Grant of Rothiemurcus and generally an example of great charity and goodness of heart, commented scornfully on one example in Irish politics: 'no Lord Chancellor – Sir Edward Sugden the most fitted by far would have been but for his wife, the follies of youth paid for most amply in mature age. She was his cook and bore him several children before he married her, of course not presentable and he is weak enough to wish to present her. I think there is a coarseness of mind in a man who could *marry*, entail as his companion for life, so inferior a person as one of Lady Sugden's degree must be.'[7] In fact, he went on to be appointed Lord Chancellor again later that same year.

A similar marriage that turned out well took place between the 71-year-old Sir Harry Fetherstonhaugh and the 20-year-old Mary Ann Bullock despite the fact that 'County' folk were reluctant to receive her and 'Society' laughed at his folly. The story goes that one day Sir Harry heard a girl singing in the Uppark dairy; after a while that same girl became the dairymaid. What happened next was handed down through succeeding generations of dairymaids: apparently, Sir Harry had appeared in the doorway and asked Mary Ann to marry him. Not surprisingly, she was rendered speechless so he suggested that, if she decided to accept him, she should cut a slice from the leg of mutton to be served at dinner. When the mutton arrived, the slice was cut. Contemporaries were scandalised at the misalliance but Sir Harry set about educating his wife-to-be, sending her to Paris to learn to read, write in an attractive style and do fashionable embroidery. Lady Fetherstonhaugh turned out to be kindly, capable and industrious. They took in and educated her little sister and established and built the school in Harting village. After twenty-four years of marriage Sir Harry died and his widow carried out many good works, restored Harting church and was remembered for her legendary generosity to her dependants each Christmas. When she died she bequeathed the house to her sister who adopted the name and arms of Fetherstonhaugh and continued to live there with Miss Sutherland, an illegitimate daughter of Sir Harry's, as her companion. In 1880 they took on as housekeeper a former maidservant who had married one of the gardeners and their son was H.G. Wells, the author.

A link between Uppark and a one-time domestic servant already existed. Sir Harry had taken Emma Hart, later Hamilton, into the house, although she was not employed as a domestic servant. That way of life had been left behind after she moved on to wider acclaim as a scantily clad participant in the various tableaux staged in Dr Graham's 'Temple of Health' in Pall Mall, London. She stayed at Uppark for almost a year, entertaining Sir Harry and his friends; she may indeed have danced naked on the dining-room table, as tradition says, but no evidence remains, either way. She left very suddenly, heavily pregnant, and had to petition a former lover for funds, but her questionable early years did not prevent her becoming the second wife of the British Minister to Naples and mistress to Admiral Lord Nelson thereafter.

Prostitution was very much a reality for any domestic servant without a job, and those who left their previous employers with no suitable reference were doubly insecure. Wages were minimal and few could save enough in the short term to tide them over unless family or friends took them in. One domestic servant who went willingly into prostitution to make money emerges from the diaries of Arthur Munby. When he had first come across her Sarah Tanner had been a maid-of-all-work but some years later when he met her again she was dressed quietly, 'as if she were an upper servant' he wrote. It transpired she had worked as a prostitute for three years and then sunk her savings into buying 'the Hampshire Coffee House, just across Waterloo Bridge'.[8] She managed it herself, she said, doing all the work that had to be done.

Servants mostly remain in the background and only become known to a wider audience on the publication of their employer's diaries, letters or other memorials such as wills. Nancy Lady Astor, Member of Parliament for Plymouth and the first woman to take her seat in the House of Commons, was looked after by her maid Rose; Angela Burdett-Coutts' companion was her former governess, Mrs Meredith; Jane Digby, that amazing personality and traveller, was accompanied for many years by her maid and chief organiser, Eugénie, whose death was keenly felt. A century earlier the two women nicknamed 'the Ladies of Llangollen' were accompanied on the flight from their parental homes by Mary Carryll, a maidservant, who stayed with this unconventional household for the rest of her days. Another century, another elopement, and Robert Browning thought it madness to set out with Elizabeth Barrett unless she took her maid Wilson to Italy with them. Loyalty could be found in conventional circumstances too: Lady Grisell Baillie might have found some of her servants troublesome but her daughters' governess May Menzies was appointed in 1705 and was still with the family some forty-five years later.

Other servants are remembered because employers, at no matter what social level, registered their gratitude on a memorial plaque or gravestone. Some epitaphs give only brief details of name, age at death and length of time in service, while others contain far greater detail:

> To the Glory of God and the Blessed Memory of Elizabeth Painter for 55 years a friend and servant in the family of the Hon. and Rev. Gerard Noel. She died Dec. 15th 1859 Aged 94 Years.
> Charlotte Rosine Sander died 11th December 1813 aged 56, faithful servant to the Princess of Wales. She left Brunswick with Her Royal Highness and was with her for 19 years.
> Mary Nye, aged 61, 38 years in the family, as Nurse then Housekeeper.

Housekeepers, cooks, chambermaids, much-loved nurses and innumerable 'servants' were all commemorated by adjectives such as faithful, honourable, devoted, trusted, of great worth, valued, beloved and many expressions of a sense of loss. Some memorials briefly refer to 'housekeeper at the Priory', 'a most excellent worthy servant', 'a faithful servant and devoted friend', 'the affectionate and deeply lamented servant' or 'a useful and honourable life'. Other headstones, though, might be graced with a verse or two, such as these inscribed in memory of

Sarah Williams who died in 1855 aged eighty-five, after sixty years of service to one man and his wife:

> Beneath, a faithful Servant lies,
> For this on earth was she,
> Her Soul is now above the skies
> Where dwells fidelity.
> Oh Mortal Reader whatso'er
> Thy lot in Life may be,
> Be thou a faithfull follower,
> Of Him who died for thee.[9]

The Yorke family at Erddig commemorated their servants in a manner unusual for the age: the servants' portraits were painted and hung in the house and lines of verse composed to reflect their particular qualities. Whichever form such memorials took they are a record to the many domestic servants who spent their lives in the service of others, using the skills they had perfected over the years. What happened to the ones who did not stay in domestic service for their whole lives? What sort of career could be based on knowledge of such everyday domestic matters as were required in the care of the home?

Mrs Raffald was a woman of formidable energy and a wealth of experience. After her marriage and departure from Arley Hall in Cheshire she set up a Registry for Domestic Servants, the first the town had known, in addition to her other numerous food-related activities in Manchester. Mrs Raffald advertised that she charged 1*s* (5p) for supplying servants of whatever sort and could supply them at short notice; servants wanting a job should also apply to her but she would only take on those with a good reference. It would be possible to interpret the Registry Office as a blow for feminism since a woman out of a job or denied a fair reference was very vulnerable and prostitution one of the few alternatives to starvation. However, Mrs Raffald was probably just taking the existing situation one step further. Before this, local shopkeepers were often approached by the Mrs Purefroys of the world in need of a servant or else the hopeful employer asked around among friends; servants wanting a change would attend the local fair and stand in line with others, each holding an implement to denote their trade – a broom for a housemaid and so on. A central venue where both sides could make enquiries would seem logical.

Not a means of obtaining servants but of knowing precisely what to expect of them was the objective of Mr and Mrs Adams's book, aimed at the less-experienced housewife. In their own careers they personify the professional servant. Sarah started out as the lowly maid-of-all-work, progressed through housemaid, laundrymaid, undercook, housekeeper and lady's maid and ended up 'as housekeeper in a very large establishment'. Her husband, meanwhile, 'had entered service as a footboy' and was successively groom, footman, valet, butler and, reaching the top of his profession, 'House Steward'. In 1825 they claimed to have been 'Fifty years Servants in different Families'.[10] So, if Samuel was correct when he said he had started in 1770 and Sarah accurate in saying she had finished her career by spending twenty years as a housekeeper after a string of other appointments, it would seem that they had clocked up no less than fifty years apiece.

The Complete Servant was published in 1825 and the Adams described it as being 'a Practical Guide to the Peculiar [i.e., individual] Duties and Business of all Descriptions of Servants, from the Housekeeper to the Servant of All-Work, and from the Land Steward to the Foot Boy'. They start with suggestions regarding the number of servants to be employed relative to the family income, then turn to 'Hints to the Mistress: Firstly, the attention due to her husband and children . . . to make home, "sweet home" the pleasing refuge of a husband, fatigued, perhaps, by his intercourse with a jarring world, – to be his enlightened companion, and the chosen friend of his bosom'. The housewife is then advised as to her relationship with her servants; how she should 'be firm without being severe and kind without being familiar . . . be consistent and reasonable . . . praise and reward them when you can'.[11] After that the servants are counselled on their general behaviour with an emphasis on the need for total honesty, fidelity and industry. Only then was each servant's duties, wages and any 'perks' outlined and recipes relevant to their work given. Thus, the housekeeper received hints on the storage of various commodities, while the scullerymaid was instructed in the cleaning of pewter pots and the lady's maid on making up 'A grape lotion for the sunburn'.

The Adams's volume had been foreshadowed by Hannah Glasse, of cookbook fame, whose manual on domestic servants was published in 1760, although she limited herself to the female staff, 'the chamber-maid, nurserymaid, housemaid, laundrymaid, scullion or undercook and housekeeper' and claimed to have explained their duties 'fully and distinctly'. The books were similar in format but Glasse's *The Servants' Directory* provided greater detail about the work expected of each servant and methods to accomplish the multiplicity of tasks. Mrs Glasse also gave many recipes for making up cleaning fluids for particular problems.

Both before and after these two publications came a plethora of authors expounding on similar themes, either exhorting the housewife to accept the serious nature of her calling or preaching to the servants on their (Christian) duties and the dignity of service. Some adopted a practical approach while others read like an extended sermon. The writers came from assorted backgrounds and among them could be found the novelist, political economist, teacher, journalist; the Countess, dramatist, 'lady', mistress of the household and, indeed, the domestic servant. However, most were overshadowed by Mrs Beeton's *Book of Household Management* of 1861. Although primarily considered as a cookery book, it also provided information on servants, their work and related matters.

Although these authors were dealing with the broader picture of domestic management, others were writing on specific subjects such as furnishing the home, cleaning it, thrifty housekeeping, etiquette or household hygiene, often in connection with courses taught at various schools of domestic economy being established up and down the country. Miss F.B. Jack was Principal of Edinburgh's School of Domestic Arts and a prolific author on the topic of cookery, laundry work and housekeeping in general. Her manual on *The Art of Laundrywork*, 'Practically Demonstrated for use in Homes and Schools', proved popular and continued in print for some twenty-five years after its first publication in 1896. In Liverpool Margaret Rankin was Head Teacher in Laundrywork at the Technical College of Domestic Science and highly qualified in most branches of the domestic arts: *A Manual of the Science of Laundry Work for Students and Teachers* stressed the scientific aspects involved and included details on the chemical composition of soap, borax, bleaches, starch and similar substances. The book proved extremely popular, swiftly going through numerous editions. These are just two examples of a wide-ranging genre; many others could be mentioned such as Louise Wetenhall's *Laundry-Work Note Book* of 1925 with its illustrations and photographs depicting electric and flat irons and how to starch, pleat and fold items correctly.

Many women earned a living from laundering, either by going out to different households or, latterly, into the commercial laundries being established in all the major cities, university towns and seaports. In 1861 a survey found that of the 167,607 laundry workers 99 per cent were female and that it came eleventh in the table of principal occupations in England and Wales.[12] For households without their own laundrymaids it was sufficient for one or two women to go in once a month or so to tackle the accumulation. It was customary to save up the washing for several weeks as to do it more frequently argued an inadequate supply of clothing and table linen; it was only in Victorian days that a once-a-week routine became commonplace. Late in the eighteenth century Parson Woodeford's household 'washed' every six weeks or so, whereas fifty years earlier Lady Grisell Baillie was unusual for the time in following a three-week routine.[13]

The housewife preferred the laundry work to be done on the premises so that she could keep an eye on what was going on; the washerwoman would work for a day, or however long it took, and would be given her meals as well as payment. In some areas it was more usual for the dirty clothing to be taken away to be dealt with in the washerwoman's own home. Other women set themselves up with a mangle and advertised their services – it was hard work but required little capital to start up and fitted in with their own domestic commitments. Increasingly, from the 1860s onwards, laundry work became industrialised and centralised. In Brighton's Black Rock district Lucy Mills and her daughter established a laundering business in a basement in 1850 which continued as a family concern well past its centenary; in its heyday there were 5 receiving shops and a staff of 180.

Laundry work generally involved the use of heavy machinery, steam and boiling water, chemicals and a range of hazardous components and required a number of workers to be gathered under one roof. This gave it a status similar to other service industries which, by the 1890s, saw the start of legislation to regulate health and safety, working hours and wages. The campaigns to improve women's working conditions were bound up with employment opportunities, welfare matters and the suffrage movement and will be looked at again in Chapter Fourteen.

It was not only women engaged in investigative research who wrote, nor those producing manuals on domestic subjects for use in home or school: the servants themselves also began to tread the literary path. The books of Mr and Mrs Adams and Hannah Woolley have already been noted and former housekeepers Anne Barker, Mary Johnson and Isabella Moore also published their thoughts on domestic service.

Several memoirs purporting to be by men servants appeared over the years but relatively few by women servants, until domestic service as a career began to decline. Rose Allen published her autobiography in 1847 but Jean Rennie and Margaret Powell, for example, were not writing until midway through the twentieth century when their experiences of domestic service were woven into entertaining tales. Monica Dickens, too, gave a semi-biographical account of her life as cook-housekeeper in the 1930s and recorded a lifestyle that even then was considered somewhat quaint.

E.M. Parker was unusual for her time in that her book was not a reflection of her working life but a romantic novel. A case of wishful thinking, maybe? Sufficient examples existed, as already noted, of an employer or an aristocrat marrying a pretty young serving-maid to fuel the dreams of a host of such girls. Arthur Munby recorded one day in 1872 how he saw in a shop window near Charing Cross a novel advertised as being by 'E.M. Parker, a domestic servant'; intrigued, he went in and was told she was the 23-year-old daughter of a village innkeeper in Buckinghamshire, and she was indeed employed in a household in St James's Place but was reluctant to reveal her identity lest it upset her employers. Munby went to see her and found her eminently 'respectable and quiet' and so he bought a copy of her book. The chapter headings tell the story, working its way through 'Mr Fairlie's Bereavement . . . Harold becomes an Orphan . . . Hopes and Fears . . . Gertrude's Trouble . . . First Love . . . Sad Tidings . . . An Eventful Morning . . . Separation' and concluding with the anticipated 'Wedding Bells, Welcome Home, Joy and Peace'.[14] She had published the novel at her own expense and the bookseller was pleased with the way it was selling. In Munby's opinion, it was the first time a domestic servant had published a novel.

In the eighteenth century some women who pursued domestic trades also displayed literary talent. Anne Yearsley (1752–1806) was a milkwoman who carried milk from door to door, as had her mother who had taught her to read. Despite being the wife of a labourer and caring for her children she wrote verses, some of which were published in newspapers in the Bristol area. She also turned her hand to a four-volume novel, a historical tragedy and opened a circulating library in Bristol Hot Wells. Mary Whateley (1738–1826), a farmer's daughter from Worcestershire, was contributing poems to the *Gentleman's Magazine* at the age of twenty-one and exciting much attention. Some years later when she was acting as housekeeper to her brother in Walsall, Staffordshire, her poems were printed by public subscription and many years later a second collection of verses was also published by these means. Elizabeth Hands (fl. 1789) was counted a valued servant to one family, prior to her marriage to a blacksmith. Verses of hers had appeared in the *Coventry Mercury* under the name of 'Daphne' but a later work attracted sufficient admiration to be thought worthy of a public subscription. Mary Leapor (1722–46) was the daughter of a gardener and nurseryman near Brackley and although she learnt to read and write, her mother discouraged her attempts at poetry. After her mother's death she kept house for her father, although she was for a while cook-maid in a nearby gentleman's residence where, predictably, she is said to have spent her time writing while ignoring her kitchen duties. Her verses circulated in the neighbourhood and an admirer sent her play and some verse to London but then Fate took a hand and Mary died of measles, still only twenty-four. Although much of their poetry follows the fashion for classical allusion and difficult-to-follow references to contemporary personages, the opening lines of Mary Leapor's 'Essay on Woman' have a more direct appeal to modern-day tastes, summing up women's rather helpless status at that time.

Woman, a pleasing but a short-lived flower,
Too soft for business and too weak for power;
A wife in bondage, or neglected maid;
Despised, if ugly; if she's fair, betrayed.
Tis wealth alone inspires every grace,
And calls the raptures to her plenteous face . . .[15]

After leaving domestic service, servants of both sexes entered a wide variety of employment but, for married couples, the most popular was that of inn or tavern keeper. According to one authority they did so because they lacked the training and expertise required for entry into other occupations whereas a more charitable viewpoint accepted that the skills acquired and honed as domestic servants were ideal for the keeping of a hostelry. In 1797 a review of a survey regarding public houses called attention to the popularity of the job among former servants:

When we consider who are the sort of persons who occupy public houses of every sort, from the best inn on the Bath road to the lowest small-beer pot house, or hedge ale-house, they are servants of all descriptions; the butler and the housekeeper, the footman and the lady's maid, the coachman and the cook, the gardener and the dairy-maid, the groom, or stable boy, with the nursery-maid, or kitchen-maid, the carter and the plough-boy with maid-servants of their own rank, whether they have acquired an independent competency by cheating their masters and mistresses, or by long and faithful service, all direct to their settlement for life to a public house.'[16]

It was a career taken up by Rosa Lewis, Kate Cranston and many others proficient in culinary matters, as noted in Chapter Two. As for former servants, one of the leading hotels in London was started in the 1840s on the savings of a retired butler and his wife and to this day it attracts the rich and the royal – the couple's name? Mr and Mrs William Claridge. Not far away is the Hyde Park Hotel where a young Irish girl arrived to work in 1916, married the cellarman and worked there for sixty-one years; royalty were entertained in her still-room. At about the same time the second parlourmaid at Appleby Castle married the son of the town's mayor and together they bought a large hotel and ran it most successfully thereafter.

Numerous examples of inns and similar establishments run by former servants can be cited. Mrs Robotham had been a servant of the Purefroy's until she married the licensee of the King's Head Tavern, Islington, and they both carried out assorted commissions on behalf of her erstwhile employer. In the same way Ann Cook (fl. 1754–60), on leaving domestic service, became the wife of an innkeeper in first Morpeth, then Hexham and latterly in Newcastle upon Tyne where, in due course, her married daughter became involved in the trade. When Mrs Cook fell on hard times she proposed setting up a pastry cook shop which would also sell a range of drinks. A shop selling cooked meats and confectionery had been opened in Manchester by Elizabeth Raffald (1733–81), the former housekeeper married to a gardener, but she was in addition the licensee of the Bull's Head in the town and of the King's Head, Salford.

CHAPTER FIVE

A Patchwork of Careers

I have always had a strong persuasion that the greater part of the
sewing done in the world will ere long be done by machinery. It
appears much more easy than many things that are done by
machinery now; and when it is considered how many minute stitches
go to the making of a garment, it seems strange that some less
laborious and slow method of making joins and edges has not been
invented before this.[1]

In fact, Harriet Martineau was slightly behind the times in 1849. The first
sewing machine had already been patented in the USA by Elias Howe,
although it was to be another decade or so before Isaac Singer produced
a practical domestic model. Until that time, though, it is hard to believe
how much hand sewing used to be commonplace. For one thing a skill in
needlework was expected of every woman; it was a basic necessity of life
in the home. For those higher up the social ladder it formed a part of the
girl's education and, with the more decorative forms of embroidery, it
took on the lustre of an accomplishment which was not only a ladylike
occupation to fill the hours but had end results visible to friends in the
same way as a talent for music or drawing. Such was the emphasis put
on the skill that women had their portraits painted while engaged in
the latest and most fashionable form of stitchery. Mrs Warren and
Mrs Pullen's *Treasures in Needlework* starts with 'Instructions in Tatting' and
the section opens with the phrase: 'This art (which is among the best
adapted for showing to advantage a pretty hand) . . .'.[2] The increasing
use of the domestic sewing machine from the 1860s onwards prolonged
the practice of home dressmaking, as did the 'make do and mend'
philosophy of the Second World War when clothes were not only scarce
but rationed and 'on coupons'. Outside the home legions of women were
engaged in the manufacture of threads and fabrics, working in the mills
that were springing up as a consequence of the Industrial Revolution and
women without number were engaged in dressmaking and allied trades.

In every home there was an abundance of plain sewing to be done, as
in the hemming of sheets, tablecloths, napkins, drying cloths and so on
as well as in the making up of basic clothing, with shirts and under
garments being smocked at yoke and cuffs to ensure a better fit. In
addition there was the mending, altering and making over of garments

that had seen better days or were now required for a different purpose. There was also needlework which was generally more decorative than purposeful and required greater skill and dexterity. The familiar Victorian picture sampler had its origins at least two centuries earlier when girls worked a strip of fabric with stitches and motifs as a sample which would be of use to her in future years; later on, printed pattern books would give this information but the sampler continued to be worked to a stylised design, becoming a benchmark in a girl's education. The whitework sampler, using white thread on a plain linen ground, ultimately led to forms such as 'Ayrshire lace' and broderie anglaise. As if that was not enough, women also spent a great number of hours on knitting, crocheting and doing patchwork and quilting, as well as other ways of making items for the home.

In the earlier part of the period, it was not only the stitching of the fabric that was done at home but also the spinning of the thread to make up the cloth. Lady Grisell Baillie's maids, regardless of designation, were expected to spin of an evening or at any other time when they were free, as noted previously. When Mrs Purefroy wrote about a new maid and outlined her myriad duties she firmly said 'and when she has done her worke she sits down to spin'.[3] On the farms the maids often helped with shearing the sheep, washing the fleeces and the other processes that followed: the dying, the carding and so on prior to the actual spinning. Many years before, Gervase Markham had described 'the ordering of Wooll, Hempe, Flax, making Cloth, and Dying'[4] as one of the housewife's normal duties.

The home-spun yarn was sent off to a weaver who would return the finished cloth, woven according to the different qualities of thread provided, and it would then be made up in the house as required. The plain stitching would be done by any maid who was clever with her needle or by the housekeeper, who would monogram and date the items according to the household's practice. Larger establishments requiring vast amounts of linen and blankets of varying quality for beds in the house, whether for family, guests or servants, and copious supplies of table linen for all those eating in the house might well find it necessary to employ professional sewing women to do all the work. When Lady Grisell's household was in London, her accounts reveal a payment: 'To Babie Robison for sowing [*sic*] at half a crown a week £1.12sh.3d.'[5] A woman to wash and scour earned 1s a day (5p), a housemaid £4 per year and cooks between £6 and £8.

One rather specialised sewing woman found in wealthier homes was the lady's maid. In the previous chapter the focus of attention fell on the domestic servants yet there was a further category that comprised personal servants – in the sense they had greater contact with their employer and were engaged by him or her, rather than by the house steward or housekeeper. As well as the lady's maid there was the nurse, the governess and, on the male side, the valet.

The job description of the lady's maid was straightforward: 'It will be her business to dress, re-dress, and undress her lady . . . Her's will be the care of her lady's wardrobe, and she should make that her particular care; appropriating to each article of dress its proper place, where it always may be found when wanted. It will be her business carefully to examine every part of her dress, when taken off, and if they have sustained an injury, or acquired any spots or stains, immediately to clean and repair them; then fold them up neatly, and put them away.'[6]

A proficiency in needlework was one of the essentials for the job, allied to specialist skills in washing and ironing the finer items, a knowledge of how to pack garments for travelling and and how best to store them when not required for immediate use. It was also desirable if she was educated to a reasonable standard so that she could read aloud to her employer or converse on matters of the day and if she had 'a soft and courteous demeanour'.[7] By that stage, the job was shading into that of 'companion'; old Lady Osborne, née Penelope Verney, wrote that, at the end of the day's activities, the evenings seemed so long: 'Had God blest me with a Dau[r] [i.e., daughter] I had not kept a maid.'[8]

When not actively engaged with her employer the lady's maid occupied herself with her needle to the benefit of her mistress. She not only carried out minor repairs but made up new garments and altered clothing, hats and accessories to accord with current fashion. Alternatively, she spent her time 'in the various occupations of getting up the fine linen, gauzes, muslins, cambrics, laces &c., washing silk stockings, taking the spots and stains out of silks &c.'[9]

Hannah Glasse in a previous era had spelt out similar duties for the mistress's female attendant, in this instance called the chambermaid. She provided this individual with plenty of appropriate 'receipts', suggesting ingredients such as sal ammoniac, spirits of turpentine, lemon juice or warmed bran to lift stains from assorted materials, or talc dampened with spirits of wine to clean gold or silver lace. The correct methods of washing fine fabrics and the making up of starches for various purposes were also detailed. Helpful cosmetics – or cures, the dividing line is a fine one – were provided: 'For chapped Hands', 'For tender Feet', 'The best Wash to make the Skin smooth and fair'. A method of blackening the hair suggested using either elderberries boiled in wine; otherwise 'Combing the hair with a black-lead* Comb will make the Hair black, but then it comes off on the Linen prodigiously'.[10]

---

* A polish used on grates and kitchen ranges.

According to Hannah Woolley, who was writing almost a century earlier than Mrs Glasse: 'All sorts of needlework and plain work' were in the chambermaid's remit, which also covered many culinary skills including pastry making and the dressing of meat 'to make sauces both for fish and flesh, to garnish dishes, to make all sorts of pickles' and to supervise generally the way the food was served at table.[11] She was also responsible for the marketing and buying in of provisions and she could expect to be promoted to the rank of housekeeper if she did well in all branches of her work.

Despite the stress put on needlework, not all chambermaids were gifted with sewing skills, such as the two employed by the new Lady Verney in the 1640s. Her husband Sir Ralph, discussing the wages for her two maidservants Luce and Bess, wrote: 'You say chamber-maides will have 4 or 5 pounds wages and neither wash, nor starch; that is to say they will doo nothing but dresse you, for I doo not valew theire needle work at a groat a moneth.'[12] Luce may have lacked needlework skills but she had other attributes probably more important in the circumstances in which she found herself. Nor were all of their mistresses willing needleworkers either: Ann Fanshawe (1627–79) recalled how she had been a 'hoyting girl' (i.e., a hoyden).[13] Margaret, Duchess of Newcastle, was chided by her neighbours for the idleness of her maids and so called for flax and wheels to be brought 'for I with my maids would sit and spin'.[14] However, her gentlewoman laughed her out of such a scheme, knowing full well her ignorance of such matters, and the Duchess' plans to make silk flowers and sweetmeats met with the same discouragement and for the same reason.

Anyone with a proficiency in sewing and a reasonable education could look to be employed as a lady's maid, although it must have been an uphill struggle for someone not blessed with the correct temperament. Whatever the period, those writing on the subject were apt to hold similar views: 'In fine, her character should be remarkable for industry and moderation, – her manners and deportment, for modesty and humility – and her dress, for neatness, simplicity and frugality.'[15]

Such attendants, be they waiting women, chambermaids or lady's maids, used their sewing skills to assist their employer in their more ambitious needlework projects. In about 1717 Lady Julia Calverleigh stitched no less than ten panels in tent stitch using silk and wool which were set into the walls at Wallington, Northumberland, in 1755. It is known that the work took just three years to complete so it is assumed some teamwork was involved. Maybe Lady Julia was following the example given to a previous generation by Queen Mary, wife to Dutch William. She was a noted needlewoman and set to work to decorate Hampton Court Palace, their preferred residence, and again the scale is such to suggest a team effort. According to Celia Fiennes: 'The hangings,

Chaires, Stooles and Screen the same, all of satten stitch done in worsteads, beasts, birds, jmages and fruitts all wrought very ffinely by Queen Mary and her maids of honour.'[16] By contrast at Manderston, near Kelso, a set of four chairs with the most beautiful embroidery on corded silk were worked by the owner's wife during the Second World War.

The most skilful needlework of every description is today often displayed at houses open to the public. Mary Linwood, composer as well as artist, was winning high praise for imitating artistic works in worsted embroidery 200 years ago; her 'needlework pictures' were displayed in London and other major towns. Early in the twentieth century, lace worked by the daughter of the 7th Duke of Atholl was so exquisite that the Victoria and Albert Museum considered it to be the finest modern embroidery in Britain. Around Blair Castle are many other hand-stitched chair covers, pole screens, fire screens and similar pieces, worked by the ladies of the household over the centuries and there is also a fine four-poster bed with embroidered hangings in seventeenth-century style. They came to the Castle through the marriage of a daughter of the 7th Earl of Derby and the bed curtains were worked, apparently, by the girl's mother 'while beseiged in Lathom House during the Civil War'. An intriguing story and worth investigating.

A contemporary authority describes the drama. The Earl of Derby was called away to defend the Isle of Man for King Charles I 'and went accordingly, having first made some provisions of men, money and ammunition for the protection and defence of his incomparable Lady, at Lathom, to whose charge he committed his Children, House and his other English concerns'. The story continues: 'She being therefore thus left in that House, the enemy looked upon it as their own.' As well they might, in the circumstances. The men left for her defence were inexperienced so for training purposes they were put into divisions under their captains but Lady Derby maintained direct authority over all. She refused all requests to surrender being, as she put it, 'under a double Trust – of Faith in her Husband and Allegiance to her Sovereign'.[17] Lengthy descriptions follow of various sorties made against the beseigers, the attacks upon Lathom House, the defiant messages sent back by the Countess to the Parliamentarian commander, the number of attackers slain and other military details. Amazingly, while Lady Derby was directing all this derring-do and military activity she supposedly found the time to stitch away at the bed hangings that in due course found their way to Blair Castle!

Prince Rupert himself rode to the rescue with Lord Derby and they defeated the beseigers in a pitched battle; the captured colours were sent to Lathom and the Countess then left with the two daughters who had been with her throughout the four months. The house was refortified, the siege continued another two years and the defenders only gave up on the direct orders of the King himself. The attackers lost over 6,000 men while the garrison lost just 400. There was no happy ending to the story. Lord Derby was captured after the Battle of Worcester and executed, in defiance of all the laws governing contemporary warfare; the Countess and her children then endured imprisonment and poverty until the Restoration.

It is unrealistic to assume that Lady Derby's skills in embroidery had much bearing on the way she conducted the siege of Lathom House. Rather the reverse: perhaps she found it a soothing exercise and a way of keeping her mind occupied while the walls of her home were being blasted by the great mortar and her men killed or maimed. Throughout the ages women have found needlework a satisfying way to pass the time, as well as rewarding to do and a way of expressing their creativity. Gertrude Jekyll is nowadays best remembered for her gardening interests and her partnership with the architect Edwin Lutyens. However, her earliest training was as a painter, before turning to the applied arts and becoming highly skilled in the working of brass and copper, in wood carving and, most especially, in embroidery. It was only when her eyesight began to fail that she gave up embroidering the flowers she loved for planting the genuine article and designing the garden as well. Many have commented on the relationship between needlework and horticulture and floral motifs have always been popular as a form of decoration within the home.

For countless other women needlework has been more an obligation than an therapeutic exercise. The housewives of *Lark Rise* were thrifty out of necessity and used every scrap of clothing that came their way: 'These were worn and altered and dyed and turned and ultimately patched and darned as long as the threads hung together.'[18] Their contemporaries across the Welsh border had a reputation for being not only thrifty but industrious too: 'When not engaged in household work,' it was said, 'they devote their time to knitting, sewing and repairing, and sometimes to patchwork, in which they are generally adepts. The patchwork counterpanes are most neatly made, and quilted in fanciful designs.'[19] As further proof of their industriousness Welshwomen would walk and knit simultaneously, as they went to and fro fetching the water, balancing the water pot upon their head. Catherine Sinclair noticed a similar activity in Shetland where the women knitted while carrying home heavy loads of peats or seaweed in creels on their backs.

Patchwork, it is said, was born of poverty and a cold climate. Patchwork quilts are now regarded as things of beauty in their own right but they started out as a means of making use of every last scrap of material in order to produce something of worth from not very much. Heavier fabrics from worn-out clothing were torn into narrow strips and woven into a hessian backing with a special tool, resulting in 'hooked' or 'prodded' rugs of simple patterns, often bordered in black. In front of the hearth or set in a doorway they added a splash of colour on a stone floor and curtailed the draughts.

These activities generally benefited the home or those who lived there. There were many other households, though, where nimble fingers contributed to the family income. In certain parts of the country, such as Yorkshire, everybody knitted, the men as well as the women. A woman in Cotterdale was accustomed to knit while walking the 3 miles to her local market each week, carrying on her head the past week's output of items knitted by her family. While selling her goods she went on knitting and returned home, still knitting, having on her head a supply of worsted for the following week's labour as well as her marketing. 'She was so expeditious and so expert', continued the story, 'that the produce of the day's labour was generally a complete pair of men's stockings.'[20]

Esther Hewlett, a writer on domestic matters, agreed with knitting as a means of providing for the cottager's family, since it needed only a penny or so to get started with needles and wool, could be taken up in any spare moment and done indoors while caring for children or outdoors while walking and that the stockings so knitted by the cottager's wife 'are worth at least three pair of the best wove ones that you can buy. . . . A good knitter, too,' she continued, 'may generally get employment if she chooses to take it in. And if the scraps of time add but sixpence to her weekly income, it is not to be despised.' Needlework she thought uneconomic, although it was better than being idle and did not wear out clothes in the way more laborious work did. Lace-making she accounted a hazard to the health of all involved: 'The poor women who live by it look like walking spectres'[21] since a woman and her daughters would toil over their pillows from dawn to dusk with no time to eat and would earn a mere pittance for so doing. The poor opinion on needlework was still evident at the end of the century, as illustrated in this extract from a contemporary report: 'Needlework is quite a typical woman's trade, and there is no doubt that crowds of women follow it, for in the census of 1881 the number of needle-women returned for Great Britain was 640,000, and since that time the numbers are believed to have largely increased.' The article continues: 'Yet it is very badly paid, and there is no doubt that the vast majority of these workers are struggling with misery and want'.[22]

However, innumerable women did contribute to the family income in various ways by their sewing skills. Tambour work was introduced in about the 1760s and was so called on account of the muslin fabric being stretched taut over a tambour, or drum, while it was worked. It began as a fashionable form of needlework but in time became a popular means of decorating wedding capes and shawls, as well as frills and flounces on undergarments, petticoats and so on. By the 1830s it was turning into an industry around the Essex village of Coggleshall, from which it derived its name of Coggleshall lace, and at its peak as many as 400 women outworkers were engaged in the production of this 'English whitework' (white embroidery on white muslin). The designs were almost always floral and carried out in chain stitch worked with a hooked tool and a continuous cotton thread.

In south-west Scotland an entire industry developed around 'whitework' which was in demand as a substitute for lace during the protracted years of the wars with France. The trade gathered momentum when a refugee from northern Italy arrived in Edinburgh and received a grant from the Board of Trustees for Fisheries and Manufactures to employ a number of young girls in order to teach them the methods of stitching 'Dresden work' and tambouring. The original range of designs and patterns were extended and the fine linen fabrics that proved difficult to produce locally were replaced with the finest cotton muslins then being achieved by Scottish handloom weavers. Tambour workshops were set up throughout the area and girls worked on a daily basis, earning in a week about a quarter of the wages of a skilled weaver. In the 1790s the parish minister of Ayr wrote: 'Of late there are many female children happily engaged in the tambouring business', while his colleague in Paisley said: 'Young women, who were formerly put to the spinning wheel, now learn to flower muslin'.[23]

By the 1820s fashions in dress had moved on and the popularity of tambour work waned. A new type of embroidery was developed, on a muslin ground that was finer but firmer, and it was called 'sewed muslin' to distinguish it from tamboured work. It owed its existence to the energies of a Mrs Jamieson, wife of an Ayrshire manufacturer's agent whose job it was to distribute the cotton yarn to the weavers and collect the finished cloth. Mrs Jamieson was lent a baby's robe with lace inserts and satin-stitch embroidery which was thought to have originated in France. She analysed the stitches, taught them to some skilled needlewomen and established a new industry. At its height she controlled a thousand outworkers who did the sewing in their own homes and were paid by the piece. The designs, though, were drawn professionally in Glasgow, transferred on to wooden blocks and then stamped on to the muslin using water-soluble dyes. It became known as Ayrshire embroidery and was notable for the great variety in the needlemade lace fillings worked into the spaces. Although many articles of dress were stitched in this way, it is generally thought of today in connection with old-fashioned baby clothes. For thirty years the business flourished and Mrs Jamieson was joined by her two daughters.

There were many imitators and work of this type was also done in Ireland, introduced there to alleviate the suffering that followed the 1848 potato famine and it engaged some 300,000 women in sewed muslin work and 20,000 in making the indigenous lace.[24] By the 1860s the trade was in decline everywhere as a result of the American Civil War, changes in fashion and machine-embroidered whitework being imported from Switzerland. To earn themselves a penny or two, the remaining sewed muslin workers stitched the simpler broderie anglaise that was used on collars and flounces for petticoats.

A grounding in practical needlework and a knowledge of clothing and fashion made it possible for women to move on to related fields. As happened with domestic servants, not all who began life as seamstresses continued in that field for ever. Mary Wollstonecraft supported herself as a seamstress for a while before turning to teaching, acting as governess, writing in various genres and blazing a trail for feminism. Hertha Ayrton (born Sarah Marks) first earned her living by needlework and teaching prior to becoming an early entrant to Girton College to read Mathematics and a career thereafter as physicist, suffragette and inventor.

The example of the lady's maid and her sewing skills has already been discussed. For a few years Queen Victoria employed a young German woman as one of her dressers and the letters she wrote to friends and family back home have subsequently been edited and published. Although they concentrate more on the sights and scenes of contemporary life – in London, on the Isle of Wight, in the Highlands of Scotland and elsewhere – a flavour of the job itself can still be gathered. For many years Nancy, Lady Astor, had a maid called Rose who wrote the story of her life in service. When she decided to become a lady's maid extra care was taken with her education. After various jobs she became the 'Young Lady's Maid' at Cliveden and was then promoted to serving Lady Astor herself. The stories these women tell echo the details found in the pages of Mr and Mrs Adams, of Hannah Glasse and of Hannah Woolley as well: across the centuries the job appears to have changed little.

Some women became famous for their embroidery and the skills associated with it. Gertrude Jekyll in her craftwork was greatly influenced by the work of William Morris and his circle. Morris' wife Jane had modelled for the Pre-Raphaelite artists before her marriage and became a skilled embroiderer and designer, although much of her time was spent in working for her husband's company. Their daughter, too, was a significant embroiderer and took it up professionally.

During the same period the Glasgow School of Art was revolutionising the concept of embroidery and the little ditty about 'Those who can, do; and those who can't, teach' was singularly inappropriate; here, the doers and the teachers were one and the same. Jessie Newbery, wife of the then

Principal, introduced a class in embroidery for the full-time students at the school in 1894. She was an extremely gifted needlewoman and her artistic precepts were in line with those emanating from the school where students of the calibre of Charles Rennie Mackintosh and his wife Margaret Macdonald, her younger sister Frances and the man she married, Herbert MacNair, had trained. Under Mrs Newbery's tuition a recognisable Glasgow style evolved incorporating appliqué work with simple stylised flowers and leaves outlined in silk stitching; she was fond of adding lettering to her work. She also brought in a technique of 'needle-weaving' where threads are pulled out of the fabric and the resulting edges stitched with coloured silks to make a border. As part of their training her students were taught to cut out, sew and decorate clothes and she had decided ideas on what was suitable – preferring warm but lightweight materials and a natural shape.

Several students from the Glasgow School became noted embroiderers. Frances Macdonald assisted Mrs Newbery in her teaching while her sister Margaret developed her own distinctive styles as an integral part of the interiors designed by her husband. When Jessie Newbery retired her place was taken by a former student, Ann Macbeth. She in turn promoted an entirely new concept of teaching needlework to schoolchildren which replaced the fine hemming and the cross-stitch samplers still being taught. In her method each lesson saw the completion of an article in which decoration and construction went hand in hand. Her theories were embodied in her book *Educational Needlecraft*, published in 1911. As well as her teaching and writing she designed embroideries for Liberty's of London and fabrics for Donald Brothers of Dundee. Under successive (female) Heads the Department continued to flourish and to expand the repertoire of skills taught.

The teaching of needlework goes back across the centuries: street directories for any town of consequence generally contain the names of individual teachers or of schools where sewing was taught. The introduction of classes in needlework, dressmaking and laundrywork, followed by housewifery, millinery and tailoring at what, for twenty years, had been the National Training School of Cookery led to its name being extended to include the words 'and Other Branches of Domestic Economy'.[25]

Alongside the teachers there were also the manuals. Midway through the nineteenth century there appeared *The Sampler*, described as 'A System of Teaching Plain Needlework in Schools by The Lady Finch'. Fifty years later Elizabeth Rosevear, 'Lecturer on Needlework at the Training College, Stockwell London, SW.; Examiner to the Examination Board of the N.U.T.'[26] produced a book covering needlework, cutting out and knitting in great detail, with many illustrations to show the workings on both right and wrong side of the fabric. Guides such as these must have been superseded by Ann Macbeth's newer methods.

Women also produced countless books instructing the individual on every conceivable aspect of needlework as well, whether specialist works on home glove-making, children's clothing, church embroidery and collecting old lace or, on a more general theme, with titles like *Light Work for Leisure Hours* or *The Dictionary of Needlework*. An early example is the compilation of 1855 written by Mrs Warren and Mrs Pullen, which gives an exhaustive, if somewhat exhausting, picture of what the 'Lady Needleworker throughout the world' might achieve. Offering instruction on 'Knitting, netting, crochet, point lace, tatting "or frivolité", braiding, embroidery &c.; the Work Table for juveniles and children's dress' the authors also offer suggestions as to what a woman might do with the end products of her dexterity. Ideas on 'Presents for Gentlemen' include a pair of braces – embroidered on velvet or worked in canvas from a Berlin pattern; a cigar case which could be in crochet, in velvet and cloth appliqué, velvet or cloth braided, embroidered or worked in beads; slippers in a similar variety of materials; shaving books which were 'especially useful'; smoking caps; fronts for bridles – a crest embroidered in seed pearls; waistcoats, pen wipers, book marks, purses, comforters, sermon cases, driving mittens and scarves. As for suitable 'Bridal Presents' their imagination knows no limits: 'Chairs,' they said, 'embroidered velvet in appliqué, Berlin work ditto, braided ditto', and they move on through sofa cushions, screens, antimacassars, table covers, sets of dish mats, fancy mats for under urns or lamps, ottomans, footstools, what-nots, doyleys, watch pockets and netted curtains.[27] The bride attracted a further selection of useful or desirable objects, all hand stitched, as did the baby at its christening.

A girl with sewing skills could work for any of the multiplicity of dressmaking concerns up and down the country; to these can be added establishments for the making of millinery, gloves, shawls, coats, stockings, corsets and every other garment or accessory that can be thought of. Conditions in these places were often difficult, the workrooms badly lit and ventilated, the hours erratic. In 'the Season' the girls toiled through the night to complete orders on time but during quiet spells they would be turned off. Their health was adversely affected by some processes used on the materials they handled or from the dye stuffs on feathers or artificial flowers. In the factories and other workplaces where such materials were commonplace, industrial poisoning from dusts, chemicals or solvents was rife; workers suffered from septicaemia, eczema and bronchial problems, while accidents as a result of using high-powered machinery were frequent. Conditions were equally insalubrious for the large numbers of mill girls involved in the manufacture of threads and textiles where high levels of humidity, dusts and chemicals were also prevalent. As with the laundry workers, these trades and their attendant abuses came to the attention of the Woman Inspectorate of Factories and Workshops because so many of these establishments were staffed with female labour.

One example can be given of a former mill hand who left school aged eleven to start her working life as a silk winder, moved on to a cotton mill and rose through the hierarchy to become supervisor of a hosiery mill. This was Miss Reddish who acted as Guild Organiser of the Women's Cooperative Guild between 1893 and 1895 and was just one of the many remarkable women who came to the fore in that organisation.

Women and girls were not only making the thread, the fabric and the garments themselves but they were selling them, too. Margaret Bondfield started her working life at fourteen with an apprenticeship to an old-fashioned drapery business run by Mrs White of Church Road, Hove. Their trade was considered 'exclusive' and many a trousseau and layette was made up and posted to customers in India. Although Mrs White treated her employees as family, conditions for shop assistants generally were appalling: long hours, minimal breaks, abysmal wages and living on the premises did not make for a happy atmosphere. After five years Margaret Bondfield went to London where she joined a trade union and went from shop to shop testing living conditions on behalf of the Women's Industrial Council. She became Secretary to the Shop Assistant's Union, a lecturer with the International Labour Party and, after a lifetime of service to trade unionism, a Member of Parliament and the first woman Cabinet minister. A satisfactory career for a youngster who started out making and selling underwear and baby clothes.

Two types of clothing were regarded as being peculiarly 'women's business' – the provision of corsets and hats. Many examples of makers of both can be found in local street directories but London was generally perceived as the centre of elegance and several corsetières set up there. Mrs Bell was not only a maker of corsets but invented several types especially suited to ladies in the later weeks of pregnancy and immediately after the birth, as well as for those of a corpulent figure or with certain medical problems. She also invented one that could be loosened by means of a spring while a second spring undid the garment completely, which, she claimed, made it invaluable in cases of swooning and spasms 'and as a Bathing Corset it is equally invaluable, from the rapidity with which it can be taken off and put on'.[28] Such was the popularity of her special corsets that she had to warn her customers of counterfeits being sold under her name.

Corset-making was only one of Mrs Bell's many activities as she also ran a high-class dressmaking establishment, making and selling every type of dress, whether for weddings, family mourning, fancy dress parties or for riding, as well as a profusion of hats from her shop in St James's. In 1820 she devised a special type of hooped hood, the Chapeau Bras, that could be folded away for carrying. There was competition not only from imposters but also rival corsetières. Madame le Plaistrier on Ludgate Street combined corset-making with millinery and dressmaking and advertised that she travelled to Paris every spring to choose the most flattering and elegant garments for her customers. Further west, among the many millinery businesses run by women in Regent Street, was a Mrs Huntley who held the appointment of 'Staymaker and Corset Maker to her Majesty Queen Adelaide'. Mrs Huntley sold corsets made to both English and Parisian designs and also her very own 'washing elastic stay'; however, further along Regent Street Mrs Mills was also claiming to have invented this type of elastic corset and in 1838 was advertising her own creation of a lightly boned corset with shaped gussets, woven on a loom.

Other establishments might concentrate on either the dressmaking or the millinery side of business. In the 1780s Susanna Towsey and her sister Elizabeth ran a small haberdashery and millinery business in Chester and despite the six-day journey by stagecoach they regularly travelled to London to select the latest wares for their customers. An advertisement in the local papers announced the goods' arrival in the shop. Susanna later married, becoming Mrs Brown, and her son carried on the business, which is how the famous Brown's of Chester started.

In Windsor a similar story unfolded in the years after Waterloo. Mary Caley and her sister Mrs Nokes were running a dressmaking, millinery and haberdashery business in Castle Street and advertising widely in the local press. Because of the proximity to the Castle and the society folk that followed the Court they were most favourably placed and by 1820 had achieved the Royal warrant as 'Milliner to Her Majesty and T.R.H. the Princesses and Duchess of Gloucester'. Mrs Nokes retired but a brother joined the firm and by the 1850s his two sons were trading as Caley Brothers, describing themselves as 'Silk Mercers, Linen Drapers, Lacemen, Furriers, Florists, etc., to the QUEEN, the Prince and Princess of Wales &c., &c.'.[29] In the early twentieth century the firm established a Court dressmaking business in London's Albemarle Street under the name 'Mme Caley'.

By this time numerous establishments claimed to be 'Court dressmakers', far more than could possibly be needed to clothe the ladies that graced the social scene but the term implied that a firm was capable of making the intricate dresses required for a Court presentation. Many employed women at the highest level. There was Mme Durrant at 116 New Bond Street where the manageress was a Miss Gray who subsequently started her own firm in Brook Street. She did not claim to be an original designer herself but adapted designs bought from Paris. The noted couture house of Reville and Rossiter, in Hanover Square, was run by Mr W.W. Reville Terry and a Miss Rossiter, respectively the former buyers of mantles and teagowns at Jay's 'General Mourning Warehouse'. In their joint venture he was the designer and she the administrator; they made clothes for Queen Mary and provided the trousseau for the then Princess Royal. Victor Stiebel, a future royal dressmaker, started designing for the firm in the 1920s.

Although other Englishwomen had been notable dressmakers, the first to be known internationally as a designer was 'Lucile'. At seventeen she married a man considerably older than herself and a daughter was born, but the marriage ended in divorce. Mrs Lucy Wallace had always made her own and her daughter's clothes, so she started to make clothes for her friends and made the bridesmaids' dresses and the wedding dress for her sister Elinor's marriage to Clayton Glyn at St George's, Hanover Square. Elinor was a beauty and shortly to become the celebrated authoress of some rather racy novels. Meanwhile 'Lucile' set up her own establishment in Old Burlington Street and moved to Hanover Square when the business outgrew its premises. In 1900 she married Sir Cosmo Duff Gordon. It is said that her fashion house was the first to use decorative boxes to deliver dresses to customers and the first to develop a more congenial atmosphere in which to view the fashions. An even greater innovation was the use of the dress parade for showing off her creations; she employed the most attractive models she could find and sent them out with co-ordinating accessories. This was in contrast to the Parisian custom of dressing their models in stiff black satin underclothing from head to foot and choosing only the plainest of girls. 'Lucile' also gave fanciful names to her gowns and decribed her creations in romantic terms.

Meanwhile, across the Park in fashionable Knightsbridge a department store was developing from its linen-draper origins. New middle-class housing in the area and also in Kensington followed in the wake of the Great Exhibition, all of which benefited a small linen shop founded in 1813 in what was then called Lowndes Terrace. Miss Harvey inherited the thriving business on her father's death, along with a recommendation that she take the silk buyer, Colonel Nichols, into partnership – hence the name 'Harvey Nichols'.

By this time, ladies' fashions and accessories had become a popular topic in the proliferating magazine market but it had taken a surprisingly long time for this to happen. From the days of Queen Anne women had edited periodicals and contributed prose and poetry to them. Some of these had been aimed at a female readership, supposedly providing what women wanted to read about. But it was not until a later manifestation of the *Lady's Magazine* between 1759 and 1763 (there had been previous short-lived periodicals of the name) that an engraving of a fashionable outfit was included with some text on the subject. The editor was 'The Hon. Mrs Caroline A. Stanhope' but there are doubts about her identity and the possible pseudonym.

Other magazines took the idea further, incorporating fashion alongside wide-ranging literary offerings. Women became heavily involved in their production. During 1803 there was the monthly *Mirroir* [*sic*] *de la Mode* published for Mme Lanchester of 17 New Bond Street, its pretentions to French elegance marred by the initial spelling mistake; for three years Mrs Fiske directed the magazine, which in 1806 became the *Record of Fashions and Court Elegance.* From its inception in 1798 the *Lady's Monthly Museum* claimed to be edited by a group of women and for its fashion plates was 'indebted to the choice of Miss Pierpont, Edward Street, Portman Square',[30] although it was a man who supervised the millinery featured. By 1832 it had been amalgamated with the elegant monthly *La Belle Assemblée* and Caroline Norton took over the editorship, though she is rarely remembered in this particular context. Somewhat earlier the fashion sections of this latter publication had been in the hands of Mrs Bell, whether wife or daughter-in-law of its founder is not clear, but the same Mrs Bell who ran a high-class dressmaking business and was maker and inventor of corsets *par excellence.* After her name ceased to appear in *La Belle Assemblée* it surfaced again a year or two later in a new magazine called the *World of Fashion and Continental Feuilletons,* where her activities and views, as before, were published in the guise of editorials and her shop was prominently featured. In 1857 Isabella Beeton was contributing a weekly column on domestic topics to her husband's *Englishwoman's Domestic Magazine.* It had a problem page and a medical column like many others but Mrs Beeton included a dressmaking pattern of her own devising with each issue, in emulation of some French journals.

Women authors also addressed the subject of dress in periodicals as well as in books and other formats. Mrs Loftie was dismissive of the dressmakers of the 1870s, considering them to be 'as a class, . . . vulgar and uneducated, with little appreciation of the artistic subtleties of their art or even of its more obvious proprieties'.[31] Mrs Oliphant, by way of contrast, wrote a lengthy and considered work on the history of dress and its underlying philosophy, while a decade or so later Georgiana Hill, who is considered to be one of the first dress historians published her *History of English Dress.* Other women created collections: whether of fans (Lady Charlotte Guest at Dowlais), of fabrics (Rachel Kay Shuttleworth at Padiham) or of fashions (Doris Langley Moore at Bath).

CHAPTER SIX

It All Began with Dinner

I took my harp to the party but nobody asked me to play.

For much of the period the poignant words of the old music hall song would have been irrelevant. It was assumed that after dinner everyone, but most especially the ladies, would be able to proffer something in the way of entertainment for their fellow guests. Music, singing or recitations were all popular and a way of not only filling the hours after dinner but of showing a girl to good advantage and enhancing her prospects of marriage.

To this day dictionaries define 'dinner' as being the main meal of the day and 'supper' as the last meal, so there is some excuse for the confusion that exists over what to call the main meal eaten during the evening. Our ancestors, though, would not have been confused. They ate breakfast which was, as the word says, taken to break the overnight fast and varied in timing and content; there was dinner which was served with some formality and originally eaten about midday; and there was supper, a meal that was totally flexible depending on whether a couple were sitting alone in front of a fire with a bowl of something on their laps or were entertaining numerous guests and treating them to a lavish display of delicacies.

When Lady Grisell Baillie married in 1691 she would have eaten dinner at about noon or 1 o'clock; by the time she died in the 1740s dinner had become an early afternoon meal and by the end of the century it was being served at 4.30 or 5 p.m. These shifting times were outlined by Lord Cockburn (1779–1854) when recalling the changed social habits within his lifetime and he summed up: 'Thus within my memory, the hour has ranged from two to half past six o'clock; and a stand has been regularly made at the end of every half hour against each encroachment.'[1]

The shifting hour had certain consequences, the most noticeable being the reduction in importance of supper. After a substantial meal during the afternoon folk were not needing to eat much before they went to their beds and so supper, formerly such a focal point, became a simpler meal altogether. Lord Cockburn again: 'Early dinners begat suppers. But suppers are so delightful that they have survived long after dinners have become late . . . Supper is cheaper than dinner; shorter; less ceremonious; and more poetical. The business of the day is over; and its still fresh events interest. It is chiefly intimate associates that are drawn together at that familiar hour, of which night deepens the sociality. If there be any fun, or heart, or spirit, in a man at all, it is then, if ever, that it will appear.'[2]

As dinner became later, so the gap between breakfast and dinner expanded beyond what was acceptable. To fill the uncomfortable void the glass of Madeira wine and slice of cake eaten mid-morning were augmented with cold meats, fruit, more cake and so on on, to become the meal called nuncheon, later luncheon. The consequence of this was that dinner continued to get later as no one was ready to eat another meal so soon after their nuncheon. However, any hunger pangs that made themselves felt in the lengthening gap between the two meals were assuaged with a cup of tea and a biscuit, which in time turned into the ritual of 'afternoon tea' so that the evening meal was set back yet again until, by the 1920s, dinner for fashionable folk was 'invariably at 8 o'clock'.[3] Meanwhile, ordinary folk ate when it was convenient to fit it into the day's schedule and tended to keep to the older timings – splitting their working hours by eating dinner in the middle of the day and 'supper' or 'tea' when the day's work ended.

Although breakfast remained as the first meal of the day throughout the period, its content and timing did vary, being lighter or more substantial, earlier or later, according to practical considerations or prevailing fashion. What people ate and drank also changed. In the days before tea, coffee or chocolate were readily available adults drank beer and children might be given weak beer or milk. For servants this continued as the norm until tea became an everyday commodity. Accompanying the drink was commonly some form of bread or oatcake spread with butter or lard; it was seemingly the Scots who introduced the idea of orange marmalade as a spread for the morning bread or toast. In rural households, or where a day of open-air activity was in prospect, more substantial fare would be on offer but by Mrs Beeton's day dishes of bacon, eggs or fish for breakfast were intended as alternatives to the meat, game and pies previously eaten.

Dinner changed considerably over the period, and not only in the timing. The style of service and the foods eaten changed too. For about two-hundred years dinner was served 'à la française'. A number of assorted foodstuffs were placed on the table simultaneously and the diners served each other with some of this, some of the other; this comprised a course. For grander meals or in wealthier households the first course was followed by a second course, equally varied but comprising rather lighter or more elegant foods. This, too, would be cleared away for a dessert, the climax of the meal: fruit of every description whether fresh, dried, preserved or made into little delicacies;

71

items based on cream or eggs or fresh cheeses; small cakes or biscuits; anything, in fact, that was rare, out of season or costly was worthy of the dessert course, to be eaten off the best china and accompanied by superior wines drunk from the finest glass.

The dessert course originated in the medieval hall when the whole household dined together. Afterwards, while the hall was cleared of its tables ready for the next activity, family and guests moved to a small room nearby, to indulge in conversation while drinking a glass or two of something and nibbling a tasty morsel. The room in which they did this was called the parlour, from '*parler*' to speak, and what they ate and drank became the dessert, from '*desservir*' to clear (the table). For long enough the dessert was consumed somewhere other than where dinner had been eaten; then it became the custom to take it in the dining-room itself, but only after everything had been cleared from the table, including the cloth; not until Victorian times did the dessert course form an integral part of the dinner.

By which time the format of dinner itself had changed, to that still served on formal occasions today – 'à la russe'. One type of dish counted as a course and was handed round to each guest in turn, the soup being followed by fish, followed by meat and so on through the menu, in a careful balance of textures, colours, cooking techniques and tastes. The range of items was considerably enlarged by the increasing amounts of foods imported from around the world. Plants, too, were introduced from elsewhere and numerous fruits and vegetables regarded as an essential element of our kitchen gardens are, in truth, incomers. Horticulture, like agriculture, witnessed many advances over the years and techniques to improve growing conditions by means of glasshouses, hot beds, vineries and so on were perfected. Faster transport, whether by canals, railways or steamships, had an enormous impact on the foods available, as did the introduction of canning and refrigeration during the nineteenth century.

What talents did a housewife have at her command in connection with mealtimes in general and dinner in particular, and in what way could she turn them to advantage in the outside world?

As the etiquette of dining grew ever more complex, allied to the fact that the middle class was expanding to include many who had not previously played a part in society, so many women turned their hand to guiding others who might be uncertain of how to behave in any given situation. Information sometimes came in works on cookery and domestic management; other authors kept the topics separate. Although books on correct modes of behaviour were nothing new, there was an explosion of such works towards the end of the nineteenth century, reflecting the intricacies of contemporary social behaviour, and who better to write them but the women themselves? The majority of titles include the word 'etiquette', 'society' or 'good manners'. A further selection purported to be by members of the aristocracy: Lady Constance Howard and Lady Gertrude Campbell, for example, and Lady Agnes Geraldine Grove, whose book comprised a collection of essays on manners, politeness and social ethics previously published in the *Cornhill Magazine, Westminster Review* and the *Ladies' Realm*. Its title page carried the extraneous information that she was the author of *Seventy-one Days' Camping in Morocco &c.*

Mrs C.E. Humphry ('Madge' of *Truth*) produced a series of etiquette books and edited a six-volume compendium on home life. This contains a lengthy section on etiquette and related topics: visiting or receiving visits, invitations, the art of entertaining, table decorations, 'At Homes', dances (which includes advice on stable accommodation for guests' carriage horses and whether the coachman should be given his supper) and a section on company staying in the house with special reference to shooting parties, hints to hostess and guest, management of guest chambers and duties of servants.[4]

Other women focussed more on entertainment under titles such as *Etiquette and Entertaining* (Mrs L.H. Armstrong), *Little Entertainments and How to Manage Them* (E.W. Leverton) or *Dainty Dinner Tables* (Mrs A. Praga). Some were even more specific: *Folding Serviettes* ('Penelope') or its predecessor *Serviettes – Dinner Napkins and How to Fold Them* (G.C. Clark). Decorating the dinner table was one facet of a slim volume *Recipes for Successful Dining* by Elsie de Wolfe, an American by birth although part of her childhood had been spent in Scotland and she eventually married an Englishman, becoming Lady Mendl. She was America's first woman interior designer but was also a celebrated hostess and thus her book incorporates the different strands of her life, being a guide to the changing tastes and fashions in food during the 1930s, when simplicity and restraint were to the fore as opposed to the lavishness of the pre-war era.

Another American author was Emily Holt. The *Encyclopaedia of Etiquette* appeared in 1901 and is somewhat American in tone but the fact that it was also published in London would suggest that manners were perceived as being similar in the two countries. It covers the usual topics of dinners, table manners, opera and theatre, visiting and house parties, musical events, garden parties and the rituals of social life – christenings, marriages and funerals. Also to be found are 'bachelor hospitalities', sporting functions, correspondence and children; it concludes with a section on servants – how they should be addressed, their duties and clothing. A few years later the author continued with the parallel theme of popularity: 'For those who, while intelligent, aspiring and successful in many of their undertakings, are not social favourites, and who for that reason are puzzled, dissatisfied and unhappy.'[5] The art of conversation, the good friend, the graceful correspondent, the welcome guest, the successful hostess, the happy traveller and similar subjects are reviewed in turn and hints given as to how to achieve the desired results.

Once a woman had assured herself that all was well with her dining room, that her servants knew what was expected of them and that she could rely upon her cook, and that she herself was well drilled in the niceties of social life she could then start to put all these things to good use. For some women, dinner parties and entertainments were not just about meeting up with friends; women were often active in promoting a husband's career and revelled in their role of 'political hostess' or 'society lady'. The dinner table was an excellent venue from which to influence both people and events; examples are widespread and take on many different forms.

Elizabeth, Duchess of Lauderdale (d. 1697), was beautiful, witty and well educated despite her relatively humble birth but, as one authority puts it, 'her moral character was not, unluckily, on a par with her mental qualities'. Her name was linked to many men of the day, including Oliver Cromwell, but she eventually married her lover of many years, who was created Duke of Lauderdale in 1672. For twenty years he acted as Secretary of Scottish Affairs and their joint rapaciousness was a byword; their ill-gotten gains were spent on Ham House, inherited from her first husband. After she died it was said of her: 'Whatever her failings . . . it is an indisputable fact . . . that no stateswoman . . . has ever taken part in the domestic and political administration of Scotland with half the ability or the power displayed by Elizabeth, Duchess of Lauderdale'.[6]

Another century, another duchess, née Jane Maxwell (?1749–1812). She and her sister were brought up in Edinburgh and despite being granddaughters of a countess 'used to be sent with the tea-kettle across the street to the Fountain Well for water to make tea';[7] they were also seen riding the pigs that still roamed the Old Town. Jane married the 4th Duke of Gordon believing that the man she loved had died abroad; on her honeymoon she heard he was alive. Her husband had little interest in public affairs, preferring country pursuits, but she was tireless in the social sphere and indefatigable in politics, campaigning ceaselessly and entertaining lavishly. It was said of her that probably no woman since the Duchess of Lauderdale had wielded so much political power.[8] She was entrusted with sorting out the Prince of Wales' debts and, in 1793 when France declared war against Britain and the Netherlands, she headed north to raise volunteers, 'The Northern, or Gordon, Fencibles', and stories abound of the methods she used. Her other claims to fame include being a most successful matchmaker for her daughters, patroness of the Scottish woollen trade, of agricultural improvements and of music, and it was through the Duchess that Robert Burns visited Edinburgh. She kept her good looks until the end and such was her fascination that, after her death at Pulteney's Hotel, London, the public were allowed in at 1*s* (5p) each to view her body. She was buried near her home in the Highlands.

Georgiana, Duchess of Devonshire, was the legendary beauty and political hostess of the 1780s. She had enormous charm, a warm heart and adored children; society was scandalised when campaigning for parliamentary candidates she kissed tradesmen in order to win their votes. The following decade the hostess role was adopted by the wife of the 3rd Baron Holland, Elizabeth Fox (1770–1845), a skilful and vivacious if somewhat overbearing woman. Society had been equally scandalised when she abandoned her husband on their Continental honeymoon and returned in the company of Lord Holland. A son was born and, after an acrimonious divorce, she eventually married her lover and reigned over Holland House. Her mother-in-law, Lady Caroline Fox, née Lennox, had played a similar role in her day. Lady Hester Stanhope (1776–1839) was a niece of Prime Minister William Pitt and acted as his hostess until his death in 1806. His dying words are reputed to have been: 'If the nation thinks fit to reward my services let them take charge of my niece.'[9] She was granted a handsome pension and her life took a different direction altogether, as will be detailed later.

Similarly, another name from a different context is that of Mrs Pankhurst (1858–1928). Her husband Dr Richard Pankhurst was a celebrated radical who failed to be elected to Parliament on three separate occasions, so the family left Manchester for London and there she hosted many gatherings of socialist and progressive thinkers, among them Annie Besant and Elizabeth Cady Stanton. The Pankhursts also founded the Women's Franchise League. Overlapping with their activities was a famous political name, that of Nancy, Lady Astor: although American by birth, she was the first woman to take her seat in the House of Commons. Her first marriage ended in divorce and in 1906 she married Waldorf Astor, MP for the Sutton division of Plymouth. On inheriting his father's title he had to resign as MP, so his wife stood for election in his place. They entertained lavishly at Cliveden, their country house outside London.

Money, a suitable background and a passionate belief in a cause contributed to the success of these women, but taking the idea of the hostess one step further were several who exercised their talents in running gaming houses. Gambling was the passion of the eighteenth century and both men and women participated. In the 1740s Lady Mornington kept public gaming houses and, some years thereafter, Lady Buckinghamshire and Lady Archer were celebrated for their expertise in running a faro bank.

After giving one's guests a good meal, the party continued with the ladies leaving the table to go to a 'withdrawing room' or 'parlour' where the men would join them at some stage, the length of the interval depending on the custom of the household and/or the drinking propensity of the menfolk. It was then time for something in the way of entertainment and everyone was expected to contribute.

For folk at every level of society singing was as natural as breathing. In some localities the old habits continued well into the nineteenth century. About Wales it was written: 'Singing and song are as natural to the Welsh as to the birds that fill the woodlands of Wales. From their cradles to their graves, songs and hymns are to be heard. The Welsh mother nursing her babe in the rocking-chair, or old-fashioned oaken cradle, sings the songs of her land as she rocks to and fro. The Welsh housewife sings while she works – the men sing to their horses, the lads sing to their oxen, and the milkmaids sing to their cows.'[10]

It was not only the Welsh who were so talented. Samuel Pepys records in his *Diary* the many occasions on which, either with his wife and servants or with a group of friends, he enjoyed singing and making music – whether it was while being rowed down the river, late at night in his own garden whereupon the neighbours opened their windows to listen or his pleasure at finding the new maid had a good singing voice. His attitude was echoed many years later at Gregynog Hall in Powys, the venue for many musical events where the Davies sisters were said to advertise for domestic staff with appropriate singing abilities – a contralto housemaid and so on. It can be seen in fiction too: Flora Thompson's mother in *Lark Rise* had been the nursery maid in a country rectory and recalled how the whole household, maids and all, had been summoned into the drawing-room of an evening to sing glees and part songs.

While many were able to sing or play an instrument to a certain level, any girl with social aspirations was given lessons, a habit spreading to the lower levels of society and deplored by William Cobbett. These skills were deemed to be acceptable 'accomplishments', though some girls were naturally talented and achieved recognition well beyond the home. Cecilia Davies (?1750–1836) sang before Duke Ferdinand of Parma, taught Empress Maria Theresa's daughters, was the first Englishwoman to sing opera on the Italian stage and performed at Drury Lane. The 'Linley Larks' were the daughters of Thomas Linley, Master of Ceremonies at the Bath concerts. Mary and Maria were more than competent, but sister Elizabeth (1754–92) was exceptional both in voice and beauty, while a brother played the violin and was a friend of Mozart. By royal command they performed at Buckingham Palace in 1772 where they won high praise. Elizabeth's career was cut short when she eloped with Richard Brinsley Sheridan, whereupon he prohibited her from singing in public as it was not 'respectable'. During his career as actor-manager his wife dealt with the actresses' clothing and the accounts. The only reminder of her singing ability is a portrait by Sir Joshua Reynolds who portrayed her as St Cecilia, patron saint of music, seated on a low stool in front of a keyboard instrument with a pair of angelic children beside her.

Other women managed to circumvent any potential ban: Anne Catley (1745–89) was singing at Vauxhall while still in her teens and thereafter sang in Dublin to great acclaim and again in London; she married Major-General Francis Lascelles. Even earlier there was Cecilia Arne (1711–89), whose career started at Drury Lane, then took her to Dublin prior to performing at London's Vauxhall Gardens in 1745. Her sister-in-law Susanna Cibber, née Arne (1714–66), was accounted the most popular singer and actress of her day – the star of Drury Lane. Charlotte Pinto (d. 1802) first appeared in public in 1758 and spent the next decade at Covent Garden, creating principal parts in several operas. She then toured round Scotland and Ireland between 1770 and 1780 accompanied by her husband and her last public appearance was at Covent Garden in 1784. Sarah Bates (d. 1811) was trained by her husband and had a successful career on the concert platform, singing mainly sacred music.

A century later and both the Patti sisters were celebrated singers. Carlotta (1835–89) had a voice of exceptional range and made her debut in New York in 1861; she retired from public life on her marriage in 1879 and died some ten years later. Her sister Adelina (1843–1919) also made her debut in New York, at the extraordinarily young age of seven. By 1861 she was singing major roles at Covent Garden and reigned supreme until the 1890s, although she had a rival in Jenny Lind. Arthur Munby, husband of Hannah Cullwick, recorded: 'Went . . . to Covent Garden, to hear Patti, the new soprano, in Lucia. She is not a Jenny Lind, but she is certainly a great triumph, her voice being more powerful & of a wider range than Bosio's'.[11] After Patti's third marriage to a Swedish Baron, she retired to a castle in Wales in 1899. She is said to have fallen in love with Craig-y-nos, near Swansea, while on a picnic, and decided to settle there, to the delight of the locals. The couple built a small theatre modelled on Drury Lane and in 1905 it was there she made her first recording for HMV (His Master's Voice).

Jenny Lind (1820–87) 'the Swedish Nightingale' became a naturalised British subject in 1859. From 1838 to 1847 she sang at many European venues before coming to Britain. She retired from the operatic stage shortly afterwards but continued to perform at concerts around the world until 1883 when she was appointed Professor of Music at the Royal College of Music. As Jenny Lind was retiring from the public scene, (Dame) Clara Butt (1873–1936) was beginning her career, having trained at the Royal College. She was immensely popular, had a wonderful contralto voice, a splendid appearance and gave recitals throughout the country. Elgar wrote pieces especially for her.

Some women were known not so much for the singing but for the writing of songs or in giving new words to favourite tunes. One authority claimed that Scotland had more popular songs than anywhere else, apart from Germany, attributable to such factors as the picturesque scenery, the simplicity of peasant life, the mellifluous cadences of the dialect and so forth – all of which could surely apply equally well to parts of Wales or England. A group of Scottish ladies were prominent in this way, although some were reluctant to let their talents be made public. Lady Grisell Baillie began writing simple songs, often only fragments, while she and her parents were in Utrecht. Many years after her death further verses were found in a parcel addressed to her brother and they were published in the *Edinburgh Magazine*. Mrs Alison Cockburn (?1712–49) wrote the words 'I've seen the smiling of fortune beguiling' for the tune 'The Flowers of the Forest', which was later taken over and plagiarised by Burns. In turn, Carolina Nairne (1766–1845) endeavoured 'to rescue a good melody from impure surroundings'.[12] She excelled in humorous ballads, Jacobite verses and songs of sentiment and domestic pathos. Her works include such favourites as 'Will ye no come back again?', 'Wi' a hundred pipers', 'Charlie is my darling', 'Caller Herrin' and others but even her own husband was unaware of her authorship as they were published under the pseudonym 'Mrs Bogan of Bogan'.

In contrast, Lady Ann Barnard is immortalised by a single song. She composed the words of the ballad 'Auld Robin Gray', setting it to 'old' music and only acknowledged it as her work shortly before she died. Another Barnard, Charlotte this time, was a prolific ballad writer, producing around one hundred between 1858 and 1869 under the pseudonym 'Claribel'. Helen Selina Sheridan, later Countess of Dufferin and of Gifford, was a song writer and a collection of her works was published in 1894. In the early twentieth century Marjorie Kennedy-Fraser (1857–1930) was the singer and collector of Hebridean songs, of which three volumes were published. The melodies were introduced into the libretto she wrote for the opera *The Seal Woman*.

Singers and song writers formed just part of the expression of women's musical talent. There were also the musicians and the composers, many of whom were teachers too. Among the more recent Imogen Holst (1907–84) was conductor, writer and teacher. She wrote a two-volume account of her father, Gustav, and was closely associated with the Aldeburgh Festival. Her works include orchestral and vocal works, piano pieces and folk-song arrangements. Elisabeth Lutyens (1906–83), her contemporary, was a daughter of the well-known architect. She studied viola and composition in Paris and became a most innovative composer, though her works were rarely performed until the 1950s. However, she has had considerable influence on later generations and has also composed many film scores. In 1931 she co-founded the MacNaughton-Lemar concerts in London with the objective of promoting modern music. Of an earlier generation Augusta Holmès, originally Holmes (1847–1903), was an Irish composer and pianist, a pupil of César Franck and she later took French nationality. Between 1882 and 1891 she composed four operas and a series of symphonic poems. (Dame) Ethel Smyth (1858–1944) was both composer and suffragette; the two strands came together in a march tune, adopted as the suffragettes' anthem, which came from her 1916 opera *The Boatswain's Mate.*

Many women played an instrument as it was considered to be a ladylike accomplishment which showed a girl to her best advantage. In the same way that artists might depict their subjects engaged in knotting or tambour work, so some portray them at an instrument. Some had a natural talent, others rather less, but all were made to practise assiduously. Elizabeth Grant had much to say on the misery of an hour's enforced piano playing before breakfast in an unheated room during the Highland winter.[13]

Catherine Barlow was the first wife of Sir William Hamilton, the diplomat who later married Emma Hart. Catherine, the daughter of a wealthy gentleman farmer, was brought up in a remote part of Wales and became an accomplished player on both the harpsichord and 'forte piano'. When she and Sir William were in London they paid a noted musician to give them and their friends a weekly 'master-class'; in Naples, they maintained a band of musicians in the house and Catherine would join in their playing. She also invited notable singers, musicians and composers to entertain their house guests.

Numerous women took their talents into the public sphere. Marianna Davies (1744–1816) travelled widely, giving public performances on the 'armorica', invented by Benjamin Franklin. Esther Burney (1749–1832), the diarist's eldest sister, was an accomplished pianist and harpsichordist who played in public from an early age; their father was organist at St Margaret's, King's Lynn and a noted teacher. Lucy Anderson (1790–1878) was a pianist who regularly played in public and introduced many works by Beethoven, Hummel and other composers to English audiences. Louisa Mary Barwell (1800–85) not only played but contributed articles on education to various journals and helped to edit the *Quarterly Musical Magazine.* Fanny Davies (1861–1934) excelled in the music of Schumann and Brahms and also played much early keyboard music, while (Dame) Myra Hess (1890–1965) was a notable exponent of Beethoven. She toured extensively and became a household name during the Second World War with her daily lunchtime concerts in London's National Gallery.

If music making or singing failed to appeal to the home circle then an alternative might consist of readings from popular works, recitations of poetry or something in the way of amateur dramatics. In 1879 Lady Pollock was the co-author of a little book that opens: 'There is perhaps no form of entertainment more generally popular at the present day than that of private theatricals, and although at first sight it may appear strange that people should take great delight in seeing their friends play at acting, when with less trouble they could see the thing done by trained actors, it is actually not difficult to find an explanation for the enjoyment which attaches to the performances.'[14] Lady Pollock then guides her readers through every aspect of the topic, including the choice of play, historical anecdotes, make-up and scenic effects. 'Charades' and its variants were always popular, especially for anyone with a penchant for acting, although others regarded such things along with the acting out of tableaux as being suitable for keeping children occupied when home for the school holidays.[15]

Needing much less in the way of preparation was the recital of some favourite poem or speech from a play; for some, the step from amateur dramatics to the professional circuit was a short one. Prior to her stage debut Sarah Siddons, née Kemble (1755–1831), was sent off to be a lady's maid to keep her out of the way of a young actor who had joined her father's company; she recited Milton, Shakespeare and other popular pieces in the servants' hall and sometimes entertained 'upstairs' too. She was eventually allowed to marry the young man and, in 1775, made a disastrous appearance on the London stage; however, the following year she triumphed in Manchester. She went on to tour the country, winning ecstatic acclaim wherever she went. Whether she acted in Liverpool, Dublin, Cork, Bristol or Edinburgh people travelled huge distances to see her. She returned to the London stage in 1782 where some of her audience actually fainted while she acted out a scene of madness. Thereafter she tended to spend winters in London and summers touring though, it was said: 'The regularity of her appearances was disturbed by the birth of her children.'[16] Others suffered similar 'disturbances': if Sarah Siddons was accounted the greatest tragedienne of the day, Dora Jordan (1762–1816) was her equal in comedy and won adultation from her adoring public. For many years she lived with the Duke of Clarence (the future William IV) and gave birth to an inordinate number of children.

The pattern had been set many years before and an actress was generally regarded as immoral and no lady. Nell Gwyn's time on the stage and her subsequent career as (royal) mistress was typical; many performers followed a similar lifestyle and careers were short, 'hardly more than a prelude to the social and domestic irregularities of their later lives'.[17] Not all, though. Mrs Betterton, one of the first women on the stage, was the only actress who was not the mistress of someone at Court, while her protégée Ann Bracegirdle (*c.* 1673–1748) excited incredulous surprise for the reputed purity of her life and in recognition of this was presented with the enormous sum of 800 guineas by her admirers. Her lifestyle slipped somewhat thereafter as she became Congreve's mistress for some years.

It was Charles II, accustomed to seeing women acting in France and wishing to see them on the English stage, who licensed them: 'We do permit and give leave from this time to come that all women's parts be acted by women' runs the famous clause.[18] Samuel Pepys recorded in his *Diary*: 'the first time that ever I saw women come upon the stage',[19] though he missed the very first performance of an actress playing Desdemona in December 1660. Since that date innumerable women have gone on the stage and many have become household names, far too many to mention individually.

Until the Restoration female characters had been played by men; a hundred years later the roles had been reversed and women were playing 'breeches parts' which showed off their legs and figures to advantage. Dublin-born 'Peg' Woffington was an early exponent, though not the first, as both Nell Gwyn and Mrs Bracegirdle had donned male attire and a Mrs Mountfort had been especially successful, as indeed had the noted comedienne Kitty Clive (1711–85), whose stage career spanned forty years. Dora Jordan was celebrated for these breeches parts, pregnancies or no, and there were some, like Charlotte Cushman and Sarah Bernhardt, who played the male leads in Shakespeare's tragedies. The part became an essential of Regency and Victorian extravaganzas and led in turn to the role of the principal boy in pantomime.

A parallel form of male impersonator developed in the music hall – a famous exponent being Vesta Tilley (1864–1952) who made her theatrical debut at the age of three and appeared on stage in boy's clothing aged five. She was a celebrated principal boy and popularised the song 'Burlington Bertie', along with many others. A music-hall comic for most of her life, Nellie Wallace (1870–1948) was a Glaswegian who toured extensively, while from London's East End came Marie Lloyd (1870–1922) whose stage career started at fourteen and who had become the star of the show by sixteen, earning the almost unheard-of sum of £100 per week. Florence Desmond (b. 1905) had a top-hat-and-tails song-and-dance routine, as did Hetty King, Ella Shields and others. And then, of course, there was 'Our Gracie': (Dame) Gracie Fields (1898–1979) began her career in the music halls around Rochdale aged thirteen and two years later had become a full-time singer and comedienne. She entered films in the 1920s and a Hollywood contract in 1938 made her the world's best-paid film star. A list of names from the early days of film could include Madeleine Carroll, Margot Graham, Nora Swinburne, Jessie Matthews, Gertrude Lawrence, Hermione Baddeley, Alison Skipworth, (Dame) Anna Neagle and many, many more.

There were other entertainers too, aside from actresses, singers and musicians, who were working professionally. Lottie Collins, famous in the music halls, started as a child skipping-rope dancer; Jenny Hill, aged seven, played a pantomime goose at 6*d* the performance (2.5p decimal) and after marrying an acrobat in 1868 shared his act. There were dancers of all sorts and those working in the circus – the tightrope walker, the juggler, the clown and the equestrienne. The group of women called 'the pretty horse-breakers' who rode up and down Rotten Row during the London Season, attracting attention by their skilful riding and their dashing dress, form a rather different aspect of the story, to be taken up later.

Arthur Munby reported seeing Catherine Parkes as 'a clown at the London Pavilion',' which was situated at the top end of Haymarket. Her face was bedaubed, he said, and she was grinning broadly but otherwise 'she seemed respectable and pretty'.[20] Many years before this Mme Violante had been a famous rope dancer and had engaged the young Peg Woffington for a children's production of *The Beggar's Opera*. She was probably the same person as 'an Italian Lady styled Signora Violante' who is recorded as managing a group of actors that twice visited Edinburgh in about 1720.[21] In the 1740s Peg Woffington and actor-manager David Garrick had a three-year liaison and she continued to act with his Drury Lane company despite his marriage to Eva Maria Veigel, a Viennese dancer professionally known as Mlle Violette.

In 1759 it was *The Beggar's Opera* that made the name of Nancy Dawson (?1730–67) when she danced the hornpipe, thereby popularising the tune, although she had previously been a figure dancer at Sadler's Wells. If the theatre-going public flocked to watch David Garrick and his company, they fell heavily for the charms of an Italian dancer some years later – 'La Bacelli', otherwise known as Giovanni Francesca Antonia Zernini. She danced at the King's Theatre and won all hearts with her lovely personality and talent for entertaining. Within a few years she had become an aristocrat's mistress and it was probably then that Gainsborough was commissioned to paint her.

Adeline Génee (1878–1970) was born in Denmark and although her dancing took her around the world her career was centred on London; · she was the first President of the Association of Operatic Dancing (later the Royal Academy of Dancing), formed to improve standards of teaching. (Dame) Marie Rambert (1888–1982) was Polish by birth but, again, her career was based in London. She first earned her living dancing barefoot in the style promoted by Isadora Duncan and then joined Diaghilev's company in Monte Carlo. She arrived in London in 1915, married Ashley Dukes, playwright and translator, in 1918 and two years later founded the highly influential Ballet Rambert School. The Ballet Rambert was established some years later.

Lilian Alice Marks (b. 1910) is generally considered to be Britain's first great prima ballerina, though better known as Alicia Markova; she believed that success in her career would be impossible without a Russian-sounding name. She, too, danced with Diaghilev's company and went on to form what became the London Festival Ballet Company with her partner, Anton Dolin. Latterly, she took to teaching. Likewise, Peggy Hookham (1919–91) changed her name and as Margot Fonteyn is celebrated as one of the greatest ballerinas of all time.

A century or so earlier, Mme Vestris (?1797–1856) was a dancer, singer and actress who not only excelled in 'breeches parts' but also took the lead roles in operettas at Drury Lane and Covent Garden. In 1831 she became the first female theatrical lessee when she took over the management of the Royal Olympic Theatre and, subsequently, the Lyceum and Covent Garden. She proved an excellent manageress, initiating a number of administrative reforms and many improvements in scenery and effects. Some years later the Lyceum was taken over by Hezekiah Bateman who introduced the then unknown Henry Irving to Londoners; after her husband died Mrs Bateman ran the theatre for three years with her son, until it was taken over by Irving himself and he engaged Ellen Terry to be his leading lady. Mrs Bateman then re-opened Sadler's Wells, Islington, as a house of melodrama and ran it until her death in 1881.

In the next decade, Annie Horniman (1860–1937) was not content to be merely a patron of the theatre, financing productions of Yeats and Shaw when no one else would take them on, but she herself undertook various chores at Dublin's Abbey Theatre. She then took over the Gaiety Theatre in Manchester and formed her own repertory company which concentrated on modern productions. She was a very dramatic figure and on gala evenings would appear in magnificent brocade dresses, smoking a cigar and sporting a monocle.

If the Lyceum was managed by women at different periods so Sadler's Wells was connected to two women and another theatre developed under the auspices of a woman. Across the Thames in Lambeth, Emma Cons became involved in the housing projects of her friend Octavia Hill, and bought some property which she decided to manage herself. Wishing to discourage her tenants from over-use of alcohol she bought an old music hall and put on concerts and lectures where nothing stronger than coffee was served. The lecture programme developed into a separate entity for adult education, becoming Morley College. The theatre side blossomed when her niece Lilian Bayliss took over in 1898; ballet and opera were also staged here until, in 1931, she established them in the new purpose-built Sadler's Wells. The old music hall she bought was originally called The Royal Victoria Coffee Music Hall but to later generations it became known as 'The Old Vic'.

It would have been nice to record that the first pieces staged at the new South Bank complex had been written by a woman but that was not to be. From the time the first actresses were appearing on the stage, women were writing for the theatre and many of their pieces were produced though they were up against strong male prejudice on several counts. In the first place they were considered 'unlearned' as they had no Latin, and in addition they were damned for using similar language to that being used by their male contemporaries to amuse their audiences and they were castigated for employing romantic and imaginative plots which were considered too far removed from 'real' life. Aphra Behn is generally taken to be the first, although it was as an actress she was buried in Westminster Abbey. Susanna Centilivre, Mary Pix, Mary Delarivière Manley and Catherine Cockburn supplied a considerable portion of the Restoration repertoire. Catherine was only fifteen when her first tragedy was performed at the Theatre Royal and she went on to write four more stage works, poetry and other pieces.

Other successful female dramatists followed, though theatrical work was often only a part of their varied literary output. Hannah More (1745–1833) was encouraged to write by Garrick himself and her tragedy *Percy* was produced at Covent Garden in December 1777; it ran for 21 nights and sold 4,000 copies in a fortnight. Two years later a second tragedy was staged but by that time Garrick was dead. Hannah More gradually turned to religion and social reform but not before writing 'Sacred Dramas' for young persons. Charges of plagiarism were brought against her by Hannah Cowley, a fellow playwright, who brought out thirteen dramatic pieces between 1776 and 1795; she also published poetry and contributed verses to a periodical under a pseudonym. The Duchess of Gordon's sister Eglantine Maxwell (Lady Wallace) wrote verse, three comedies and other pieces but one play produced at Covent Garden was accounted as dull, while a second was refused the Lord Chamberlain's licence as some passages were 'so freely expressed'.[22] At much the same time Mariana Starke (?1762–1838), whose early life in India provided material for her dramatic works, had one comedy acted at the Haymarket Theatre in 1788, a three-act tragedy in verse at Covent Garden in 1798 and another tragedy in 1800, though it must be admitted that one authority claims that 'all were of slight interest'.[23] Joanna Baillie (1762–1851) became well known for her poetry which encouraged her to try her hand at writing a series of plays intended to show the passions of the human mind. *De Montfort*, a play in the Gothic style, proved popular, with Fanny Kemble and her aunt Sarah Siddons in the leading parts, but the most successful was *The Family Legend* produced at Drury Lane in 1810.

The women engaged in writing plays were likely to be producing verses, novels, biographies and other forms of literary work. Bringing the story into the twentieth century, some women had their life stories made into films, such as Anna Leonowens in Siam and Gladys Aylward in China; others, like Rumer Godden in 1947, saw their books turned into films. One of the first to take advantage of the new medium was Elinor Glyn (1864–1943), sister to 'Lucile' the couturière, who was the author of numerous 'society' novels and passionate romances, including *Three Weeks*, a tale featuring illicit passion on a tiger skin in Venice. Later, in Hollywood, she wrote many filmscripts for silent films, some of which were based on her own books. It was of her that 'Anon.' penned the evocative ditty:

> Would you like to sin,
> With Elinor Glyn,
> On a tiger skin?
> Or would you prefer
> to err
> with her
> on some other fur?[24]

CHAPTER SEVEN

A is for Art

'A' is for art and 'A' is also for accomplishment and one can add architecture and acquisition to the list as well: drawing, sketching, painting in watercolours and other skills in the artistic line were regarded as part of a girl's education, to be included in the repertoire along with the sewing and music, the singing and dancing considered appropriate for a girl aspiring to a place in society. It goes without saying that the attainment of all such skills depended on being given the opportunity to learn them, the money to be taught them and the leisure in which to practise them. Many women were blessed with a natural talent or became proficient by dint of long practice. That a number were able to take that talent not just one step forward but several steps further and become celebrated exponents in a particular form might come as a surprise. For those without the wherewithal to indulge in leisure pursuits, painting on china and similar activities were a means of earning a bare living, employed in factory work for the mass market. As in the textile trades, conditions in the workplace and the substances used were often injurious to the women's health.

Until early in the seventeenth century the housewife was directly engaged in her housewifely duties and would teach her daughters her methods so as to enable them to carry out their own far-ranging responsibilities in due course. By the mid-eighteenth century opinion had changed to the extent that domestic talents were increasingly regarded as old fashioned and, instead, girls were taught 'accomplishments'. A book of the 1760s sets the tone: it begins with the making of 'Gum-Flowers' and works its way through the painting of ribbons, japanning and gilding, shell work, limning, mosaics, 'to preserve Birds with their Plumage' and the dying of Silks and Thread, to the making of Wax Candles. Only then does Mrs Robertson tackle the topics of 'Cosmeticks &c., Jellies &c' and other items of confectionery and home-made wines. It is Part II that contains 'a great Variety of practical Receipts in Cookery, Pastry, Puddings, Marketing &c'. In other words, the showy accomplishments were more important to the young lady than a knowledge of practical work in the kitchen; so far had the objectives of a girl's education wandered off into the sideline of accomplishments.[1]

Another fifty years and the wheel of fashion had turned so far that numerous authors were emphasising that a housewife's Christian duty lay in the care of her household but there was no pretence that she should do the work herself. Instead, with servants to carry out the domestic tasks the manuals instructed her how to fill her leisure hours with schemes for self-improvement and pastimes. Skills of this nature supposedly made a girl more attractive to a potential husband. To remain unmarried was regarded as a disaster, as well as being a drain on her family's resources. It was unthinkable, as well as being most unladylike, that she should go out and earn her own living, other than in disastrous circumstances; it was even worse for a girl to have 'book learning' as that might well scare away any husband-to-be!

How is it possible to account for such a swing in attitude from dedication to the housewifely virtues to an emphasis on genteel pastimes? After the upheavals of the Civil War, when many families lost estates and income, society was in a state of flux; the Restoration of Charles II introduced different values at Court which gradually percolated downwards through the social levels. As society became less dominated by the long-established codes of behaviour, so new means, other than the somewhat unspectacular skills of housewifery, had to be devised to make a girl an attractive proposition on the marriage market – hence the increasing emphasis on a girl's appearance and behaviour, as well as her ability to embroider, to sing or play a musical instrument and to do something 'artistic', in the drawing or painting line. The end results of her accomplishments were likely to be displayed to visitors in the drawing-room after dinner.

Many women excelled in artistic work and few found anything to criticise in their employment. Anne Killigrew was a Maid of Honour to James II's second wife, Mary of Modena, and was noted for her portraits, though she is generally remembered for her poetry. She died from small pox in 1685 at an early age. Someone who died just a few years earlier was Elizabeth, Countess of Carnavon; she and her sister Mary, Duchess of Beaufort, did much to promote the cause of botany, but it was Elizabeth who excelled in flower painting. The links between embroidery, painting and gardening have often been noted and 200 years later the twinned elements were still flourishing. Flower paintings and embroideries to the highest standard were being created by Anne Nasmyth, a daughter-in-law of Alexander, the Scottish watercolourist and portrait painter. Her husband retired to a property in Kent and there she grew the flowers she delighted to portray in paint and silken thread.

Between the painter and the embroiderer sits Mrs Delany (1700–88) with her 'paper mosaic flowers' which she initiated entirely by accident: a piece of paper beside her exactly matched the colour of the geraniums across the room and she amused herself by cutting out some petals and assembling them on a black background into the shape of the flower head. Leaves, stems and calyx were added in shades of green and thus her very own art form was born. Cutting out shapes in paper was not in itself a new pastime but the incredibly fine detail Mrs Delany put into her flower silhouettes coupled with their botanical accuracy had not been seen before. Ten volumes of these shapes were the result of her endeavours which she subtitled 'A Catalogue of Plants copied from Nature in Paper Mosaick, finished in the year 1778, and disposed of in alphabetical order, according to the Generic and Specific names of Linnaeus.'[2]

Moving from the gifted amateur to the professional it is possible to make use of only a limited number of examples from the many available. It is noteworthy that several successful exponents were the daughters of men with art-related careers, though as many again were not. Mary Moser (d. 1819), a celebrated painter of flowers, was the daughter of a prominent enameller who was drawing master to George III and the first Keeper of the Royal Academy. Anne Forbes (1745–1834) was a granddaughter of William Aikman, the Scottish portraitist, and Angelica Kauffmann (1741–1807), the daughter of an obscure artist. Into the next century and the father of Ann Mary Severn (1832–66) was Joseph Severn, painter and British Consul in Rome and the man who befriended Keats in his dying days. Kate Greenaway's father was a draughtsman, while Alexander Nasmyth trained all five of his daughters. By way of contrast Mary Beale (1637–97) was the daughter of a Suffolk rector. Elizabeth Blackwell (fl. 1737), who drew, engraved and coloured a catalogue of medicinal plants, was either the daughter of a poor farmer or of a worthy merchant. J.M. King (1875–1949) was the daughter of a Scots divine and Gwen John (1876–1939) of a lawyer.

To take their talent beyond the home was fraught with problems: the majority of girls were taught within the feminine environment of school or home and it was difficult for them to obtain further training in the way that a man could. In the early days few studios were willing to accept them as apprentices so it was a challenge to gain access to high-calibre material for copying purposes, nor were they allowed to attend classes to draw a nude figure of either sex. Mary Beale, an early success story, was accepted into the studios of Peter Lely and Ann Killigrew is thought to have studied there too. In turn Mary Beale trained Sarah Curtis (d. 1743) and examples of their work are in the National Portrait Gallery in London. Celia Lucy Brightwell (1811–75), etcher and authoress, became a pupil of John Sell Cotman. Angelica Kauffmann, Maria Cosway and Anne Forbes studied in Italy; Ann Mary Severn and Gwen John went to Paris, while Catherine Read studied in both cities. At the turn of the century Jessie Mary King won a travelling scholarship to Italy and Germany and Ann Redpath (1895–1965) was able to travel in Europe by the same means.

Assorted cookbooks written by women including, from left to right, a manuscript collection (1940s), Eliza Acton's Modern Cookery *(1856) and* Domestic Cookery *'by a Lady' (1824).*

A fishwife carrying oysters in a creel on her back. Fish and shellfish were just some of the many goods hawked through the streets of Edinburgh. (From the Book of the Old Edinburgh Club, *Vol. 2)*

The staff of Lowe's the Florist, in Edinburgh's Canongate, c. 1900. The shop appears well stocked and the hand-written sign over the doorway announces 'Cheapest in Town'. (By kind permission of The People's Story Museum, City of Edinburgh Council Museums)

The female employees of J.W. Mackie's, a high-class grocer's shop and restaurant in Princes Street, posing in the gardens opposite, c. 1905/6. Some worked in the office looking after the accounts. (By kind permission of The People's Story Museum, City of Edinburgh Council Museums)

Playtime in the nursery, c. 1904. This shows a light, bright room with suitable child-sized furniture. The nurse might well look exhausted but she is actually holding another infant in her arms. (Drawing by A. Rackham from Mrs C.E. Humphry (ed.), Book of the Home, *Vol. 5)*

A fashion plate of 1828 showing dresses 'invented by Miss Pierpoint Edwards of Portman Square'. The court dress is white with touches of yellow, repeated in the headdress; the carriage dress is peacock-blue, with ribbons of blue, yellow and pink in the hat. (From J.M. Price, Dame Fashion, *1913)*

Seventeenth-century bed curtains worked by Lady Derby during the siege of Lathom House in 1650. A daughter married the 1st Marquis of Atholl which is how the embroideries come to be in Blair Castle. (From the Blair Castle Collection, Perthshire)

The Ladies Waldegrave *by Joshua Reynolds, 1771. The sisters are engaged in tambour work, a fashionable form of embroidery. In time, numerous women earned their living this way, though few in such elegant surroundings. (By kind permission of The National Gallery of Scotland)*

Women and girls who worked at the New Lanark Cotton Mills, c. 1890. The great majority of the large workforce was female; many worked bare-foot in the damp, humid conditions. (By kind permission of the New Lanark Conservation Trust)

Statue commemorating Sarah Siddons (1755–1831) in the grounds of St Mary's Church, Paddington Green, where she was buried. She was accounted the greatest tragic actress of her day.

Examples of 'Bad Style' (left) and of 'Good Style' (right) on the dance floor. The etiquette books took such matters seriously but the couple on the left are obviously having far more fun! (From Mrs C.E. Humphry (ed.), Book of the Home, *Vol. 6)*

Coade Stone figures on St Pancras Church, London. In the 1770s Mrs Coade perfected a technique for manufacturing a species of terracotta that was widely used for about fifty years.

The 'Kirkleatham Centrepiece' created by Huguenot silversmiths Anne Tanqueray and her brother
David Willaume II. It was commissioned by Chomley Turner of Kirkleatham, Yorkshire, in 1731.
(By kind permission of Leeds Museum and Galleries (Temple Newsam House))

Mary Somerville (1780–1872) by Thomas Phillips. Largely self-taught, she was a mathematician, astronomer and gifted writer on scientific matters. (By kind permission of The Scottish National Portrait Gallery)

On the other hand, Margaret Gillies (1803–87), miniaturist and watercolourist, had little in the way of formal training at all but quickly established a reputation for herself. The parents of Beatrix Potter (1866–1943) only permitted her to visit the museums around London, although she was allowed to keep a menagerie of small furry animals which she drew, endlessly. By this time the art colleges were beginning to accept female students and, indeed, some, such as the Glasgow School of Art, were appointing women teachers. Kate Greenaway (1846–1901), illustrator of childrens' books, spent ten years at art schools in and around London, while (Dame) Laura Knight enrolled at the Nottingham School of Art in 1890 when she was only thirteen years of age.

It was also significant if a woman's career was supported by a male relative. For Anne Forbes (1745–1834) the lack of a man in the background hampered her output and on her earnings she was unable to employ the assistants to paint backgrounds or clothing with the result that she completed fewer commissions and so her popularity dwindled. Mary Beale's husband Charles was exemplary: he not only entertained the clients and kept the accounts but also mixed her colours for her and latterly her two sons painted in the draperies so that she could concentrate on getting the likeness of her sitter. Angelica Kauffmann, too, had assistance from her father in the early days and then from her second husband, who acted in much the same way as Charles Beale. However, for some it did not quite work out so well. In the case of Jane Nasmyth, the eldest of the five daughters taught by their father, she acquired a style so similar to her father's that many of her landscapes were probably completed by him, signed and passed off as his own. Fanny Reynolds' efforts were scorned by her famous brother: her miniatures, he said, 'made others laugh and me cry'[3] and so she was his housekeeper for many years. The women not only travelled to Rome or to Paris in order to perfect techniques and styles but some also set off in search of patrons and commissions. The Scots-born Catherine Read's work was highly prized while she was still studying in Rome, whereas Angelica Kauffmann and Maria Cosway went the other way, leaving Italy for London. In time, India came to be regarded as a potential source of wealthy patrons, so to India the adventurous painters went, including Catherine Read. She was an outstanding user of pastels and her charming portraits and family groups were much admired. Some women were downright adventurous and their botanical paintings made a cloak for their travels. Marianne North (1830–90) kept house for her widowed father and, like Anne Nasmyth, had her own glass houses in which she grew the specimens she wished to paint. She took trips with her father, painting and sketching local scenes, but after his death she travelled the world.

Marianne North's speciality was flowers, especially tropical flowers and vegetation, although landscapes and figures appear in her backgrounds; the resulting collection of her botanical work is housed in its own gallery in Kew Gardens. Mary Moser was also a flower painter and a founder member of the Royal Academy of Arts where her work was frequently exhibited. In an earlier era Elizabeth Blackwell had produced *The Curious Herbal* in order to pay off her husband's debts; her illustrations were all taken from specimens in the Chelsea Physic Garden and she then engraved the plates on to copper and coloured them herself. Celia Lucy Brightwell drew and lithographed figures to accompany her father's book on the fauna of East Norfolk. Catherine Read and Anne Forbes, Joan (sometimes called Ann) Carlisle, Mary Beale and others were portraitists, although family groups or conversation pieces might be included under that head. Some were miniaturists such as Maria Cosway and M.A. Knight. Angelica Kauffmann specialised in large-scale historical or allegorical scenes and Elizabeth Butler (*c.* 1850–1933) in equally large-scale and detailed battle scenes, while it was landscapes for Jane Nasmyth and 'genre' paintings with stories based on legend or folklore for the Scottish duo of Fanny MacIan and Jessie McGeehan.

Women painters or 'limners' were around in Tudor times but from the mid-seventeenth century onwards their names are more frequently recorded. One such was Joan (or Ann) Carlisle who died in about 1680. She was noted for her portraits and conversation pieces, though she was chiefly occupied in copying Italian masters or reproducing them as miniatures. Charles II so admired her work, it was said, that he presented her with ultramarine to a considerable value and an annuity of £200. A near neighbour of hers was Mary Beale who made good money from her artistic talents. 'No other English portrait painter of the period', claimed one authority, 'had so distinguished a clientele or is represented by so many canvases in English galleries.' She painted in oils, watercolours and pastels and charged £5 for a head, £10 for half-length. Her success can be measured by the financial returns recorded in her husband's pocket book: '1672. Received this year, for pictures done by my dearest heart, 202l. 5s.' In 1674 that sum was rather greater and three years later had all but doubled to 429l.[4] In fact, her husband gave up his own job as an artist's colourman in order to assist his wife in her career.

Angelica Kauffmann was probably being paid for her paintings from the age of twelve onwards, although she still went to Rome to study and engage in further copying. In 1766 she was persuaded to work in England since portraiture was at that time much in demand and Londoners found her charm and dignity most attractive; Dr Johnson, though, thought it was bad for women to study men's faces so closely.[5] In 1768 she joined Mary Moser in being among the forty founder members of the Royal

Academy of Arts; the ceiling she was commissioned to paint for the Academy's Council Room at Somerset House was later shifted to Burlington House and many other houses were decorated by her. Her designs also featured on Wedgwood and Meissen china, although it is chiefly for her large historical and allegorical paintings that she is remembered.

It was Angelica Kauffmann who fostered the talents of the young Maria Hadfield (1759–1838) and introduced her to English artistic and social circles. Maria married Richard Cosway, the fashionable miniaturist of the day, but the marriage was not particularly successful and she lived abroad for much of the time. After the death of her husband and her daughter she returned to Italy and kept a school there for the rest of her days. A contemporary and fellow miniaturist was Mary Anne Knight who was exhibiting at the Royal Academy from 1807 onwards.

Both Italy and the Royal Academy feature in the short career of Ann Mary Severn. Taught by her father she was employed as a copyist by George Richmond R.A. and, having painted a much-admired portrait of the Countess of Eglinton, she received a number of commissions including some from the Royal family. A delightful glimpse of her comes from Arthur Munby who described her as that 'exquisite artist. Her drawings, especially her portraits, in pencil and in water-colour are charming. She painted the Duchess of Kent & the younger princesses: & the Queen would sit by her for hours looking on, or go & fetch clean water for her colours.'[6] During the 1850s her work was exhibited in the Royal Academy but after her marriage in 1861 to Charles Newton, keeper of classical antiquities at the British Museum, she illustrated many of her husband's books and lectures and made copious sketches for him during their travels in Greece and Asia Minor. She died of measles in 1866.

Book illustration seems a career particularly favoured by women. The speciality of Ellen Carter (1762–1815) lay in drawing the human figure and her work often featured in the *Gentleman's Magazine* and similar journals. The *Botanical Magazine* was another publication to employ illustrators such as Miss Drake (fl. 1818–47), Mrs Withers (fl. 1827–64) and Anne Pratt (1806–93). Though Maria Cosway was primarily a miniaturist, she was also a prolific etcher and book illustrator. The instantly recognisable Kate Greenaway figures first appeared in the 1870s and her drawings of little girls wearing the high-waisted dresses and mob caps of an earlier era became the fashionable wear for (real) children. Helen Allingham (1842–1926) painted 'traditional' English scenes with children and flowers, country lanes and thatched cottages which were inspired by the villages of rural Surrey where she lived. Beatrix Potter's inimitable stories for children would not have enchanted so many generations without the illustrations she painted to accompany them.

Jessie Mary King was not only an internationally renowned and sought-after illustrator of books but was very varied in her talents: she was a designer of jewellery for Liberty's of London, devised furniture and wallpaper and decorated pottery. Her near contemporaries at the Glasgow College of Art were the Macdonald sisters, Frances (1873–1921) and Margaret (1865–1933), and their husbands-to-be, respectively Herbert MacNair and Charles Rennie Mackintosh, who were the most influential exponents of art noveau in Scotland. Frances was a noted embroiderer, while Margaret excelled in watercolour and stained glass and collaborated with her husband in the decorative schemes for his buildings.

Innumerable women must have had their say in the planning or decorating of their homes, although it is generally difficult to evaluate the extent of their influence. In 1752, Lord Lyttelton wrote to the architect while improvements were still at the planning stage: 'Lady Lyttelton wishes for a room of separation between the eating room and the drawing room, to hinder [i.e., protect] the ladies from the noise and talk of the men when left to their bottle, which must sometimes happen, even at Hagley.'[7] Elsewhere it becomes apparent that women initiated the work themselves. The rebuilding of Hamilton Palace was set in motion by the Duke and Duchess but the Duchess inaugurated the next two phases after her husband's death in 1694. Margaret Hamilton, widow of John Hope of Hopetoun, was one of the three signatories to the contract with William Bruce in 1699 for the new residence for her son, the others being the boy's legal guardians. Sarah, Duchess of Marlborough, deplored the way Blenheim Palace was developing and considered it an impossible place to live in; both she and the Duke preferred their own Marlborough House in London and, having dismissed Wren, their architect, the Duchess saw to the finishing of it herself. At a later date Montagu House, Portman Square, with decorations by Angelica Kauffmann was commissioned by Mrs Montagu, the Society hostess.

In the nineteenth century the Blunts, notable travellers and breeders of Arab horses, are described as owner-designers of their home Crabbets Park, Sussex. At Wallington, Northumberland, Pauline, Lady Trevelyan, supervised the major alterations made to the house and commissioned works from her friends among the Pre-Raphaelites; she herself contributed designs of flowers and foliage to the pillars in the new central hall. Nearby Ford Castle was remodelled by the widowed Louisa, Marchioness of Waterford who lived there from 1859 until her death in 1891; she also saw to many other improvements on the estate including the building of a schoolhouse decorated with her own mural paintings which took her twenty-one years to complete.

Two early women architects and interior designers were the Parminter cousins, Jane (d. 1811) and Mary (d. 1841) of Exmouth, Devon. They travelled extensively on the Continent, making a study of architecture, and their buildings included almshouses, a sixteen-sided house with an octagonal centre and a church in which they are both buried. As late as the 1890s the claim was made that 'Architecture as a profession is generally regarded with great favour by parents who are on the look-out for a "gentlemanly" career for their sons.'[8] Writing in 1922 one authority announced: 'Architecture is a comparatively new profession for women, and it is only in quite recent years that they have entered it in any numbers.' The situation was slow to change, since two years later the profession's year book lists only 2 female students out of a total of 141 and just 1 female Member whose address was in Australia.[9]

During the later eighteenth century the contemporary building style demanded classical ornamentation around doorways, under windows or along the string course and architects were keen to find an alternative to carved stone; many versions of artifical stone were developed but there was one that outshone and outlasted them all – Coade stone. Its inventor was the daughter of a wool merchant who had to earn her living after her father's bankruptcy. Elinor Coade began as a linen draper in the City of London and then went into partnership with a maker of artifical stone in Lambeth. Within a few years she had taken over the business and perfected a building material which proved to be both durable and malleable. Decorative items were supplied to houses all over the country, and not only for the houses, either; it was also used for garden follies, funerary monuments, churches and occasionally for sculpting. The material was widely exported. Mrs Coade died in 1821 without revealing the secrets of its composition or manufacture and within twenty years the business had closed, largely due to changes in architectural fashion. There is a twist to the story, though, in that the excavations for the Festival of Britain of 1951 revealed the site of the factory and many artefacts were rescued. Modern analysis revealed the stone's secrets; the ingredients were simple enough but the thoroughness of the grinding process together with the very high temperature of the firing gave the material its hardness and capacity to accept detail.

Coade stone was occasionally used for sculpture. Anne Damer (d. 1828) employed it for her life-size statue of George III, which was noted by a German visitor to Edinburgh: 'We must honour her good intention, but, alas, the statue is a formless piece of work.'[10] Mrs Damer began modelling after a conversation in which she claimed she could make better figurines than those being sold in the street below; she studied anatomy and marble carving and went on to make a name for herself in portrait sculpture and animal pieces. She had a small studio in the garden of Strawberry Hill, Twickenham, the home of her cousin Horace Walpole, and inherited the house and an income for its upkeep after his death.

(Dame) Ethel Walker (1861–1951) was a sculptress and painter who divided her time between studios in Yorkshire and in London but she is best known for her portraits of girls, flower paintings and seascapes. Clare Sheridan (1885–1970) took up an artistic career after being widowed in the First World War, specialising in portraiture in clay and sculpture and, later, in wood carving. She was also a journalist and writer who travelled the world interviewing many important figures of the day, a number of whom sat for her. A contemporary was (Dame) Barbara Hepworth (1903–1975), who trained at the Leeds School of Art and at the Royal College of Art in London; she won a travelling scholarship to Italy and, after her first marriage, lived there for a while, learning how to carve stone.

Another form of modelling used wax as the principal material. Mrs Damer had started with wax before moving on to marble or bronze but one woman made wax modelling an art form in its own right. Marie Tussaud's widowed mother went as housekeeper to a Dr Curtius who set up a wax museum in Paris and among the models on show were some of the French Royal family. Marie (1761–1850) learnt the modelling trade from him and spent several years at Versailles teaching art to the French King's sister, a strong contrast to the years that followed the Revolution when she was involved in taking death masks of numerous victims of the guillotine. The museum made a fortune from the public curiosity over the victims' appearance. Marie inherited the museum on the death of its owner but after various ups and downs she left her husband and younger son in France and set off for England. For thirty years she travelled the country with her exhibits, continually expanding the stock, until she had raised enough money to establish herself in London where Madame Tussaud's continues to attract the crowds.

The 'Chamber of Horrors' may have fascinated the visitors but it is not a room the average housewife would desire as a decorative scheme within her own home. 'We take it for granted', said one authority 'that every woman is interested in houses – that she either has a house in course of construction, or dreams of having one, or has had a house for long enough to wish it were right. . . . a man may build and decorate a beautiful house but it remains for a woman to make a home of it for him. It is the personality of the mistress that the home expresses.'[11] A sweeping generalisation, perhaps, but the sentiments would be recognisable to the women writing on many aspects of houses and their decoration in the preceding forty years or so and by innumerable housewives up and down the country.

Flora Thompson describes how the young housewives in the hamlet of Lark Rise would decorate their cottage homes with ideas picked up from their days in service. There was a preference for small 'parlour' chairs with upholstered seats, rather than the wooden wheel-backs of former days; the central table would be covered by a brightly coloured woollen cloth when not being used; the wicker chairs by the hearth would have hand-made antimacassars and cushions, while a vase or two of flowers might be seen on a shelf. There were those who were concerned about more than just the decoration of the home and wanted such girls to be knowledgeable about every aspect of domestic life: Mrs Buckton considered it essential, partly to give them the knowledge to help their own parents and families, partly to equip them for domestic service and her efforts in this direction have already been noted. These principles were recommended by the Royal Commission on Technical Education of 1881, with the suggested syllabuses embracing such topics as the laws of health and the human body; the general treatment of animals, especially horses; heating and ventilation; the composition and nutritive value of different foods and their functions; cookery, cleaning and laundrywork; as well as instruction in 'kitchen flues, boilers, cisterns and every sanitary appliance found in a cottage dwelling'.[12]

Such down-to-earth matters as greasetraps, cleaning of 'The Artisan Water Closet' and the disposal of old rags and matches were less likely to feature in books with titles such as *Bedroom & Boudoir* (Lady Barker) or *The Drawing Room* (Mrs L. Orrinsmith), which were followed by *The Art of Decoration* (Mrs R.H. Haweis), *The Art of the House* (R.M. Watson), *The Decoration of Houses* (E. Wharton and O. Codman jnr) and *The House in Good Taste* (E. de Wolfe). Articles, many written by women, also featured in periodicals such as the *Pall Mall Gazette* or in domestic encyclopaedias such as that edited by Mrs Humphry, mentioned earlier. Women proffered advice as to how rooms should be furnished to achieve the best in appearance and comfort and to promote the desired effect. Books, for example, had no place in a drawing-room, although a few, 'well-bound and costly', might be placed to hand to encourage conversation among visitors.[13] The half-worn drawing-room carpet should not be put into a bedroom as the colours would be wrong and the carpet itself would be 'frowsy and fusty',[14] while the best flooring for a dining-room was considered to be bare stone or marble.[15]

A little DIY* was envisaged when one author admitted that women rarely had the luxury of choosing where or even what they lived in, which was, she explained, to be treated as a challenge: 'As long as a woman possesses a pair of hands and her work-basket, a little hammer and a few tin tacks, it is hard if she need live in a room which is actually ugly.'[16] Painting, varnishing, staining and graining were to be encouraged, seeing that by the later nineteenth century it was claimed: 'Everything is nowadays made so easy for the amateur . . . that many people think far less of the trouble of

---

*   DIY: do-it-yourself handiwork.

decorating a room in all its details than of that involved by the arrival of a small army of workmen to execute the task for them'. However, a warning was issued, too: 'The beginner must not be disappointed if his [!] first attempts do not equal the work done by a professional decorator.'[17] One encouraged women to embroider their own quilts, while another announced: 'Design and embroider your own curtains'.[18]

Mrs H.R. Haweis gave a comprehensive over-view of the subject of domestic decor, with a historical analysis of the way rooms evolved, styles of decoration and furniture, alongside the *objets d'art* that provided the finishing touches. She was not alone in deploring recent fashions in interior design and begged women to think for themselves. Similar sentiments were reiterated by R.M. Watson, whose book was a collection of her essays previously published in the *Pall Mall Gazette,* and by the prolific American novelist and cosmopolitan socialite Edith Wharton.

Suitability, proportion and simplicity were the watchwords of Elsie de Wolfe (Lady Mendl), the first professional woman decorator in the USA. Although American by birth, she had spent some years in Scotland and was 'presented' at Court; she maintained her links with Europe, with a house in the park at Versailles and frequent buying trips to satisfy her clients. *The House in Good Taste* is full of her personal likes and dislikes, mixed in with anecdotes about high-powered commissions and famous people, but it also has useful advice on what to look for in a house and emphasises the need for restraint in colour and decoration.

From the general decoration of rooms to the decorative objects within them is but a step. A celebrated practitioner in the medium of glass was Mary Beilby (1749–97) who, with her brother William, worked as a glass enameller in Newcastle on Tyne. Surface decoration on glassware became increasingly popular after the Excise Act of 1745 decreed that material lost in the cutting of lead crystal was still liable for duty and so embellishments in the form of air twists, threads of enamel and surface painting came to replace the cutting technique. The Beilby's early work made use of armorial devices in white and coloured enamels, the later ones taking the more naturalistic shapes of birds, plants and landscapes in opaque white. The work of the two are indistinguishable as items are only signed 'Beilby'. Thomas Bewick, the wood engraver, was apprenticed to one of their brothers and boarded in the house; he would have married Miss Beilby but, as an apprentice, the family looked down on him and he had never approached her: 'Before I was out of my time . . . Miss Beilby had a paralytic stroke, which very greatly altered her look, and rendered her for some time unhappy. Long after this she went with her eldest brother into Fifeshire where she died.'[19]

No well-set dining-room was complete without a display of silverware and a number of influential women are known in this connection. Anne Willaume was the daughter of a Huguenot goldsmith from Metz who was well established in London by the end of the seventeenth century. In 1717 she married a fellow goldsmith David Tanqueray and, after his death, she continued to run the business, entered her own marks and produced pieces of the highest quality. Hester Bateman's name is well known, partly on account of her own work as a silversmith, partly as the founder of a dynasty. She was born in about 1709 and seemingly never learnt to read or write; she married John Bateman, a gold-chain worker, and bore him five children. On his death in 1760 he left all his property to his wife and the following year she entered her own mark as a silversmith; in 1763 she entered her mark as a goldsmith. For the next thirty years she created a wide range of the most elegant items, primarily for use on the tea or dinner table, although she also produced religious pieces. It was a family enterprise in that three sons and a daughter-in-law were working in it and when Hester retired in 1790 the business passed to her surviving son and Ann, her widowed daughter-in-law, who was herself a gifted silversmith. Ann took her own sons into the firm and it continued until one of them sold it in about 1840, having become heavily involved in the Chartered Gas, Light & Coke Company.

Although many silversmith's widows took over their late husband's trade and entered their own mark, it did not necessarily mean that they were practising silversmiths themselves. To take a single example: after John Emes died in 1808 his widow Rebecca went into partnership with Edward Barnard, his leading journeyman, and the firm became one of the largest concerns of the time, supplying well-known London retailers such as Rundell & Bridges.

No well-dressed dinner table would be without its service of ceramic wares to complement the glass and silverware and here, too, widows can be found taking over an enterprise. An early example is Mrs Warburton, whose husband John ran one of the most extensive concerns of the early eighteenth century: under her supervision significant improvements were made in the production of cream ware, which predate the experiments of Josiah Wedgwood. In time, the widow's son Jacob succeeded to the business; he died in 1828 at the advanced age of eighty-six and the firm ceased trading the next year. Earthernware manufacturers included Maria Lockers in Burslem in about 1750; Sarah Bell, Stoke-on-Trent, in 1786; while listed in the Staffordshire Potteries of 1802 there was Mrs Mellor at Hanley, Dorothy Whitehead at Shelton, Mrs Ratcliffe at Stoke Lane and Mary Syples at Lane End. The situation could be replicated at a number of potteries around the country: at Yarmouth Mrs Dyball ran the business, and at Portobello, outside Edinburgh, the widowed Mrs Rathbone was in charge of the Buchan Pottery. Numerous women around the country were selling such products in what were termed 'china, glass and earthernware ware houses'.

   Individual women can also be found engaged in the decoration of these wares: John and Ann Warburton of Hot Lane (now Cobridge) took up enamelling soon after its introduction and are thought to have decorated some of the earlier Wedgwood wares. Ann Wilson was another enameller who was working in Burslem. These named individuals were very much in the minority as innumerable women and children had been employed in the various decorating processes ever since designs in blue and white had been used in imitation of the Chinese porcelain imported into the country; many also did a wide range of jobs as unskilled assistants to the (male) potters and craftsmen. In 1861 it was calculated that women and girls made up some 31 per cent of the workforce in the pottery trade; by 1959 that figure had all but doubled to 61 per cent. Their jobs were mostly in the least-skilled, lower-paid work, but there were some women designers and paintresses who enjoyed enhanced working conditions and higher rates of pay and status. Three influential designers of the twentieth century are Charlotte Rhead (1885–1947), Clarice Cliff (1899–1972) and Susie Cooper (b. 1902) but they, innovative as they were, were following in the footsteps of an earlier generation. The best known of these were probably Hannah Barlow and Eliza Simmance at Doulton, while Helen Miles worked for Wedgwood, but others were working for the smaller potteries. Earlier again and Lady Templetown was providing designs for the decoration of Wedgwood's jasper ware. She had considerable artistic talents and specialised in the then fashionable pastime of cutting out silhouettes, freehand, many of which were used as models for the jasper. It was said of her: 'Had Lady Templetown been a poorer woman she might have made a fortune by her wonderful gifts.'[20] After her husband's death in 1785 she turned her back on art and ran his extensive estates instead. Her contemporary in the design field was Lady Diana Beauclerk (1734–1808) who supposedly worked with ceramics, although it is her paintings and book illustrations that are generally on record. A hundred years later the Dunmore Pottery near Stirling achieved considerable popularity after the Prince of Wales' visit in 1871 and by that time Lady Dunmore herself was designing rustic vases and ornaments for the firm.

   Finally, there have been those who have collected such items just for the pleasure of owning them. One of the earliest collections of blue and white porcelain was put together by Queen Mary, wife of William III, at a time when it was being imported into the country from China, along with the tea. Much later, it was English ceramics that attracted Lady Charlotte Guest of the Dowlais Iron Works and she donated her collection to the Victoria and Albert Museum.

   In the 1860s John Bowes (1811–85) and his French wife Josephine (1825–74), a former actress, possibly because there were no children of the marriage, did not limit themselves to porcelain but set about extending their private collection of *objets d'art* to transform it into a collection for public viewing. The idea was said to have been Josephine's: she certainly sold her property in France in order to buy land at Barnard Castle as a site for their joint museum. Their collection, numbering some 15,000 items, was amassed within fifteen years and the building was specifically designed to house the museum. Although Josephine died long before either the collection or the building was complete (it opened in 1892), her will detailed the way she wished the museum to be run.

The Grosvenor Gallery at 135–7 New Bond Street was the joint venture of Sir Coutts Lindsay (1824–1913) and his wife Blanche, Lady Fitzroy (1844–1912). In its fourteen-year existence, from 1877–90, it proved to be the most progressive exhibition space of the era, staging the work of avant-garde artists in the summer and the more conventional, or a mix of old and new, in the winter. Both husband and wife were keen amateur painters and exhibited their own paintings there. Her connections served to attract a great deal of fashionable attention as well as patronage, so that the gallery conferred great prestige on those who exhibited there.

At a less exalted level women have been concerned in collecting and arranging for public display ordinary, everyday artefacts that have gone out of use. Items no longer needed from around the home, the farm, the school, the local shops or anything else pertaining to the local way of life have carefully been rescued and, eventually, put on show. The Angus Folk Museum at Glamis was the work of Jean, Lady Maitland (1890–1981), and it opened in 1953, although it moved to its present site a few years later. Similarly, in the 1930s Dr Isobel Grant recognised that the rural way of life was vanishing and so rescued many discarded items for what is now the Highland Folk Museum at Kingussie. Joan Ingleby and Marie Hartley saw the same process happening in Wensleydale and the result of their labours is the Upper Dales Folk Museum at Hawes, North Yorkshire.

Meanwhile, it was not only the rural way of life that was perceived as being in need of preservation but a concern over maintaining open spaces for people to enjoy that led to the founding of the National Trust. Octavia Hill (1838–1912) was deeply concerned with the welfare of the poorest levels of society and she initiated far-reaching improvements in housing and other aspects of their life. This included endeavouring to maintain public spaces, referred to as 'open-air sitting rooms for the poor', in which they could enjoy fresh air and life outdoors. The need was not only in London but applied to any of the fast-growing cities of the day, all of which called for an overall plan. From this sprang the concept of a more comprehensive scheme altogether. In 1895 Octavia Hill, in conjunction with Sir Robert Hunter and Canon H.D. Rawnsley, established The National Trust, their object being to preserve as much as possible of the country's history and beauty for the benefit of the people.

CHAPTER EIGHT

Literary and Learned Ladies

Why, when housewives were engaged for the most part in very practical matters all day and every day, did they actually need to read, write and do a little arithmetic? In what way could such skills make them better housewives and then, again, how could those skills be harnessed to be of benefit outwith the domestic situation? It has been suggested that women favoured literary pursuits because so many other avenues were closed to them, although they faced considerable hostility from some quarters by so doing.

Many managed without the three Rs. For girls, education tended to be expendable and, where money was scarce, the boys would get the benefit of what was available while the girls helped their mothers around the house or earned a few pence helping someone else. Even after the beginnings of compulsory education in the 1870s girls would be kept at home on washday, either to help with the heavy workload or to mind their siblings so that mother could get on with the chores. At a higher social level some ability in reading, writing and arithmetic was deemed an asset for a girl, though too much was not to be encouraged as mothers feared husbands-to-be would be scared off, while men feared that a 'clever' wife would neglect her household duties and his comfort.

The housewife might employ her writing skills to keep track of information of a domestic nature, passed on to her verbally, or of household expenditure; to keep in touch with family and friends living at a distance or to order goods and services for the home; to keep a journal of day-to-day activities or of major events, as an aide-memoire to the family's welfare or of her thoughts on the Sunday's sermon or other religious theme. In fact, such private and personal activities could easily be turned around and put into a format suitable for public reading and examples of their writing have already been seen in previous chapters; others will be found relevant to the chapters that follow. Meantime, some women revelled in the education they were given and continued to learn as much as they could of a given subject or to amass new skills or information.

Much of what is known about women in the past and their private preoccupations is due to the subsequent publication of material that was never intended for anything other than personal record keeping or for use within the family circle. It is therefore necessary to keep clear in the mind the fine line that divides this form of evidence from that written intentionally for public consumption.

It was noted earlier how, over the years, commentators from Gervase Markham to Isabella Beeton and beyond described the pivotal role of the housewife, seeing her as 'the mother and mistris' whose example was all-important to those with whom she came into contact. Hers was the responsibility for the moral education of her servants as well as of her children and the teaching of Christian principles was underlined in many households by daily prayers and Bible reading for all: late in Victorian times it was still maintained that 'Private prayer and family prayers morning and evening are common amongst all Christians'.[1] Mothers would instruct their children from an early age to say their prayers and learn their catechism and would then, if they themselves could read, progress to teaching them to read the Bible and to learn passages from it by heart. Some housewives followed this routine with their servants too.

The reading housewife was not only able to impart the technique to others and help them along the path of life, but she also gained access to a wider range of information. Mothers taught their daughters and they in turn would teach the next generation; there is nothing wrong with oral information and local tradition but printed material could well open up new horizons. During the period, the market for books on cookery, needlework, medical and devotional matter and similar subjects expanded, as did the area of what might be termed 'recreational' reading – many works in both sections were written by women for women. The converse of this was that many a housewife came to complain that their daughters' and housemaids' heads were being stuffed with romantic nonsense from all the novels being churned out to satisfy the new reading public.

The housewife able to do simple sums could keep track of domestic expenditure, thereby ensuring there was nothing untoward in the outgoings. Many housewives, though, had no need to keep accounts; they knew to the last halfpenny exactly where the week's money had gone, and there was never enough to go round. Countless domestic account books survive in manuscript form among family archives and they are the raw material of the domestic historian's trade. One of the best known of those subsequently printed covers the years 1692 to 1733 and pertains to the household of Lady Grisell Baillie while based in Edinburgh, in London and at Mellerstain near Kelso, and it includes mention of their travels around Britain and a lengthy sojourn in Italy. An earlier example survives in Sarah Fell's accounts for Swarthmoor Hall, near Ulverston. Quaker commitments meant her mother Margaret Fell and step-father George Fox were often absent for long periods and so the three unmarried daughters saw to the running of the household and kept records of the farm work.

Housewives were apt to jot down bits and pieces of information, sometimes on loose scraps of paper, sometimes in a book. Many of these notes survive in manuscript form: some relate solely to cookery while others embrace a wider range of subject matter. The collections assembled by Lady Castlehill, Elinor Fettiplace and Rebecca Price, since edited and published, were discussed earlier. Into this category come instructions drawn up by some housewives for the use of their servants, such as those by Lady Grisell herself and Susanna Whatman or, later, by the Ladies Hippisley and Breadalbane, prior to being given over to the house steward or butler and the housekeeper. This avoided misunderstandings over the domestic routine and did away with constant repetition due to the frequent turnover in lower servants.

Women who could write comfortably, regardless of whether they could spell consistently, might write out a sermon they had heard or their thoughts on immortality, Christian duty and so on. Some went further, keeping an account of their spiritual progress, their personal 'journal of the soul'. Willielma, Lady Glenorchy (1741–86), and her sister were both beauties, accomplished, and married in the year 1761; the sister and her husband died suddenly in Bath, leaving one daughter, and Willielma herself became a childless widow some ten years after her marriage. 'About her twenty third year Lady Glenorchy came under religious influences of the deepest kind . . . she was so absorbed with the spiritual bearings of life that its more human aspects were somewhat overlooked'.[2] She was celebrated for her charity, established several chapels and kept a diary relating to both her daily and her spiritual life.

Another Grisell Baillie (1822–91), a descendant of *the* Lady Grisell Baillie, dedicated herself 'To lead a life of devotion to God, and to give all her energy and all her strength to His direct service in the path which he seemed to point out to her, [was] . . . the realisation of her brightest hopes and most earnest desires'.[3] She carried on the religious instruction of the young for most of her life, cared for her less fortunate neighbours and raised money for foreign missions; in addition, she instituted the Young Women's Christian Association, as well as a local Band of Hope to promote temperance and a 'Mothers' Meeting' for which she built a hall as a memorial to a beloved brother. It was in connection with these latter gatherings that she wrote down her thoughts on various aspects of the Church's teaching; the principal points as an aide-memoire for while she was speaking and then elaborating on them afterwards from memory and writing them down for the benefit of others. After her death they were published in the hope that 'those who did not hear them spoken may glean golden grain from them'.[4]

Not only a 'journal of the soul' with biblical references and devotional experiences but a diary, albeit incomplete but kept by a woman, survives from the seventeenth century. Lady Anne Clifford (1590–1676) was the heiress to great estates in the north of England but she had to fight for many years before she gained access to her inheritance and so her diary records much in the way of family history and actions taken for future reference.

Two equally formidable contemporaries commemorated their husbands for the sake of their children but reveal details of their own personalities in so doing. Lucy Hutchinson wrote the *Memoirs* after her husband's death: 'To moderate my woe, and if it were possible to augment my love'. The Colonel had sided with the Parliament and was one of King Charles' judges but after the King was beheaded he played little further part in politics. After the Restoration he was imprisoned on a trumped-up charge and died shortly afterwards. To be nearer the prison Lucy and two children moved to Deal in Kent 'from whence they walk'd every day on foote to dinner and back againe at night, with horrible toyle and inconvenience'.[5]

In 1644 Ann Harrison married a relation, Richard Fanshawe, just as the Civil War was gathering momentum and, after the Battle of Worcester and her husband's imprisonment, she, too, suffered 'toyle and inconvenience'. She would walk through the streets at 4 a.m. in order to visit him: 'There I would goe under his window and softly call him: he, after the first time excepted, never failed to put out his head at the first call: thus we talked together, and sometimes I was so wet with the rain that it went in at my neck and out at my heels.'[6] Instead of staying put quietly in the country, she shared in all his wanderings and on his missions abroad, as witnessed by the variety of places in which their children were born, and just as often died. As a widow she wrote her husband's biography for her only surviving son Sir Richard Fanshawe, 2nd Baronet, who had been rendered deaf and dumb through illness.

The approaching birth of her first child and the departure of a faithful servant caused a farmer's wife to leave off writing her diary: 'So now I say goodbye to my book, for I shall have too much work to do to write agen.' Anne Hughes kept 'her boke in wiche I write what I doe, when I hav thee tyme, and beginnen wyth this daye, Feb ye 6 1796' and for eighteen months recorded her everyday activities and relationships within the household.[7] This is possibly not the original format. Back in 1896 Jeanne Preston listened to an old woman reading from her mother's 'boke' and telling stories of long ago and the youngster jotted them down as she thought she herself might make use of them one day. She grew up to contribute articles to *Farmers Weekly* and it was there that the story of Anne Hughes, allied to her own mother's recipes, first appeared. With regard to other diaries Hannah Cullwick's record of her life as a maidservant is almost unique and has already been mentioned while some of the early members of the Cooperative Women's Guild also preserved details of their working lives but at a slightly later date.

Anne Hughes' life may have overlapped chronologically with that of Fanny Burney's (1752–1840) but the two women were poles apart in most respects. Fanny was born into a close-knit, well-educated, musical and intellectually active family and while still in her teens she began keeping a diary and started the voluminous correspondence that continued to the end of her life. There are also her journals, often composed many years after the events portrayed, which she based on letters, notebooks and her own memories. Her husband, General D'Arblay, before he died had made her promise to write a record of their life together for their only son Alexander who, in fact, predeceased her.

A specialised form of diary was kept by women while on their travels. Celia Fiennes journeyed the length and breadth of England between 1685 and 1703 and also crossed into Scotland and into Wales, though she thought poorly of both and stayed only briefly. So much caught her eye: the towns she passed through, sites of interest, local legends, innovative technology, the food she ate, market-places, significant houses, roads, industries and the latest in gardening styles – the list is almost endless. Scotland and its people was the focal point of a day-to-day journal kept by Dorothy Wordsworth as she travelled with her brother William and their friend Coleridge in 1803. The Highlands feature prominently in the *Memoirs* of Elizabeth Grant of Rothiemurchus (1797–1885) which, while not exactly being a tale of travel, recalled a byegone way of life contrasted with periods spent in London and Edinburgh. The *Memoirs* were written between 1846 and 1854 'for her own children and the daughter of her sister . . . with no thought but to interest them in the scenes of her early life which she recalled so vividly',[8] and they were not published until a decade or so after her death. The journal she kept of her married life on her husband's estate in Ireland has also been published, as has an account of a two-year stay in France during the 1840s. In the same way, Eleanor Sillar began to write down memories of her Victorian childhood for her own pleasure and as a reminder of the happiness of early days; it was only as the theme developed that she thought they might be of interest 'to my children and my friends' and at that point she was persuaded to consider publication.[9]

It was generally the womenfolk who were the letter writers but few could have foreseen their correspondence being published for the world to read. The *Memoirs of the Verney Family* contain a wealth of detail about life at the time of the Civil War. Sir Ralph preferred a seven-year exile in France rather than commit himself to a cause he did not fully believe in. His wife Mary returned to England to negotiate with the authorities on his behalf and died aged only thirty-three, worn out by her endeavours and privations, on her return to France.

The young William Temple met Dorothy Osborne (1627–95) by chance on the Isle of Wight and their subsequent courtship was long drawn out and beset with problems. Her *Letters* to him have survived the years and are filled with wonderful, everyday details of contemporary life and attitudes. Before he leaves for Ireland she asks him to bring back an Irish greyhound; she airs her views on marriage in general and discusses her other suitors in the event that the two of them are unable to marry; she apologises for a letter that fails to arrive, is happy after a quarrel has been sorted out, mourns the death of her father, expresses anxieties over her future and much, much more.

By way of contrast Mrs Purefroy of Shalstone in Buckinghamshire was a widow who shared the estate with her bachelor son Henry and the two of them wrote numerous letters regarding the everyday needs of the household as well as commissioning a wide range of purchases from the two men who acted as their agents in London, some 60 miles away. Today, much of this would be done over the telephone but at that time it was committed to paper and the results have since been edited and published. Half a century later Catherine Hutton's literary talents overflowed into her correspondence with family and friends, her letters containing graphic accounts of places, modes of travelling, manners and customs, fashions and characters, as well as comments on their fellow guests in the sparsely populated resort of Blackpool and a request to a male friend to purchase a new hat in London for her.

Many others were writing to inform, entertain, console or to ask for advice or re-assurance. The letters intended for the perusal of Fanny Burney's siblings and friends, those written by Mrs Delany, along with those of two nineteenth-century Janes – Austen and Carlyle – have reached a far wider audience than could ever have been envisaged by their authors, while it was a letter to a sick child, telling the tale of a rabbit accompanied by sketches, that started Beatrix Potter's career as a children's writer. From Ireland comes the correspondence of Emilia Lennox, Duchess of Leinster (1731–1814), and from further afield, from central Africa, the letters of Jane Moir.

First of all, though, the women had to learn how to use a pen. The practice of writing in a beautiful script was a discipline that was fading, even at the end of the seventeenth century, but several women were noted for their calligraphy. Esther Inglis (1571–1624) was renowned for her exquisite work and taught the royal families of Scotland and England. In the 1690s Elizabeth Penistone, herself the daughter of a writing master, kept a writing school in London, as did her contemporary Mrs Royer. Later again, Mary Johns (b. 1725), daughter of a Bermondsay cooper, was described as 'a very curious Englishwoman who surpasses many writing masters in the dextrous use of the pen'[10] and she was still active in the 1760s. Although writing continued to be taught to girls at most schools, it would rarely attain the same levels of expertise.

Once a woman had acquired the knack of writing, whether artistically or not, she also needed the paper and ink with which to record her thoughts and some time to herself in which to set them down. It is said that women preferred poetry because it needed less in the way of writing materials than, say, a biography or a novel and it was easier to turn the rhythms around in the mind while doing repetitive tasks around the home. Once organised, there were few areas in which they did not venture, seeing that most formats used by women for personal reasons adapted easily to publication. Their published writings on matters relating to the kitchen, the dining-room, the routine of servants and domestic management in general are legion and have featured in earlier chapters. Almost as prolific are those who emphasised the sacred nature of the housewife's calling and the moral duties involved in leading a household, while also stressing to the servants their responsibilities. Achievements in the way of personal accomplishments such as needlework, entertainment, music and art have also been outlined but their works under the all-embracing headings of childcare, health, religion, education, horticulture, travel and campaigning will be found in the chapters that follow. The scale of the problem is brought into focus when one author, in specifically discussing the development of the novel, could sub-title the work '100 good women writers before Jane Austen' and there has certainly been no lack of 'good women writers' in the years since.[11]

The letter format was one that was easy to modify for a public readership, as many authors found. Mary Delarivière Manley (1663–1724) was an early example with her witty observations on *A Stage Coach Journey to Exeter*. A question mark hangs over the publication of Lady Mary Wortley Montagu's (1689–1762) *Letters* in 1763. Written half a century earlier during her time in Constantinople where her husband was Ambassador, she claimed that she wrote only for herself but her actions would suggest she intended them to be published after her death. Mary Wollstonecraft's *Letters Written during a Short Residence in Sweden, Norway and Denmark* appeared in 1796 and, in due course, her widowed daughter Mary Shelley earned some money to support herself and her son by writing of her travels with her poet husband. Mrs Grant of Laggan, Inverness-shire, when widowed was left homeless, penniless and with eight children to support and it was the publication of her correspondence with friends under the title of *Letters from the Mountains* that set her on the literary path. The format was followed by Maria Graham who published many accounts of her travels, ranging from her *Letters on India with etchings and a map* to her *Letter to the Geological Society regarding the earthquake witnessed in Chile in 1822*, while 1864 saw the publication of *Letters from the Cape* by Lucy Duff Gordon (1821–69), followed the next year by her *Letters from Egypt.*

Alongside the memoirs intended for family perusal can be set Margaret, Duchess of Newcastle's published biography of her husband in which she sang his praises to the world. As Master of the King's Horse he had taught Charles II when Prince of Wales the art of horsemanship and written two books on the subject. She married the then Marquess (later Duke) in Paris in 1645 as his second wife. After the Restoration the couple returned to England to lead a retired life in the country and she employed herself in writing, copiously, on diverse topics. She said of her husband: 'His behaviour is such that it might be a pattern for all gentlemen; courtly, civil, easy and free, without formality or constraint: and yet hath something in it of grandeur, that causes an awful respect towards him.'[12] Contemporaries were not very polite about her literary efforts and styled her 'Mad Madge of Newcastle' and Samuel Pepys recorded: 'Reading the ridiculous History of my Lord Newcastle, wrote by his wife, which shows her to be a mad, conceited, ridiculous woman, and he an asse to suffer her to write what she writes to him, and of him.'[13] The Duke must have thought otherwise, as on his wife's death in 1673 he described her thus: 'A wise, witty and learned lady, which her many books do well testify; she was a most virtuous and a loving and careful wife, and was with her lord all the time of his banishment and miseries, and when he came home never parted from him in his solitary retirements.'[14]

Anna Bradstreet (?1612–72), America's first published woman poet, was another who publicly declared her love for her husband, including one poem entitled 'To my dear and loving husband' with its opening lines:

> If ever two were one, then surely we.
> If ever man were lov'd by wife, then thee;
> If ever wife was happy in a man,
> Compare with me ye woman if you can . . .[15]

Anna Bradstreet claimed her poetry was published without her consent but the paean of praise for a marriage of true minds can be found in most eras. Almost two-hundred years later Elizabeth Barrett Browning (1806–61) was demanding:

> How do I love thee? Let me count the ways.
> I love thee to the depth and breadth and height
> My soul can reach, when feeling out of sight
> For the ends of Being and ideal Grace.[16]

However, other women, saddled with less than ideal partners and trapped in the marriage by their lack of legal status, were looking at their relationships with somewhat cynical eyes. Elizabeth Thomas (1675–1731) in 'The Forsaken Wife' rebukes the unfaithful husband for his lack of humanity and insists that she herself will not change. The poem ends:

> . . . Show me a man that dare be true,
> That dares to suffer what I do;
> That can for ever sigh unheard,
> And ever love without regard:
> I then will own your prior claim
> To love, to honour, and to fame;
> But till that time, my dear, adieu,
> I yet superior am to you.[17]

Biography as a genre attracted many women authors. Fanny Burney (1752–1840), novelist and diarist, composed a *Memoir* of her father, although it proved to be disappointing due to its pompous style of writing. Catherine Hutton (1756–1846) commemorated her father, who was described as the historian of Birmingham. Ann Hope (1809–87) wrote a biography of her husband, the physician James Hope. Mrs Gaskell (1810–65) was commissioned to write a biography of Charlotte Brontë which provoked a scandalised response in certain quarters. C.L. Brightwell (1811–75) wrote a *Life of Amelia Opie* and there was Charlotte M. Yonge's (1823–1901) *Hannah More*. Mrs Oliphant (1824–97) included four full-length biographies of prominent men and a life of St Francis of Assissi among her copious output, whereas it was significant women of bygone days who filled the six volumes produced by Mary Hays (1760–1843). In 1919 it was not the illustrious of either sex who concerned Alice Clark but the working life of seventeenth-century women.

Catherine Macaulay (1731–91) wrote an acclaimed eight-volume *History of England* (1763–83) but her public credibility slipped when she married a man considerably younger than herself. Maria Graham (1785–1842) translated several historical tomes and also includes her own *History of Spain* and *Essays towards the History of Painting* among her considerable output. M.A.E. Wood (1818–95) worked on *Letters of Royal Ladies down to Mary's Reign* (1846), six volumes of *The Lives of the Princesses of England* (1849–55) and the *Life and Letters of Henrietta Maria* (1857) before spending the rest of her days editing no less than forty-one volumes of Calendars of Domestic State Papers in the Public Record Office. Lady Lucy Duff Gordon (1821–69) was another translator of historical tomes from their original German and an editor of other works. Catherine Sinclair (1800–64) wrote several volumes relating to

Scottish life and history. Alison Hay Dunlop concentrated on the history of old Edinburgh, while Elizabeth Penrose, 'Mrs Markham', focused on writing history for the young.

It has been said that the letter format at which women excelled and the biography were the basis of the novel and that, over the period, the letter/novel would evolve into the different forms familiar today. Some of the authors are well known and equally well documented: the three Brontës – Anne, Charlotte and Emily – for example, Jane Austen, Mrs Gaskell, George Eliot (Mary Ann Evans), Rebecca West, Virginia Woolf, Agatha Christie and children's writers Frances Hodgson Burnett, Enid Blyton and Beatrix Potter, to mention a mere fraction of a lengthy rollcall. Fanny Burney, whose novel *Evelina* was published in 1778, is often counted the first Englishwoman to write a popular novel, though alternative claimants of the calibre of Eliza Haywood (1693–1756), Sarah Fielding (1710–68) or Charlotte Lennox (?1727–1804) could easily be put forward. Mary Shelley's *Frankenstein* is considered one of the original works of science fiction and Ann Radcliffe did much to form the public taste for 'Gothic' novels.

Other authors have dropped out of the public eye, despite being popular during their lifetime. Who reads Frances Brook (1724–89), author of the first Canadian novel? Amelia Opie (1769–1853), a prolific novelist prior to her conversion to Quakerism? Eliza Parsons, who produced sixty novels, Charlotte Smith, Mary Pilkington or the Scots-born writers Mrs C.I. Johnstone (1781–1857), Susan Ferrier (1782–1854) and Mary Brunton (1778–1818)?

Mrs A.B. Jameson (1794–1860) first came to notice in 1826 after publication of *A Lady's Diary* (retitled *Diary of an Ennuyée*) and for the rest of her days she continued writing on diverse themes including art history and her travels, 'Latterly giving public expression', it was said, 'to her opinions about the position, education and utilitarian training of women'[18] and investigating the work of the Sisters of Charity around Europe. For over fifty years Mrs Oliphant (1828–97) supported her family by her writing and produced over one-hundred books, including novels, biographies needing much detailed research and innumerable short stories, articles and reviews. She could command an advance of £400 for a novel. 'Miss Braddon' (M.E. Maxwell, 1837–1915) wrote about eighty novels, a number of plays, edited several magazines and contributed articles to others but the novel that made her fortune was *Lady Audley's Secret*, published in 1862. Maria Corelli, pseudonym of Mary Mackay (1855–1924), was the flamboyant writer of sensational romantic novels whose later career did not match her earlier successes, while Winifred Holtby (1895–1935) had a considerable following in her day but her reputation waned after her early death.

Women known for writing in a particular genre can often be found writing in others too, as well as refining their feelings into poetry and already some of the names will be sounding familiar: Margaret, Duchess of Newcastle, for example, of whose *Poems & Fancies* Dorothy Osborne wrote to her lover: 'For God's sake if you meet with it send it to me; they say 'tis ten times more extravagant than her dress.' Later she wrote: 'You need not send me my Lady Newcastle's book at all, for I have seen it, and am satisfied there are many soberer people in Bedlam.'[19] However, Charles Lamb was to prove a kindlier critic. There are verses from Lady Mary Wortley Montagu, Elizabeth Rowe (1674–1737), Elizabeth Carter (1717–1806), Hester Piozzi (1741–1821), the Brontës, especially Anne and Emily, Caroline Norton, defined in the *DNB* as 'poetess' rather than for any of her other activities, Alice Meynell (1847–1922) and (Dame) Edith Sitwell (1887–1964).

Many other names could be added to the list, like those of early exponents Katherine Philips (1631–64), Anne Finch, Countess of Winchilsea (?1661–1720), and not forgetting the American Anna Bradstreet. Georgiana, Duchess of Devonshire, Hannah More, Elizabeth Barrett who was even more famous at the time than her husband Robert Browning and Christina Rossetti (1830–94), regarded as one of the great Victorian poets and composer of a popular Christmas hymn. Mary Beale and Ann Killigrew were not only poets but also accomplished artists. Mary Robinson was an actress and novelist and Joanna Baillie a playwright, while Eliza Acton wrote her cookbook at her publisher's suggestion after he rejected her offering of 'further fugitive verses'.

There is also the work of that prolific author and old friend 'Anon' to consider. Virginia Woolf declared: 'When one reads of a witch being ducked, of a woman possessed by devils, of a wise woman selling herbs, or even of a very remarkable man who had a mother, then I think we are on the track of a lost novelist, a suppressed poet, of some mute and inglorious Jane Austen, some Emily Brontë who dashed her brains out on the moor or mopped and mowed about the highways crazed with the torture her gift had put her to. Indeed I would venture that Anon, who wrote so many poems without signing them, was a woman.'[20]

In the earlier part of the period, the fashion for overlong verses brim full of innumerable classical allusions put women at a disadvantage, seeing that few had received a grounding in Latin or Greek and so they often found it necessary to apologise for their 'lack of learning'. Their shorter poems, which make use of domestic imagery and everyday themes, need no apologies and are more to the taste of our own age seeing that relatively few women today are given a grounding in the classics. Some exhibit a wry sense of humour such as Esther Johnson (1681–1728):

> If it be true, celestial Powers,
> That you have formed me fair,
> And yet in all my vainest hours
> My mind has been my care;
> Then in return I beg this grace,
> As you were ever kind:
> What envious Time take from my face,
> Bestow upon my mind.[21]

Women were frequently aware that a lack of education was at the root of their problems and that until girls could gain access to schooling comparable to their brothers' they would remain at a disadvantage. Examples are to be found of individual women who, against the odds, did acquire an education of higher calibre than was normal, either through their own initiative or because their fathers saw no reason to differentiate between sons and daughters. Where there were brothers and a tutor was employed, a girl might be allowed to share in the lessons, while others badgered male relatives for information.

During Tudor times women had benefited from the new attitudes to learning that were evolving but the situation had regressed by the later seventeenth century. The disruptions of the Civil War and the emphasis on marriage as the only career for a woman were implicated in the changing attitudes, though some girls were brought up in what was increasingly seen as an outmoded style. The daughters of John Milton (1608–74) were able to read aloud to their blind father in Hebrew, Greek, Latin, Italian, Spanish and French and though they did it unwillingly they were, nevertheless, efficient. Anna Bradstreet was encouraged to use her father's employer's library; Lady Mary Wortley Montagu, as the daughter of a duke, was educated according to the tenets of the time but she also read extensively the English and French works in her father's library and taught herself Latin with the aid of dictionaries and grammars.

Elizabeth Elstob (1683–1756) was orphaned at an early age and her uncle was horrified at the child's request to learn French, although the aunt was more amenable and helped her in her studies. Next, Elizabeth taught herself Latin and Greek, then set to work on Anglo-Saxon and, aged eighteen, became housekeeper to an older brother, a London vicar. Together they pursued their studies, attracting the attention of men of learning and Elizabeth became known as a brilliant scholar and writer. Her brother's death stopped further publications and she turned to teaching to save herself from starving, initially running a dame school in Evesham and later becoming governess to the Duchess of Portland's children.

Although 'the Saxon Lady' did not live to see the days when women would defy social attitudes to parade their learning, those days were not far off. Mrs Montagu and Mrs Carter were eminent members of a group nicknamed the 'Blue Stockings' who met regularly to discuss intellectual matters and to display their own erudition. The name was said to derive from the blue worsted stockings worn by Edward Stillingfleet who was too poor to wear the correct black silk stockings for attending salons. Mrs Montagu (1720–1800) was accounted the first 'Blue Stocking', an indefatigable correspondent, an essayist in dispute with Voltaire and a brilliant hostess who held literary salons in her mansion in Portman Square. Doctor Johnson called her 'Queen of the Blues',[22] while of their mutual friend Elizabeth Carter (1717–1806) he said: 'A man is in general better pleased when he has a good dinner on the table than when his wife talks Greek. My old friend Mrs Carter', he added, 'could make a pudding as well as translate Epictetus from the Greek, and work a handkerchief as well as compose a poem.'[23] Mrs Carter had been taught by her father but she was so slow in learning that he implored her to desist, a plea she ignored. She read early and late, keeping herself awake with green tea and tobacco; she mastered Latin and Greek, then Hebrew, French, Italian, Spanish and German; later in life she learnt Portuguese and Arabic following her interests in astronomy, ancient geography and ancient and modern history. She was an accomplished player on the spinet and German flute and a skilled needlewoman.

Other women in the group included Mrs Vesey from Ireland and Mrs Boscawen, the admiral's wife, who are respectively credited with originating the concept of literary salons and with coining the name for the group; Mrs Chapone, essayist, poet and writer on education; Mrs Delany of the 'paper mosaics' and a wide-ranging circle of correspondents; and Hannah More, playright, educationalist and social reformer. Meanwhile, there were others outwith the charmed circle who aspired to emulate them by specialising in abstruse topics or forming collections of natural history or botanical specimens. Inevitably, the 'Blue Stockings' attracted hostility and criticism and the name came to carry a derogatory aura about it. They were not confined to London as it was said, in connection with two Scottish novelists, Mrs Elizabeth Hamilton and Mrs Grant of Laggan: 'They were excellent women, and not too blue', while Francis Jeffrey, an eminent Scottish judge and literary editor, remarked 'that there was no objection to the blue stocking, providing the petticoat came low enough down'.[24] Generally, though, the prevailing attitude throughout the period was that a girl should disguise her learning for fear of frightening away a potential husband.

Mary Somerville (1780–1872) found her childhood and first marriage frustrating in the extreme and it was only after her second marriage that she achieved her potential as mathematician, astronomer and writer on scientific subjects. Of her it was said: 'Although her books were popular Mary Somerville was not a populariser of science. Rather she was an expositor, describing and explaining the current state of science in terms understandable to the well-educated reader. She emphasised experimental findings and used precise scientific vocabulary. She presented both sides of controversial issues; but once an idea was discredited, it disappeared from subsequent editions.'[25] From the 1840s onwards, the Somervilles were living in Italy and she was elected to numerous academic institutions in Italy as well as in the USA and was awarded several gold medals for her work: the Victoria Gold Medal of the Royal Geographical Society, The Victor Emmanuel Gold Medal and the first Gold Medal of the Geographical Society of Florence.

In 1835 Mary Somerville was one of the first two women to be elected to honorary membership of the Royal Astronomical Society, the other being her gifted predecessor in the field of astronomy, Caroline Herschel (1750–1848). Born into a family of musicians in Hanover and expected to be the family housekeeper, Caroline travelled to England at the behest of two brothers and trained with them as an opera singer. However, when brother William turned to astronomy she abandoned her music to become his assistant: 'I did nothing for my brother', she later wrote, 'but what a well-trained puppy dog would have done: that is to say I did what he commanded me. I was a mere tool which *he* had the trouble of sharpening.'[26] In this she failed to do herself justice. In 1782 William was appointed astronomer to George III and five years later Caroline was given her own salary of £50 a year in recognition of her work as his assistant. In the next ten years she independently found 3 stars and 8 comets (another 10 comets were to come) and presented the Royal Society with a list of no less than 561 stars omitted from their official records. After her brother's death in 1822 she returned to Hanover and, at the age of 75, completed her work on the positions of 2,500 nebulae. In 1828 she received the Gold Medal of the Royal Astronomical Society and the honorary membership followed some years later.

Someone who made a particular study of mathematics and foresaw the beginnings of computer science was Ada Lovelace (1815–52), Lord Byron's only legitimate child. By the age of fourteen she was competent in mathematics, astronomy, geometry and astronomy and was befriended by Mary Somerville. In 1834 Ada attended lectures on the 'difference engine' designed by Charles Babbage and studied its mathematical basis. Some years later she translated from the original Italian a theoretical and practical description of Babbage's next concept, an 'analytical engine', adding copious notes of her own on the programming of this machine, which was far more sophisticated than its predecessor and capable of performing advanced mathematical calculations. Her later years were disastrous. To raise money for the manufacture of Babbage's 'engine' she devised a supposedly infallible system for betting on the horses and fell heavily into debt; following a serious illness she became drug-dependent and turned away from mathematics in favour of electricity and chemistry. When she was only thirty-six she died of cancer.

Another whose final days were clouded was the engineer Henrietta Vansittart (1833–83), eldest daughter of a smoke-jack maker who devised a screw propeller trialled by the Royal Navy in 1857. Following her father's death some years later she continued his pioneering work and took out a patent for the Lowe-Vansittart Propellor which, in 1871 and thereafter, won numerous awards around the world. The propellor was fitted to many warships and to liners including the *Scandinavian* and the *Lusitania*. Henrietta's life ended in a lunatic asylum near Newcastle upon Tyne. Her obituary spoke warmly of her achievements and personality and, in referring to a scientific paper she had presented in 1876, claimed that, to date, she was the only woman who had ever written and read a scientific paper, illustrated by her own diagrams, to a scientific institution.[27]

Hertha Ayrton (1854–1923) was the first full female member of the Institute of Electrical Engineers and a founder member of the National Union of Scientific Workers. Initially she had earned her living as a seamstress and teacher but she attended Girton College to read mathematics (helped financially by the founders Emily Davies and Barbara Bodichon), became a lecturer and married an eminent professor of electricity. Her researches into the electric arc and her solutions to the problems encountered led in turn to her work for the Admiralty on searchlights and, later, to the development of a fan to disperse poisonous gases.

As women slowly gained access to higher education and were appointed to positions within the academic institutions, so they were able to benefit not only from such instruction but some went on to make distinctive and influential contributions in the sphere of education itself, while others, in their chosen fields of research, went on to win the highest academic recognition in the world.

CHAPTER NINE

Body and Soul

The preceding chapters have covered domestic topics such as cookery, the production and purveying of foods, the management of servants and the making of clothing and household linens and looked at how some women were able to use their skills in the wider world: the next chapters focussed on personal talents, such as a flair for entertaining or abilities in music, art or literature and then followed up the way in which women moved beyond the home in the exercise of their talents.

In contrast this chapter looks at women as they were, not necessarily exercising any one particular talent but acting only as themselves, within their own personalities – the heroine, the strong-minded, the half of a partnership, the dispenser of charity and the firm believer in Christian observance. That such women existed always seems in strong contrast to the generally accepted view of womanhood which implied they were in a permanent state of ill-health, frail, vapid, lacking financial resources and education, submissive if not intimidated, and without any means of improving their lot. Did it mean that the heroines, explorers, missionaries and women with personality-plus were unique, despite the numbers to be met with, or was it rather that the generalised picture of womanhood was flawed?

Some of the women who feature here have been met with already but in a different guise. The Countess of Derby, for example, embroiderer of bed hangings while under seige; Lady Fanshawe, biographer and constant companion of an adored husband; Lucy Hutchinson who suffered such 'toyle and inconvenience' when her husband was incarcerated; and Lady Grisell Baillie who nowadays is counted as a paragon of the domestic virtues, rather than for her childhood heroism in aiding her father's escape by carrying food to him each evening while he lay hidden in the local churchyard.

Staying north of the Border, the seventeenth century was a tumultuous one as folk fought for and against the establishment of Presbyterianism; religion, politics and family ambition all tangled together and the struggles brought in their wake disruption and hardship to many which, in so doing, revealed a host of strong-minded and fearless women on both sides of the debate. Dunnottar Castle, by Stonehaven, is spectacular even in its ruined condition. In 1650 it succumbed after an eight-month seige but the beseigers found no trace of the 'Honours of Scotland' – the

Crown, Sceptre and Sword denoting the sovereign's authority – nor of the private papers of Charles II. The story of the rescue varies but one version pays credit to the local minister's wife, Mrs Christian Grainger, who was sometimes able to enter the Castle. After one such visit she took away with her the regalia hidden about her person and the Cromwellian commander, it is said, assisted her to mount her horse. Another story credits the Grainger's servant who was often to be seen gathering seaweed at the base of the cliffs; one day she gathered up the regalia lowered to her in a basket. Either way the regalia spent the years until the Restoration stored in the pulpit of the local church at Kinneff, except for being taken out for monthly airings – a housewifely touch here, surely?

The Covenanters derived their name from the signing of The National Covenant in 1638 which demonstrated the widespread opposition to Charles I's anglicisation of Scottish worship and the introduction of bishops into the presbyterian system. Feelings ran high on both sides, and the women were as involved as the men, whether actively helping to carry earth and stones to fortify the port of Leith, assisting their menfolk to evade capture, suffering heartbreak at the loss of loved ones and trauma of being dispossessed of home, belongings and means of livelihood at the hands of the opposing soldiery. Whatever their religious convictions the women had their own ways of dealing with a problem. An anecdote relates how the women in a certain parish were rebuked for their non-attendance on the Sabbath by the minister, annoyed at his scanty congregation; the following week they all attended the kirk, each with a squalling infant in their arms and, rebuked again, the women replied with perfect logic that if they themselves were to be at the service their babies would be left untended.[1]

In 1661 the Marchioness of Argyll laid plans to rescue her husband from imprisonment within Edinburgh Castle. Accustoming the guards to seeing her sedan chair (the first recorded on the city's streets) carried in and out of the Castle, the Marchioness persuaded her husband to change places with her and he was already dressed in her clothes and head-dress when he abandoned the attempt. He was executed for treason shortly afterwards. Some twenty years later his son found himself in a similar predicament and was offered a means of escape by his step-daughter, Lady Sophia Lindsay, who smuggled in a suit of page's clothes. 'The Earl', says one account, 'was so agitated that he dropt the lady's gown when about to pass the sentinel at the gate; but she, with admirable presence of mind, snatched up her train from the mud, and in a pretend rage threw it in the Earl's face, with many reproaches of "Careless loon", which so besmeared him that his features were not recognised.'[2]

Helen Alexander (1654–1729) was another Covenanting heroine who assisted many of her co-religionists to evade capture. Lady Earlston, author of the widely read *Soliloquies*, voluntarily shared her husband's prison though she was not kept in irons. The widow of William Mure of Caldwell, spent three years incarcerated in Blackness Castle on the shores of the Firth of Forth due to an unsupported charge of listening to a sermon in her own home. The first year her eldest daughter was with her but was then freed. Hearing that her second daughter was close to death, only 2 miles away, Lady Caldwell tried everything to get permission to go to her 'tho' but for an hour; which she could not obtain; tho' she willingly offered to take the whole garrison along with her if they pleased as her guard, and maintain them upon her own proper cost, whilst she should be there doing the last duty of a Christian and tender-hearted mother'.[3] Even this feminine solution to the problem was rejected.

Among the zealous could be found the Duchess of Rothes, the Countess of Wigtown, Lady Kenmure, Lady Colville and many others. Anne, Duchess of Hamilton, refused to let Monmouth's troops search through her woods for defeated Covenanters after the Battle of Bothwell Bridge (1679), the excuse being 'lest the soldiers disturb the game in the parks'.[4] In this she was following the opinions of her grandmother who evinced formidable resistance to the imposition of English episcopacy: in 1639 Charles I had sent a fleet to Leith to enforce his views and Lady Hamilton 'whose son was in command of the King's Naval force, appeared on the sea shore with a brace of pistols at her saddlebow, loaded with balls of gold – it was supposed that lead bullets could not pierce the magic armour of the devil's agents – and personally opposed his landing'.[5]

Women on the other side also took up arms in defence of their beliefs. Ann, Lady Methven, on hearing that in her husband's absence a thousand Covenanters were holding a field meeting on his estate, proceeded to assemble a company of sixty men and led the way, 'with a light horseman's carbine ready cocked over her arm and a drawn sword in the other hand'.[6] After some debate, the Covenanters retreated. Another, whose husband was charged in the Glasgow courts for his religious activities, arrived in person and demanded the death penalty for him: 'He is a rebel! Hang him, my Lords!' The judges let the man go free, on the grounds that 'The poor man suffers enough at home already'.[7]

Scotland was not the only country to produce heroines in such troubled times: other women put their lives, their households and their husband's entire property at risk in assisting Charles II after the Battle of Worcester. A delightful story details the reactions of one such family faced with the news that the fugitive King needed shelter for the night and, not surprisingly, they were thrown into confusion at the thought. There were two main problems to sort out: 'And so . . . they contrive how his Majesty might be brought into the house, without any suspicion to their family [i.e., household], consisting of above twenty persons. Among them therefore, Mrs Julian Coningsby (the Lady Wyndham's Neice [*sic*]), Eleanor Withers, Joan Halsenoth . . . are made privy to their design. Next they consider what Chambers are fittest for his Majesty's reception.'[8]

Lady Derby's determination to save her husband's property at Lathom House was described earlier. Her heroism was matched by that of the Marchioness of Winchester who refused to quit Basing House despite frequent demands for its surrender. These women who declined to follow the patterns set for seige warfare were a problem: not only was Lady Winchester related to certain powerful families but she was also half-sister to the Parliamentary commander Lord Essex. Once the siege was under way she and her ladies set to work, moulding bullets from lead stripped off the roof. Eventually the house was surrendered and razed to the ground, though Lady Winchester herself survived. Corfe Castle in Dorset was also defended by a woman, Lady Bankes, who in the latter days of the seige 'to her eternal honour be it spoken'[9] defended the castle's upper ward with her waiting women and five soldiers who all heaved stones and hot embers over the battlements, thereby preventing the attackers from gaining entry. That terminated the first seige; the second was ended by treachery but Lady Bankes and her children were allowed to leave unmolested though the castle was razed and its contents looted. The Parliamentary side had a heroine of their own in Brilliana, Lady Harley, who was similarly related to families on both sides; however, despite being publicly defiant she differed from those highborn ladies and their scornful refusals to surrender in being privately anxious and uncertain how to proceed. Her weakness and prevarications acted in her favour; the seige of Brampton Bryan Castle was lifted, only to be resumed; but then Brilliana herself fell ill and died, leaving the garrison bereft and unable to continue. Later, it was said of her: 'That noble Lady and Phoenix of Women dyed in peace; though surrounded with drums and noyse of war, yet she took her leave in peace. The sword had no force against her, as long as God preserved her, He preserved the place where she was.'[10]

The story of women's bravery in time of war continues across the years. Mrs Smith, one of only four soldiers' wives present at the Battle of Balaclava, two-hundred years later, was seen laying about the fleeing Turkish soldiers with a stave and berating them in no uncertain terms in the broadest of Scots for abandoning their allies in the face of the oncoming Russian troops.

In times of war and its aftermath so many of the menfolk would be absent from home – through death, exile or imprisonment – that courage of another sort was demanded from the women left behind, who must continue day by day to do their utmost for their absent husband or orphaned children and for the welfare of their whole household. Indeed, such courage is a living memory for those who were caught up in the two world wars when, in the absence of the menfolk, women worked in the factories, on the farms and in the forests, operating heavy machinery and felling timber. This was not unique to the twentieth century. The Verney *Memoirs* reveal how the women of the family coped in the absence of their menfolk; both Lady Verney and Margaret, Duchess of Newcastle, returned from exile for a year or more in an attempt to sort out their husbands' affairs and obtain relief on the estates. Anne, Duchess of Hamilton, inherited her title in 1651 when her lands had been forfeited, crops, livestock and timber plundered and estates given over to others and she had to negotiate for loans with which to pay off the fines imposed and gradually buy back the estates; it was 1656 before she married and had the support of a husband. The wives of the early Quaker preachers, too, 'willingly shared with their husband's loss of income and social position, and lengthy separations',[11] though just as often it was the Quaker women who were absent from their homes.

A hundred years later, another period of turmoil in Scotland produced a group of exceptional women. After the Battle of Culloden punitive measures were enforced against the Highlanders; clan chiefs and property owners went into exile and some estates were forfeited. It was often the womenfolk who struggled to regain control of the property and oversaw its workings, who kept in touch with the exiles and sent money abroad if they could. They argued with government officials against every imposition of taxes and were not afraid to take their grievances to the King, if they could gain access to him, pleading on behalf of their 'fatherless bairns' even though those same 'bairns' had grown to adulthood meanwhile. One outstanding act of bravery is well known. It was not the Honours of Scotland that Flora Macdonald (1722–90) smuggled away but the claimant to the throne itself, Prince Charles Edward Stewart. After Culloden the Prince was hunted across Scotland and Flora was persuaded to escort him, disguised as an Irish serving girl, from Benbecula to the Isle of Skye. After Flora's part in the escape became known she was sent to a prison ship in the Firth of Forth and was then held in the Tower of London but was released under the 1747 Act of Indemnity. The sea played its part in another act of heroism in 1838 when Grace Darling (1815–42) and her father, keeper of the Longstone lighthouse on the Farne Islands, carried out a daring rescue of survivors of the storm-hit steamship *Forfarshire* which had gone aground in atrocious conditions. She was honoured by the nation for her bravery but died just a few years afterwards and is buried in Bamburgh.

On the other hand, some women are remembered nowadays largely due to their force of personality. Lady Anne Clifford (1590–1676) and her struggles over a thirty-eight year period to regain her inheritance belong to an earlier era but her stubbornness ensured her success. Margaret,

Duchess of Newcastle, is now recalled more for the person she was than for the writings that flowed from her pen. The commanding personality of Sarah, Duchess of Marlborough, dominated the friendship with Princess (later Queen) Anne, the two women taking on the pseudonyms of Mrs Morley and Mrs Freeman in order to banish the differences in rank. Born Sarah Jennings, she followed her sister as Maid of Honour to the Princess and then married a young soldier, John Churchill, in about 1678. As his career progressed so he advanced in the peerage, receiving his Dukedom in 1702. Meanwhile, Sarah assisted the Princess with her tangled finances and endeavoured to clamp down on the widespread cheating and bribery within the Household; she sorted out the Princess's wardrobe, worked on her politics and to promote better relationships with her father, James II, and her brother-in-law, William of Orange. After losing the Queen's favour and the dismissal of her husband from office the couple travelled abroad, only returning to England the day after the Queen's death.

The name of Lady Mary Wortley Montagu (1689–1762) may still strike a chord, although the reasons why have generally been forgotten. Yet, in her day, she was eminently newsworthy. She eloped; she accompanied her husband, the Ambassador, to Turkey; and on her return introduced their custom of inoculation for smallpox into England. After her marriage broke down she travelled widely and lived abroad for much of the time. She was a writer and a poet, concerned with the status of women and strongly in favour of education for women although, as she wrote to her daughter, a girl should disguise her learning as she would a physical deformity or she might become an object of envy and hatred.

As newsworthy in their day were the two 'Ladies of Llangollen' who eloped from their homes in Ireland because they enjoyed each other's company and wished to spend the rest of their lives together. As was to be expected, their action caused a major sensation and they aroused intense curiosity for the rest of their lives. Lady Eleanor Butler (1739–1829) and Sarah Ponsonby (1755–1831) settled in Llangollen where they planned to lead a quiet existence, reading and studying, gardening and walking, and overseeing a small farm. They acquired a wide circle of friends, welcomed many visitors to their house over the years and were well spoken of by the local community. References to 'the Ladies' can be found in a number of contemporary journals.

Many other women were also 'personalities' within the meaning of the term but their names tend to be connected with a specific cause that they worked for – fighting for improvements within the prisons, the nursing service, for a better deal for married women or to curtail working hours for children. Otherwise, they are remembered for some particular line of action that they took, whether at home or abroad, and will therefore be found elsewhere in this book.

Personality allied to feminine charms contributed to the social advance of many women, all the more so if they managed to become the mistresses of men of high rank or substance. At the top of the scale must come the Royal mistresses for which Charles II can lay claim to a goodly number, though his brother James was almost as busy. Lucy Walter (1630–58) had been the mistress of various men before she gave birth to two of the King's children after he had fled from England. Rumours of a marriage between them were always strenuously denied by the King. After the Restoration Barbara Villiers (1641–1709) bore the King five children in as many years and, once cast off by the King, had a three-year liaison with John Churchill before he met and married Sarah Jennings. John Churchill's sister Arabella (1648–1730), meantime, was mistress to the King's brother James, Duke of York and bore him four children in quick sucession. She was supplanted by Catherine Smedley who is interesting in that, as an heiress in her own right, she could have expected 'a good marriage' but obviously considered life as a mistress more rewarding. Arabella herself married a colonel and produced two more daughters. In 1671 Charles established Louise de Keroualle as his mistress '*en titre*' and she used her influence to ensure his dependence on France. Meanwhile, a serious rival in the King's affections was Eleanor Gwyn (1650–87), 'pretty, witty Nell', orange seller and comedienne at the Theatre Royal, Drury Lane, who won the King's heart by standing on stage reciting a witty ditty while wearing a hat the size of a coachwheel; he took her home for supper, she became his mistress and gave birth to two of his sons. It was of her that the King said as he lay dying: 'Let not poor Nelly starve'.[12] Royal mistresses were rarely out of fashion in the years that followed, most monarchs preferring the company of somebody other than their wife, which was maybe not so surprising when royalty married for political expediency and with little regard for their feelings.

Nell Gwyn was just one actress whose life on stage was a springboard for an alternative career and actresses for long enough carried an aura of immorality about them, whether justified or not. Dora Jordan, the foremost comedienne of her day, was the long-term mistress of the Duke of Clarence (later William IV) and mother of innumerable children but she was abruptly ousted from both his affections and his household when it was decided he should marry and produce some legitimate heirs. Marriage to Adelaide of Saxe-Meiningen followed but there were no children of the union.

An actress of another sort, Emma Hart or Lyon, after a chequered career lived as the mistress and then the wife of Sir William Hamilton, ambassador, music lover and collector of antiquities. Like Dora Jordan and some of her colleagues, Emma was painted several times by the foremost artists of the day. However, she is better known to history as the mistress of Admiral Lord Nelson and the mother of his child, Horatia, and was supposedly 'bequeathed to the nation' when Lord Nelson died. At a somewhat later date, Catherine Walters, nicknamed 'Skittles', is called 'the last Victorian courtesan' and was regarded as an absolute charmer who could hold her own in any society. However, 'Society' was outraged when she appeared at the 1862 Derby on the arm of Lord Hartington, son and heir to the Duke of Devonshire; he was sent off to the USA for six months while she fled to Germany, to continue her career elsewhere.

The line between kept mistress and paid prostitute is a narrow one and many women must have found themselves switching from one category to the other as circumstances dictated. It was said that whereas the occasional prostitute might be lucky and persuade someone to marry her, 'the vast majority accomplish the full curriculum of the Harlot's Progress. From the house at St John's Wood, the brougham and pair, the diamonds, the gay parties and gayer suppers, to Regent Street and the Strand, the gin shop and the kennel, there are very few steps indeed . . .'.[13] Many were driven into prostitution through lack of employment or means of support: when a servant, shop girl, factory hand or any female employee was dismissed with little or no warning without a family to support her it was almost inevitable she would end up on the streets and the chances were high that she would become pregnant, thereby obliterating her chance of regaining 'respectable' employment. When women themselves began to campaign against the double standards inherent in social attitudes, they pointed out that the moral code should operate on behalf of all women, not merely women of the middle classes, otherwise an entire sub-class of women 'made up of other men's daughters and other men's sisters . . . "God forbid they should be our own"' would need to be 'set aside for men's vices'.[14] Prostitution and the hypocritical attitudes towards it were one of the principal campaigns of the later nineteenth century and will be referred to again in a later chapter.

'Lucy Locket lost her pocket, Kitty Fisher found it' run the opening lines of a nursery rhyme. 'Kitty Fisher' is thought by some to refer to Catherine Maria Fisher or Fischer (d. 1767), a notorious courtesan of the day, witty and beautiful and a daring horsewoman; she was painted several times by Reynolds. After her marriage to John Norris of Benenden, sometime MP for Rye, she devoted herself to building up his dilapidated fortunes. At one time she was forced to advertise, to state that memoirs in circulation purporting to be hers were no such thing. On the other hand, Harriette Wilson's *Memoirs* of 1825 were not false and it was to her that the Duke of Wellington supposedly replied 'Publish and be damned' when a blackmailing letter came prior to publication.[15] An earlier example, probably written with blackmail in mind seeing that their author was imprisoned for debt in London's Marshalsea, were by Dublin-born Laetitia Pilkington, though she included her poetical writings in the work; her memoirs proved popular and were reprinted several times in quick succession.

Laetitia is described not as 'courtesan' but 'adventuress' and several other women could fall into this category. Lola Montez, whose real name was Marie Dolores Eliza Rosanna Gilbert (1818–61) was another Irish lass. In 1837, while on the way to India and a possible marriage, she eloped with a ship's officer and when the marriage failed she took up a career as a 'Spanish dancer'. She was extremely popular in Dresden, Berlin, Warsaw, St Petersburg and Paris; there were various lovers and one or two children as well and, within a few days of arriving in Bavaria, she was the mistress of Ludwig I and meddling in the country's politics. Having been banished from that country, she toured the USA with fifty cases of clothes and worked in Australia before settling in the States and devoting herself to helping 'fallen women'.

Prior to meeting with Lola Montez, the Bavarian King had had an affair with an Englishwoman, Jane Digby (1807–81), who was certainly 'adventurous' though not necessarily an 'adventuress'. Born into an aristocratic family and considered one of the most beautiful woman of her time, at seventeen she married a much older man who neglected her for his political career – with inevitable results. The divorce in 1830 was spectacular for its news coverage of intimate details and Jane escaped to Europe with her Austrian prince. Thereafter, she stayed abroad and over the years had a number of love affairs with members of the European aristocracy, two more marriages and several children, and she travelled widely. It was in Syria that she met and married the man who was to be the love of her life for over twenty years – a Bedouin sheikh very much younger than herself, of a different culture and with a wife and children already. Stories of their life together in Damascus and in the Syrian desert filtered through to England and lost nothing in the telling.

Comparisons were inevitably made between Jane Digby and Hester Stanhope (1776–1839), niece and hostess to her uncle William Pitt. On his death he asked the nation to look after her as a reward for his services. When a favourite brother and Sir John Moore, the man she hoped to marry, were both killed at Corunna she set off on her travels to fulfil a fortune-teller's prophecy that she would be 'Queen in the East'.[16] After some exciting times wandering through Europe, being shipwrecked off Rhodes and undertaking a pilgrimage to Jerusalem, she settled on the slopes of Mount Lebanon, converting the ruins of a convent and village into the semblance of a fortress. Her small retinue gradually deserted her but there were innumerable inquisitive visitors; she adopted Eastern customs and manners, became steeped in oriental mysticism and astrology, dabbled in local politics and supported a rabble of beggars. She ran up enormous debts and when her government pension was stopped in order to pay them off, she shut herself within her fortress with five attendants and refused access to everyone. Her death occured a year later and although the British Consul and an American missionary arrived just after she died, the servants had fled and the place had been looted. At midnight, the two men buried her, by torchlight, in her own garden.

If Hester Stanhope was a bequest to the nation, other women were on the receiving end of rather more solid inheritances of their own. Throughout the period any heiress was much sought after as a wife, whatever her looks might have been, seeing that control of her property and the income derived from it passed to the husband on marriage. One prominent example concerns the Grosvenor Estates in London which were brought into the family by twelve-year-old Mary Davies on her marriage to Sir Thomas Grosvenor in 1677. Her inheritance included about 100 acres in Mayfair, where building began in 1720, and some 400 acres in Belgravia and Pimlico where the main developments date from the 1820s to the 1850s. Further examples are provided by the daughters of wealthy Americans who married into certain aristocratic families later in the nineteenth century and were their financial salvation.

An inheritor of great wealth in her own right was the philanthropist Angela Burdett Coutts (1814–1906), whose grandfather was Thomas Coutts, the banker. She, too, was called 'Queen' but in this instance the title was 'Queen of the Poor'. She spent her money wisely, supporting innumerable worthy causes which included housing schemes, evening classes, social clubs, 'fallen women', training for sailors, the rebuilding of churches, the provision of stables for donkeys and drinking fountains for horses and dogs and a bishopric in New Zealand. When she died, many thousands of people gathered to watch her funeral procession go past. An inheritance of a different kind was that of the Dowlais iron and steel works in Wales, owned by Sir Josiah John Guest. On his death in 1852 Lady Charlotte Guest (1812–95) took over its running, having been accustomed to helping in the management of the business, despite being the mother of ten children. Thereafter she effectively ran the enterprise and took a close interest in the welfare of those who worked for her. In addition she was a writer, translator of an ancient Welsh saga and collector of *objets d'art*, including fans and porcelain.

At the commercial level, some of the women who took over the running of a business following the death of father or husband have already been noted: Miss Harvey, for example, who inherited a linen draper's shop; Hester Bateman, the silversmith; and Mrs Hepplewhite who, two years after her husband's death, published *The Cabinet Maker*, on which much of his fame rests. If these women could run a venture then it has to be assumed that many others were similarly engaged, a situation confirmed by reference to the street directories of numerous towns.

Welfare tended to be a woman's concern, whether it concerned the employees at an ironworks or a couple of domestic servants. This was partly due to their natural aptitude as carers, partly to their religious convictions. Charity and the giving of alms, the care of one's neighbours and of those less able to look after themselves were all part of the Christian teaching and many women followed its tenets with generosity of spirit. Their benevolence took many forms. Lady Anne Clifford provided almshouses for old women, rebuilt several parish churches and commissioned elaborate memorials to her mother. Lady Glenorchy established chapels in Carlisle, Matlock, Edinburgh and Strathfillan and in her will left large sums to the Society for the Propagation of Christian Knowledge, primarily for the maintenance of schools. Lady Anne Halkett was skilled in medical practices and people travelled immense distances to visit her. Nell Gwyn, actress and royal mistress, was reputedly behind the setting up of the Royal Hospital, Chelsea, for the care of veteran soldiers. Selina, Lady Huntingdon (1707–91), put her money at the disposal of the Methodists to support preachers, build chapels and establish a training college. Mrs Sarah Trimmer was an influential educationalist and, among her other projects, fostered Sunday schools in the Brentford area. Hannah More, dramatist, educationalist and philanthropist, was instrumental in promoting schools around the Cheddar Gorge area where, her sister Martha said: 'There is as much knowledge of Christ as in the wilds of Africa.'[17] Catherine Sinclair (1800–64) was equally distinguished for her numerous writings and for her deeds of benevolence, while her compatriot, the former Elizabeth Grant of Rothiemurchus and her husband, in the midst of the Irish potato famine of the 1840s, did everything they could to mitigate the problems of the tenants on their estate. Even Queen Victoria knitted comforts for the soldiers in the Crimea.

Caroline Norton, along with her other campaigns, focussed attention on the appalling conditions that faced young children in factories. Agnes Weston worked tirelessly on behalf of seamen and established 'Sailors' Rest' homes in Devonport (1876) and in Portsmouth (1881) and when she died in 1918 was accorded a burial with full naval honours. Lady Victoria Campbell travelled tirelessly all over Scotland organising Bible classes, mothers' meetings, local branches of the Young Women's Christian Association, clothing clubs and soup kitchens. In the twentieth century Olave Baden Powell established the Girl Guide Movement, Eglantyne Jebb founded the charity Save the Children in the aftermath of the First World War and, after the Second World War, Sue Ryder devoted her energies to the relief of suffering, initially from Nazi atrocities, but latterly on a broader spectrum.

If religious principles inspired benevolence, there were fanatics, too. Elspeth Buchan (1738–91) established a sect in south-west Scotland in which everything was held in common: as the Lord's coming was imminent they saw no point in doing any work. The story was told of how she tried to persuade a gardener to leave 'Mr Copland's garden and come and work in that of the Lord.' 'Thank 'ee,' replied the dour old man, 'but the Lord was na' owre kind to the last gardener he had.'[18] Mother Buchan herself died in 1791 but the sect continued until the 1830s. Joanna Southcott (1750–1814) was another fanatic; a Devonshire farmer's daughter, she prophesied and interpreted strange dreams thereby attracting both attention and some converts, but not to the same extent as the Buchanites.

Many took up their pens to expound on aspects of the Christian religion. In the seventeenth century the Ladies Glenorchy, Brooke and Halkett were writing at length on these and related topics, as did many others. Elizabeth Rowe (1674–1737) was well known for both her prose and verse writings but her *Devout Exercises of the Heart in Meditation and Soliloquy, Praise and Prayer* appeared after her death in 1737 and was still being reprinted into the next century, as was her *Friendship in Death.* Her three-volume *Letters Moral and Entertaining* were designed to excite 'religious sentiment in the careless and the dissipated'.[19] During her long widowhood she retired to her birthplace near Frome and devoted herself to pious exercises and looking after the 'sick poor'. Grace Kennedy (1782–1825) also devoted herself to her contemplative studies and her writing, although her family remained unaware of either activity. Her books, she said, were addressed 'to the youth of the higher classes'[20] but her authorship remained anonymous until the last year of her life and then even her deathbed became the theme of a sermon. Mary Ann Burges (1763–1813) was another who preferred anonymity: educated, musical, competent in geology and botany and able to illustrate her own works, she wrote an immensely popular continuation of *The Pilgrim's Progress* which ran through several editions in London, Dublin and the USA. Lucy Hutchinson's *Memoirs* of her husband remained in manuscript until 1806 and it was a further decade before her religious writings were published. Hannah More wrote for the stage, encouraged by actor-manager David Garrick, until she came to believe this was wrong. Instead, she wrote *Sacred Dramas* for young people and works on moral reflections, while her poem against slavery was well received. Mary Ann Jevons (1795–1845) was the author of *Sonnets and Other Poems, chiefly devotional.* Eliza Acton's poetry deals with themes of abandoned love, death and desolation, whereas her cookery writing is precise and often humorous. Grisell Baillie (a descendant of Lady Grisell of Mellerstain) lived a life of such piety and good works that a niece published a biography and included many of her aunt's talks addressed to local church groups. Dorothy Sayers created her aristocratic detective Lord Peter Wimsey and wrote a series of stories about him before turning to writing religious dramas for radio.

Religious themes were expanded to include morality and humanitarian concerns: 'Charlotte Elizabeth' took the theme of flowers, one for each chapter, and from each derived many a philosophical musing and moral tale, a method that proved popular with her readership. J. Ellice Hopkins, social reformer, founder of the White Cross League and writer, pleaded with mothers to see to the moral education of their sons since it was they who would be responsible for the future health and happiness of their womenfolk.

Hymn writing was another facet of women's talents: Frances Ridley Havergal created many religious verses that were set to music. Christina Rossetti composed the words of a much-loved Christmas carol. Mrs C.F. Alexander (1818–95) contributed the words to a number of hymns still sung today, including some written especially for children. Catherine Winkworth translated several resounding hymns from the German which are equally popular. Ann Griffiths (1776–1805) was a writer of hymns in Welsh: a farmer's daughter, she spent her whole life near Llanfihangel Yng Ngwynfa, Powys, and on becoming a Methodist in 1797 expressed her faith through her verses but, being illiterate, they were written out by someone else. Her most famous work is translated as 'Bread of Heaven' and sung to the tune of 'Cwm Rhondda'.

However, for some religion went much further than looking after 'the poor', writing devotional works or hymns to be sung in church. They not only translated their religious principles into action but were active in preaching their beliefs with vigour which, in the intolerant climate of the time, took courage of enormous proportions. The fervour of the Scottish Covenanters has already been described and many were persecuted or killed in the name of religion: Margaret McLaughlan and Margaret Wilson are called the 'Wigtown Martyrs' since the story is that they were tied to a stake in the river estuary and left to drown as the tide came in. Two others were hanged for attending a field preaching and remarking on the barbarity of the soldiers. As they waited at the gallows they sang the 13th Psalm so loudly that the minister sent to preach at them could not make himself heard. For similar offences others were branded and transported to New Jersey.

Mary Fisher was an early Quaker of awesome courage. She was one of the first to take Quakerism to America and was flogged before being banished. She preached in East Anglia, was stoned, whipped and imprisoned in York Jail. In 1657 she set off with a few others on a mission to Jerusalem and they decided to convert the Turkish ruler while they were about it; the British Consul sent them back by sea to Venice but Mary somehow left the party and, all alone, walked 500 miles and more through Greece, Macedonia and Thrace until she arrived at the Sultan's Court, then at Adrianople. It was ironic that, given the humble status of women in the East generally, Mary Fisher was treated politely and accorded a respect noticeably lacking in the treatment she and other women received in much of western Europe and America. Having arrived at the Court of the 'Great Turk', she was listened to attentively; she was then invited to stay on or offered a guard for the return journey. Both offers were declined and she returned in safety 'without the least hurt or scoff'. Other Quaker women were similarly courageous in their suffering while putting their beliefs into practice.

The Quaker movement was gathering momentum in the 1650s. Margaret Fell first heard George Fox preaching in Ulverston church and she became thereafter a source of guidance and inspiration to the developing Society of Friends. At first she was kept at home by her domestic and family duties – eight of her children survived – but during this period she offered hospitality to all, provided spiritual and material help to wandering preachers, wrote innumerable letters expressing sympathy and encouragement to individuals as well as to groups and expounded on the fundamental principles of Quakerism. Particularly did she give support to the women and children left behind by the itinerant preachers: 'The sturdy independence of these wives is truly remarkable: they were left to carry on the farm, or the shop, or the estate, often caring for little children as well.'[21] It was on her initiative that the 'Swarthmore Fund' was started, to assist preachers, those in prison and others in need. The Quakers' beliefs brought them into conflict with the State and with both the Puritans and the Episcopalian Church and they became snared in legislation designed to deter Catholics and other Dissenters, which caused severe suffering to many. Some ten years after the death of her husband Judge Fell, Margaret married George Fox in 1669 and together they formed a stimulating partnership.

Catholics were persecuted in the sixteenth century and women had died for their beliefs; thereafter, many young Catholics were sent abroad for their education, despite fines if it became known. In 1686 a Catholic sympathiser gifted and endowed a house in York and invited Frances Bedingfield, who belonged to an order of nuns founded in St Omer by Yorkshirewoman Mary Ward, to open a school for girls of Catholic families. The timing was particularly delicate being so soon after the accession of James II, when fears of a Catholic resurgence abounded, and the school first opened at Hammersmith, outside London, before moving north to a site by the Micklegate Bar. The locals were seemingly unaware of the true nature of the concern, merely accepting that the ladies of the Bar 'had an interest in education', even though the head of the school was imprisoned on several occasions. There is also the tradition that on one occasion when an angry mob attacked the house a sudden silence fell and the crowd dispersed when St Michael himself was seen riding to the rescue of the nuns. Would the locals really keep quiet about such a sight? The Bar Convent flourished as a day school and in 1929 was recognised by the government as a direct grant school. A similar enterprise was set up in Edinburgh by Lady Elizabeth Howard, who, it was said, 'openly kept a kind of college for instructing young people in Jesuitism and Jacobitism together. In this labour she seems to have been assisted by the Duchess of Perth, a kindred soul, whose enthusiasm afterwards caused the ruin of her family, by sending her son into the insurrection of 1745.'[22]

As a result of the Reformation, any gathering of men or women within the Anglican communion was immediately suspected of 'Romish' tendencies – as witnessed by the rejection of intermittent proposals for educational 'colleges' for girls. Individual households were another matter and some families were devout, saying or singing matins and evensong daily. The community at Little Gidding, established by Nicholas Ferrar and his mother in about 1626, proposed to follow a simple life and a routine of praise and worship around the clock. It survived the death of its founder but, as a result of Charles I's visit to the community, the Puritans in revenge destroyed everything in 1647.

There was little thereafter in this line. Women wishing the religious life either went abroad or lived in seclusion at home until, as a result of the French Revolution, several houses of nuns were re-sited in England and it came to be realised just how much these women could achieve. Following a change in public opinion and the passing of the Catholic Emancipation Act in 1829, Robert Southey, the then Poet Laureate, called for the setting up of an order of 'Anglican Sisters of Mercy' to undertake what was called 'religious charity' in prisons, hospitals and other venues. After his death in 1843 the Sisterhood of the Holy Cross was established at 17 Park Village West, London, in his memory and this is considered to be the first Anglican community. Later on, it was merged into the Devonport Community founded by Priscilla Lydia Sellon who became Abbess of the united house in 1857. A few years before this she had answered a call from the local bishop to tackle the appalling conditions in Plymouth: within two years homes had been established for orphans, for sailor boys, for training girls for domestic service, for old sailors and their wives, along with an industrial school and its lodging houses, a soup kitchen for those too old to work and no less than five 'ragged' schools. Her sphere of influence spread elsewhere in the south-west but throughout she faced much opposition, persecution, suspicion and interference. Meanwhile, the foundation stone had been laid for the building of St Mary the Virgin, Wantage, which would in time become one of the largest communities of women within the Church of England. Here, mental prayer and private devotions were fostered as, indeed, were the arts; a well-maintained library, well-tended gardens and a world-famous embroidery room, printing room, modelling room and exceptional music followed in due course.

Meanwhile, small groups of women were already working in slum areas. One group, trained in Ireland with the Sisters of Mercy and founded in 1828 by Catherine McAuley, had returned to work in the slums of Bermondsey and Birmingham, winning high praise for their heroic endeavours; most Catholic houses were enclosed orders, although some taught girls, but the 'Faithful Companions of Jesus' was founded as a teaching community. In fact, one religious foundation had survived Henry VIII's purge. St Katherine's was founded by Queen Mathilda in 1148 for the maintenance of 'thirteen poor persons' and for prayers to be said in perpetuity for herself and her family; in time, its scope widened to cover education, hospitality for strangers, and care for the old and the ill. It remained under the direct patronage of the Queens of England. However, it was forced to leave its original site in Aldgate when that district of London was developed as St Katherine Dock but it moved back to the area after the Second World War when the community undertook a wide range of social and educational work.

Another organisation of dedicated men and women working within the East End of London was founded by General Booth and his wife Catherine Mumford. Together, they started preaching at street corners then, with a nucleus of reformed criminals, formed a Halleluja Band and by 1878 had become known as the Salvation Army. Meetings were held in any available space, indoors or outdoors, and visits were made to factories, prisons, public houses or wherever folk gathered together. The Regulations that Mrs Booth helped to draw up state: 'The Army, believing that God never intended to make any spiritual difference between man and woman, allows women equally with men to take part publicly in its meetings, and to occupy equally with men any posts for which they prove themselves qualified.'[23] From starting in London's East End the 'Sally Ann', as it is affectionately known, had spread to many other British cities and to Australia and the USA before the turn of the century.

A movement started in the USA in 1875 under the leadership of Madame Blavatsky was led, from 1907 onwards, by Annie Besant (1847–1927) who had long been a convert to its belief in universal brotherhood. The Theosophical Society continued to flourish both there and in India, which was where Annie decided to settle. She worked towards establishing schools for Hindu girls, was active in Indian politics and in 1918 presided over the Indian National Congress. Prior to dedicating herself to Theosophy, Annie Besant had lived a full and adventurous life in widely diverse spheres of activity and her name crops up in relation to other events and campaigns of her times.

CHAPTER TEN

The Hand that Rocks the Cradle

The words of the popular song have 'love and marriage' going together like 'a horse and carriage' but, until relatively recently, it was more a case of marriage and motherhood. There are two sides to most stories and marriage, motherhood and the rearing of children is no exception, as exemplified in the following stories of events that both took place in 1780 within a matter of months. The *Newcastle Courant* wrote of a shoemaker in Kirkoswald whose wife had given birth to 16 children in 17 years, of whom 13 were living, with another babe well on the way. They were reported to be remarkably fine children and were well cared for but, as they all resembled each other, the neighbours had difficulty in telling them apart. The other side of the coin was the harrowing story in the *Stamford News*: within the space of little more than a month a local farmer had buried 5 of his children (and 3 of them within 6 days) aged 3, 9, 11, 13 and 18 years old, the cause of death being a malignant fever, prevalent in the town for some time.[1]

It is not all that long since motherhood was no longer the almost inevitable consequence of marriage; not for every woman but for the majority. Children were certainly looked for and anticipated with pleasure; sons were always hoped for, especially if property or a family name was involved and also as potential bread winners; daughters were welcomed as helpers around the house, as carers of the sick and the elderly at any time and, in the lower social levels, as contributors to the family income prior to their own marriage. Within living memory there were communities, even in Presbyterian Scotland, where girls did not 'walk up the aisle' until they were pregnant since children were the equivalent of the state pension. Before Lloyd George and his Old Age Pensions Act of 1908, old age was not a time that folk without savings could look forward to with any equanimity. Without savings and without children to care for them the only alternative was the workhouse where the husband and wife would be separated – into different ends of the building or into different buildings altogether. Hence the initial response of the elderly to the idea of a guaranteed weekly sum was to consider it as a blessing of indescribable munificence. Until such time though, it was the children who were expected to undertake the support of their parents.

Marriage and motherhood went together. Girls were taught that it was their duty to marry, to produce the next generation and to bring them up in a Christian fashion. The marriage service in the Book of Common Prayer is quite clear on this point, when considering the causes for which matrimony was ordained: 'First, it was ordained for the procreation of children, to be brought up in the fear and nurture of the Lord, and to the praise of his Holy name.' Secondly, 'as a remedy against sin, and to avoid fornication', while the third and final cause speaks of 'the mutual society, help and comfort that the one ought to have of the other, both in prosperity and adversity'. Until later in the eighteenth century it was the parents' duty to negotiate the marriages of their children, especially where a title or property were concerned, and to check the financial settlements made for the support of a daughter during marriage and, should it occur, in her widowhood. Obedience was expected of children but they were generally given some leeway in the matter and instances are on record where a child flatly refused to follow the parents' arrangements. The concept of love as a prior requirement was reserved for novelists and play actors; all being well, love would follow in due course and, in many instances, it did. Attitudes then changed and love became of greater importance in the choice of partners, although it was best, especially for the woman's future financial security, if parental approval could be obtained. Where inheritance and a family name were not at stake, practical considerations might well be uppermost: in Cheshire, for example, farmers would choose the strongest girls as it saved the costs of extra labour if the wife could turn the heavy cheeses single-handed.

The marriage of parents was of importance to their offspring because it conferred legitimacy on them; illegitimate children could not inherit. For this reason it was not unknown for a man to live with the mother of his children for many years without benefit of matrimony even though a marriage would take place eventually, the reason being that they would wait until after she was of child-bearing age so that subsequent, legitimate children would not oust the earlier illegitimate family. Scottish law differed in this aspect, in that the subsequent marriage of parents legitimised the bastard child.

The situation as regards illegitimate children was variable, society generally turning a blind eye to men who fathered children by their mistresses but employing the 'double standard' when a woman became pregnant by a man not her husband. One of the more extreme examples was the household of the Duke of Devonshire and his Duchess, the enchanting Georgiana; the Duke installed his mistress in the house and their children were included in the (legitimate) nursery party of two daughters and a son but when the Duchess became pregnant by her lover, she was banished to the Continent for two years.

What often comes as a surprise is that so many of the women whose names are known to history – whether by way of being religious leader, traveller, royalty, craftswoman or novelist, whatever the category might be – were so often mothers as well and spent much of their married lives in being pregnant or recovering from childbirth. Many would be giving birth every year or so for twelve or fifteen years, maybe longer, which must have made things very difficult for those women who did not conceive at all or who lost the children they had at a later stage. Few mothers would see all their children reach adulthood and even then some would predecease their parents, death commonly being occasioned by accidents involving horses or carriages, malignant fevers, smallpox or consumption and, for daughters, death in childbed. Belief in the Will of God and Life hereafter might help cushion the blow but every childhood death was sincerely mourned.

In case the worst happened the baby was christened as quickly as possible after the birth but it would be a month before the mother would go to be 'churched' – to return thanks for her safe delivery and render donations to the parish clergy and the poor. The custom of 'swaddling' the infant continued well into the eighteenth century as it was thought to encourage straight limbs; its necessity, though, was increasingly questioned and the evidence would suggest that babies were being released from their bonds at an earlier stage. The fact that advice to mothers early in the twentieth century specifically warns against binding an infant's limbs too tightly would argue that the practice continued to be widespread. Many women breast fed their babies but where artificial feeding was necessary a hollowed out cow's-horn was utilised as a feeding bottle and, later on, a soft mash of bread mixed with water or milk would be given with a horn spoon from a silver or pewter pap-boat. After weaning, the baby was fed on bread crusts, milk and soups and given a chicken bone to gnaw on to help the teeth coming through. Teething rings of coral were also provided at this stage, as were rattles and simple rag dolls.

For long enough cradles were made of wood with high sides and, in some areas of the country, a hood at the head, and were set on rockers – which in time suggested the possibility of putting a butter churn on rockers so that a woman could churn the butter with her foot while using her hands for another task. Bassinets were lighter constructions based on wickerwork which the mother-to-be was expected to trim; it was described as 'pretty work and not so difficult as it appears at first sight'.[2] Until the invention of the 'baby carriage' or 'Bassinet perambulator' in the 1850s, babies were taken outdoors for an airing in the arms of mother or nursemaid. After Queen Victoria had given the new vehicles the seal of royal approval by buying three of them, their use spread rapidly as the latest fashionable childcare accessory. By the 1880s even Flora Thompson's mother in the hamlet of Lark Rise had a baby carriage 'made of black wickerwork, . . . running on three wheels and pushed from behind. It wobbled and creaked and rattled over the stones, for rubber tyres were not yet invented and its springs, if springs it had, were of the most primitive kind. Yet,' the author continues, 'it was one of the most cherished of family possessions, for there was only one other baby carriage in the hamlet, the up-to-date new bassinet which the young wife at the inn had recently purchased. The other mothers carried their babies on one arm, tightly rolled in shawls, with only the face showing.'[3]

It was about this time, too, that newer ideas on child raising were being adopted; for long enough children's special needs had generally been ignored. Now, fresh air and exercise, suitable foods, lighter more appropriate clothing and books with illustrations and easy words were advocated, as was the concept that a nursery could be prettily decorated with its own furniture and pictures on the walls rather than with cast-off bits and pieces from elsewhere in the house. Some thought was also given to providing, and decorating, separate rooms for the nurse and nursemaids; previously all had shared the day nursery and night nursery.

Examples of motherhood can be found everywhere, from the highest in the land to the stricken farmer near Stamford or that prolific shoemaker of Kirkoswald. Royal mistresses Lucy Walter, Barbara Villiers, Nell Gwyn, Louise de Keroualle and others, too, all gave birth to Charles II's bastard children, though no children resulted from his marriage to Catherine of Braganza. His brother (later James VII and II) fathered four children in quick succession by Arabella Churchill, though that did not spoil her chances of marrying thereafter and producing further, legitimate, children. Her sister-in-law Sarah, Duchess of Marlborough, removed herself from Court from time to time in order to give birth to another child and supervise the upbringing of the family. The heroines of the Civil War were mothers: both Lady Derby at Lathom and Lady Bankes at Corfe had daughters with them while besieged and Brilliana, Lady Harley, seemingly had small children with her at Brampton Bryan. Margaret Fell, 'mother of Quakerism', was also the mother of seven daughters and a son who were brought up to fulfil both domestic duties and their religious obligations.

Even though women had children it was rare for all to survive. The rate of mortality among infants was high, though some women suffered more than their fair share of bereavements. Lady Fanshawe, courageous companion and traveller, included in the paean of praise penned of her husband an account of the ten children lost out of the fourteen born, with several miscarriages in addition. Her litany of woe begins:

> Harrison, my eldest son, and Henry, my second son, Richard, my third; Henry my fourth; and Richard, my fifth, are all dead; my second lies buried in the Protestant Church-yard in Paris by the

father of the Earl of Bristol; my eldest daughter, Anne, lies buried in the Parish Church at Tankersley, in Yorkshire, where she died; Elisabeth lies in the Chapel of the French Hospital at Madrid, where she died of a fever at ten days old; my next daughter of her name lies buried in the Parish of Foot's Cray in Kent . . . and my daughter Mary lies in my father's vault in Hertford, with my first son, Henry . . .[4]

Of Sarah, Duchess of Marlborough's family of seven, a son and daughter died early, and both parents were devastated when their surviving son died of smallpox aged seventeen; two married daughters then died within a year of each other – from smallpox and 'pleuritic fever' respectively. Queen Anne was another who suffered more than the average as all her children died young, only William of Gloucester reaching the age of eleven. Lady Grisell Baillie gave birth first to a daughter and then to a son who died two years later, just days after the birth of a second daughter, cruel timing indeed. Susanna Wesley (1669–1742), 'Mother of Methodism', gave birth to 18 (or 19) children in 21 years, of whom only 10 grew to adulthood: she taught them all herself and ran a small school in her home for over 20 years, teaching in all some 200 children. Lady Janet Sinclair of Ulbster was married in 1740 and over the next 17 years gave birth to either 11 or 12 children (the records differ), of whom 5 died in infancy and 2 sons died in their teens. Lady Susan Bury (1775–1861) wrote novels, poetry and a cookery book, as well as having 9 children by her first marriage, of whom only 2 daughters survived their mother, and 2 daughters from her second marriage.

Yet some prolific mothers had fewer problems than average. The family of Sarah Trimmer (1741–1810), authoress and educationalist, comprised six daughters and six sons. Elizabeth Raffald, woman of many interests and talents, had fifteen or sixteen daughters before her own early death, aged forty-eight. Margaret Stephen was herself the mother of nine despite being held in considerable repute as a midwife, attending Queen Charlotte and publishing a textbook on her subject. The careers of Dora Jordan and Sarah Siddons continued unabated despite their frequent pregnancies. That pioneer of prison reform, Elizabeth Fry (1780–1845), had ten children in sixteen years and Lady Charlotte Guest (1812–95) was another mother of ten, even though she assisted her husband in running the Dowlais Iron Works and took over the business after his death.

What could a woman expect to do with her motherhood skills? In what direction could talents honed by maternal love and instinct be practised to good effect beyond the home? The short answer is that the repertoire garnered over the years might well qualify a woman to work in virtually every sphere imaginable whether in writing about her experiences, exercising a particular skill, teaching it to others or campaigning to improve conditions for those following on. What sort of areas might be covered? Activities relating to childbirth or its prevention, the care of infants and children and leading on to healthcare generally; education in its widest sense; the legal and financial position of women and the custody of children; welfare of any and every description which might include nutrition, housing and hygiene, employment of female labour, women in prisons, in factories, or their care in old age.

Where to start? Some women wrote about their involvement in childbirth and childcare. Lady Fanshawe's story was published long after the events she described but Anna Bradstreet's poetry appeared contemporaneously. Although much of it today seems long winded and allusions are no longer meaningful, there is no problem whatever in understanding the evocative verses on the loss of two little ones. The poem 'In memory of my dear grandchild, Elizabeth Bradstreet who deceased August 1665 being a year and a half old' opens:

> Farewel dear babe, my heart's too much content,
> Farewel sweet babe, the pleasure of mine eye,
> Farewel sweet flower that for a space was lent,
> Then ta'en away unto Eternity . . .[5]

To commemorate Anna Bradstreet who died aged three and a half she wrote:

> With troubled heart & trembling hand I write,
> The Heavens have chang'd to sorrow my delight.
> How oft with disappointment have I met,
> When I on fading things my hopes have set? . . .
>
> . . . Farewel dear child, thou ne'er shall come to me,
> But yet a while, and I shall go to thee;
> Mean time my throbbing heart's chear'd up with this
> Thou with thy Saviour art in endless bliss.[6]

It was in order to support a brood of children that the widowed Anne Grant turned to writing. Born in 1755, she spent some ten years of her childhood in America before returning to the Scottish Highlands; she married the Revd James Grant who became minister of Laggan parish. Twelve children were born, but four succumbed to tuberculosis, as did her husband. Homeless and penniless and with the family to support she tried farming but without success. A book of poems met with a lyrical review and was promoted by Jane, Duchess of Gordon, who offered unrelenting assistance. Mrs Grant retrieved her correspondence from such well-known friends as Felicia Hemans, Joanna Bailey, William

Wordsworth, Robert Southey and others, which were published to great acclaim in 1806 as *Letters from the Mountains* and this was followed by *Memoirs of an American Lady*. One by one all her children died, apart from the youngest son. She then lived in Edinburgh where she was described by Sir Walter Scott as being 'proud as a Highland-woman, vain as a poetess, and absurd as a blue-stocking'.[7]

Although Mrs Oliphant (1828–97) wrote her first novel while caring for her sick mother, she continued to exercise her talents throughout her life and, as a result 'had worn a hole in her finger which made it agony for her to write'.[8] The ability to earn a living wage from her writing was all the more necessary when her husband died after a few short years bequeathing her, as she put it: 'Three children, my two hands, and a thousand pounds worth of debts.'[9] Two children had died as infants, a daughter died aged eleven and she took in her brother's family, including her nephew whom she sent to school with her own sons. The nephew died when a young man, one son died aged thirty-four and the youngest at about the same age. By this time Mrs Oliphant had been writing for fifty years and her output was awesome. As she pointed out: 'Writers as a rule do not spring from the ranks of the rich.'[10]

Maria Rundell (1745–1828) came to writing by accident but it was because of her daughters that it happened at all. The wife of half the jewellery partnership of Rundell and Bridges she had been noted for her hospitality and for the good food served in her household; on being widowed she left London and retired to Bath. Her children had frequently suggested that she should write down some of the hundreds of recipes employed in the family home and this she began to do, intending to have identical copies written out, one for each daughter. The publisher, John Murray senior, had long been a family friend and it was his son who thought the project should be given to a wider audience. It was published as *A New System of Domestic Cookery* written 'By a Lady' – again that problem of payment being demeaning for anyone of a certain social standing.

By way of contrast, it was precisely the lack of children that drove some women to activity in the wider world: when so many of their contemporaries were in a constant cycle of pregnancy and childbirth it must have been difficult for those outside the circle. Would Margaret, Duchess of Newcastle, have written quite so much if she had had a family of her own? As a childless widow Lady Glenorchy took to religion, though that was a refuge for many whether with or without children. It was precisely because of their lack of children that John Bowes and his French actress wife decided to collect *objets d'art* during the 1860s for their museum which sits like a French château on the outskirts of Barnard Castle.

It was at about this time that an increasing number of women began writing on a topic that had concerned them for so long, that of the care of children and their upbringing. It was during the second half of the nineteenth century that a trickle of such books becomes a veritable flood, with titles that are virtually interchangeable. Earlier works include Mrs Child's *The Mother's Book* (1837) described as being useful when medical help might not be available or not really needed; *Children and How to Manage Them* (1856) by M.M. Pullan; there was Mrs Reed's *Mother's Manual* (1865), while *The Management of Children in Sickness and in Health* (1866) was published under Mrs Beeton's name and was a straight lift from sections in her earlier book on household management. Slightly different and rather more personal was Mrs Warren's book purporting to be an account of the way she had raised her own family and offering advice to mothers on a wide range of topics, both practical and moral. At this point, the care of children and their health were still a domestic concern, coming under the remit of the housewife and mother. Thereafter, it is interesting to find the influence of women with medical qualifications behind the manuals on infant health and childcare. Sophia Jex-Blake was one of the first women to study medicine and the founder of the London School of Medicine for Women. A.M. Hewer described herself as a hospital ward sister; M.M. Burgess was the former assistant house surgeon at the Victoria Hospital for Sick Children in Hull and lecturer to the London County Council (LCC) on a wide range of health matters; M. Wheeler had been superintendent of the Babies' Hospital, New York, since 1891. T.M. Brewster was on the nursing staff of the Hospital for Sick Children, Great Ormond Street, and her chosen format took the form of a series of lessons prepared according to the syllabus of domestic economy teachers and were designed for the use of elementary school teachers.

Many young girls were taken on as nursery nurses, their only qualification being that they came from large families themselves and thus were experienced in looking after their siblings. The mother in *Lark Rise* would tell her own offspring of her time as nursemaid to a rector's family with nine children, who were always held up to them as examples of good behaviour. The eldest of her former charges sent a parcel of books and toys to them every Christmas and kept in touch with her former nurse for forty years or more. In real life, though, one mother of fourteen in Bethnal Green earned a living as nurse to the local vicarage and her own children would take her current baby up to her to feed, three or four times a day.

Nannies, as opposed to the nurse or the governess, came on the scene relatively late in Victorian times and reached their apogee between 1895 and the 1930s. Memoirs would suggest that some mothers had little

138

contact with their children and left them in the care of 'Nurse' who might be a saint or a tyrant. Examples of both abound: Lord Curzon, future Viceroy of India, had a horror, as did Compton Mackenzie, and Catherine Sinclair depicts 'Mrs Crabtree' as an evil specimen in her popular novel *Holiday House* (1835). But Winston Churchill adored his nurse, Everest, who was his principal confidante and dearest friend for twenty years. Robert Louis Stevenson had his beloved 'Cummy' (Alison Cunningham) who was herself a story teller of no mean talents. In the dedication of *A Child's Garden of Verses* (1884) he summed up all that he owed to her, calling her 'The angel of my infant life'. Also in Edinburgh but somewhat later in time, Eleanor Sillar and her brothers, after the early death of their mother, were cared for thereafter by the devoted Ann Torbain, who had pledged never to leave them and she stayed on to care for the next generation too. Some hundred years earlier a similar promise had been given by a young nursemaid when Elizabeth Grant, née Raper, was dying; she placed her infant daughter in Sophy William's arms, who devoted the rest of her life to her charge. Earlier again, a similar devotion was evinced by the Verney's 'Nan Fudd' who cared for Sir Ralph's five unmarried sisters left behind in England after he and his wife and children had gone into exile in France and she cared for their children too, in due course. Lady Verney's maid, Luce, accompanied her employer when she returned to England to look into her husband's affairs and on that occasion Luce had decided to leave her job. However, she agreed to continue until a suitable replacement could be found and after Lady Verney's death stayed on in France, supervising the children and carrying out a variety of duties.

Another, intermittent, member of the household was the wet nurse. From Tudor times onwards the wealthier echelons of society often put their children into the care of a woman who had herself recently given birth but who was paid to feed her milk to another child. It seems to have been a matter of personal preference as to who breast fed their own children or who handed them over to someone else but over the years much emphasis was placed on the benefits of breast feeding and there was disapproval of those who did not do their maternal duty. Mothers preferred to install the wet nurse in their own home where they could be certain of what was going on; the fact that the woman's own baby might, in turn, have to be cared for by someone else was of secondary importance until quite late in the day. The choice of wet nurse was to be approached with care as it was thought her characteristics could be transferred along with her milk; the advice changed little during the period and was still being repeated into the twentieth century: in 1909 'Wet Nurse's Qualifications' stressed that the woman, prior to being engaged, should be 'examined and approved by an experienced doctor'.

She should be 'a strong, cheerful and healthy-looking person, with a healthy-looking child . . . A peasant woman makes an infinitely better nurse than a town-bred woman . . . It is sometimes thought that brunettes make better nurses than blondes, but all the best medical authorities agree that complexion is of no moment, so long as the woman is of sound constitution and good muscular development and in good health.'[11] By the 1930s advice on wet nurses seems to have been dropped from the baby books.

Since time immemorial and at every level of society it was women who had assisted women to give birth, the situation only changing slowly during the eighteenth century. The midwife (meaning 'with-woman') often held an honoured position in society and the best of them were well paid, not only from their fees but also from the gifts they received from godparents and guests attending the baptism. The fifteen children of George III and Queen Charlotte were generally brought into the world by the midwife Mrs Stephen; it was unfortunate therefore that Princess Charlotte, heiress to her father George IV and attended by a male accoucheur, died in giving birth. The mishap did not deter Queen Victoria who chose to have a man in attendance although the same midwife, Charlotte von Siebold, had attended both her own mother and Prince Albert's. Without the money to pay the fees, many women would be forced to rely on a kindly neighbour or two to help them when their time came.

The two Miss Willughbys were midwives in the mid-seventeenth century and daughters of a noted practioner who trained them himself. He told the story of assisting one of them in a particularly difficult case: 'At my daughter's request, unknown to the lady, I crept into the chamber on my hands and knees, and returned, and it was not perceived by the lady.'[12] In fact the birth was difficult and he paid a second visit in the same manner. Mrs Cellier, their contemporary, had an excellent reputation, was well educated and well to do but, being Catholic, was at the mercy of public opinion. She put forward proposals to improve the status of the profession by raising the standards of all midwives through a registration system based on examinations which had been suggested by her predecessors Hester Shaw and Mrs Whipp some forty years before. Mrs Cellier asked Charles II for a Charter, maybe thinking he could well have a vested interest in improving standards in the profession, but despite his promises the matter was taken no further.

In 1671 Jane Sharp, after thirty years as a practising midwife, wrote a textbook in simple language, insisting on the necessity of studying anatomy and on the good conduct of the labour, although she stressed that the subject could not really be taught by pictures alone but required long and diligent practice. The book's full title describes its contents:

The Midwives' Book or the Whole Art of Midwifery discovered, directing Child bearing Women how to behave themselves in their Conception, Breeding, Bearing and Nursing of Children. In spite of losing ground to male obstetricians and gynaecologists over this period some midwives continued to be notable practitioners: Sarah Stone in the West Country was delivering three-hundred babies a year, and by 1737 she was established in London's Piccadilly and published *A Complete Practice of Midwifery*. She queried why so many men were called in to assist when midwives were doing the real work and she also doubted the overuse of instruments during the birth. Elizabeth Niehill was a rather more political character or possibly, from the point of view she took, an early feminist since she was more than a little scornful of the male accoucheur and his dependence on instruments. Her book on midwifery was published in 1760, Mrs Margaret Stephen's book in 1795, closely followed by Martha Mears's work *The Pupil of Nature.*

The earliest lying-in hospital in the British Isles was established in 1739 'to afford an asylum for indigent females during the awful period of childbirth and also to facilitate the repentence of suffering and contrite sinners'.[13] Later, it came under the patronage of Queen Charlotte whose name it carried thereafter. In time, a number of institutions designed for the care or support of women were set up throughout the country and the scope of their activities considerably enlarged.

Following on the care of women in childbirth, there were those who taught women how to prevent the pregnancy occurring in the first place. Given the nature of the question it is difficult to establish much in the way of evidence about contraceptive practices in the past, although what is certain is that many women were totally ignorant of 'the facts of life'. When Annie Besant, who was involved with many social causes, published a pamphlet on birth control in 1877 she and her fellow editor Charles Bradlaugh were charged with obscenity and the trial that followed caused a sensation. As a result, her daughter was taken away from her which occasioned an additional campaign concerning the lack of the mother's rights, which Caroline Norton's situation had brought to the fore some years earlier.

At about the time of Annie Besant's trial a woman was born who was to be a pioneer in the field of contraception. Marie Stopes (1880–1958) was well educated with a degree in botany and zoology but even at the age of twenty-seven, as she later admitted, she was quite ignorant about relationships between the sexes. Her first marriage was annulled which led her (presumably after time to research the subject) to write her first book *Married Love*, an instant best seller, and other books followed on the subject of contraceptive practices. In 1921 she opened the first birth-control clinic in Britain where women could get free advice. She faced enormous hostility to what she was doing as well as several legal cases but, being as 'newsworthy' as she was, these helped to spread not only her fame but, with it, the knowledge of contraception.

Women came to be particularly associated with healing. The Reformation had swept away much of the religious aspect of caring for the sick, the poor and the old and these matters then fell into the category of domestic pursuits. In delineating a housewife's duties had not Gervase Markham placed 'her skill in Physick, Surgery' ahead of cookery and everything else in her repertoire?[14] At any moment, a member of household or farm might suffer serious accident or illness and prompt treatment with the housewife's home-made remedies could well save the day. Some were so skilled that their reputation spread far and wide. They learnt from their mothers, from other women or from books and some apothecaries might admit them to the trade through marriage or apprenticeship. That was in the early days; but as the associations of physicians, surgeons and apothecaries raised their standards by insisting on attendance at university and the passing of examinations, so women were excluded. Also, women with healing skills had to be careful to avoid charges of witchcraft even though it was considered a basic tenet of Christianity to care for those in need.

Anne Halkett, who as Anne Murray had aided the escape of James, Duke of York, early in the Civil War, met with some wounded soldiers after the Battle of Dunbar and suggested she could help them if they came to her at Kinross as she was well provisioned for such an eventuality. She dressed the wounds of sixty or more men and continued 'most agreeably' to help all the sick and wounded who came to her, generally on a Wednesday. She gathered and prepared her own remedies and was reknowned for her piety, producing in all some twenty-one books on theological matters. It was claimed that she was so proficient in the study of physic and in the more unfeminine science of surgery that the most eminent professional men, as well as invalids of the first rank, both in Britain and on the Continent, sought her advice. Her work among the soldiers has led her to be described, rather over-enthusiastically, as a surgeon in the Royal Army.

Among her contemporaries can be found Elizabeth Bury (1644–1720) whose reasons for taking up with the study of anatomy and medicine were a combination of her own ill health and a desire to make herself useful. Other names on record include Lady Read, who advertised her services as an eye surgeon; the bone-setter Mrs Mapp (fl. 1736), who became both celebrated and wealthy but when her husband of just two weeks ran off with her life savings she took to drink and latterly was known as 'Crazy Sally of Epsom'; and Catherine Bowles, famous for her operations for hernias, stone in the bladder and hydrocele, and for her published work. Rather than face an operation her patients might have preferred to take Joanna Stevens' pills to cure them of bladder stone. In 1739 the government presented her with the then enormous sum of £5,000 to reveal her secret remedy, which she graciously did: 'A powder made of egg-shells and smoked garden snails, a decoction of herbs and soap, . . . and held together with honey. It proved ineffective.'[15]

Two particularly efficacious introductions were made by women at about this time. Lady Mary Wortley Montagu, who accompanied her husband to Turkey, noted with approval their method of holding smallpox parties for children at which they were 'engrafted' with the virus. The children played together for the next week, were feverish and bedbound for a couple of days and then recovered; she knew of none who had died from it and had her own small son treated. In Britain alone many thousands died from the disease each year; others were disfigured for life and so a means of preventing the ravages of the disease were incalculable. On her return to England she interested the Princess of Wales who had her children inoculated, but generally acceptance was slow: as Lady Mary had feared, the doctors' opposition was considerable since smallpox patients were a source of profit to them. Later in the century a Shropshire woman, Mother Hutton, who was a botanist and pharmacist, discovered that digitalis was beneficial in the treatment of heart problems. She experimented until she found the correct way to prepare and administer the medication and patients were soon coming from far and wide. Unlike Joanna Stevens, she kept the secret to herself but eventually sold it to a Dr Withering, who is often credited with its discovery.

The spas and seaside resorts around the country employed many women to look after the visitors who flocked to these centres in search of health and some of the 'well-women' became celebrated for their services. At Brighton Martha Gunn was known as the 'Queen of the Dippers' because her job was to supervise the helpers who assisted women into the sea from the horse-drawn bathing machines. She died in 1815 at the advanced age of eighty-seven so she was a good advertisement for the treatment, while at Harrogate those who drank the waters were served for over sixty years by Betty Lupton.

Woman's role in caring for the sick was, again, very much a domestic pursuit at the start of the period but when the first institutions were established to nurse people outside their own homes the standards both of nursing and of the nurses themselves were apt to be very low indeed. Florence Nightingale's campaign to improve nursing care in the military sphere is well known; perhaps less familiar is her life thereafter when, although mainly bedbound, she went on to revolutionise the nursing profession in general. She approved plans for the new St Thomas's Hospital and established the Nightingale Training School of Nursing alongside it, demanding nothing but the highest standards from her nurses. There was 'Sister Dora', the first non-Royal woman in Britain to be commemorated by a statue which was erected in the market-place at Walsall. She founded the town's cottage hospital following a smallpox outbreak in the 1860s. She not only tended the sick brought to the hospital but went into many of the poorest homes where infection was rife, risking her life many times over. It was said in her praise: 'What Florence Nightingale did for military hospitals Dorothy Pattison accomplished in the sphere of civic duty.'[16] After a number of years as a governess Edith Cavell took up nursing and returned to Brussels where she became Matron of the Berkendael Medical Institute and transformed it into a teaching hospital. In 1914 it became a Red Cross Hospital tending wounded soldiers of all nationalities. For some eight months the hospital was part of an escape route for Allied soldiers; Edith Cavell was arrested by the Germans, court-martialled and shot on 12 October 1915.

Elsie Inglis is another name from that era, although she trained as a doctor rather than as a nurse. She founded a free hospice for women and children in the Edinburgh slums and when the war began raised money for and equipped her Scottish Women's Hospitals, staffed entirely by women. The problems facing Dr Elizabeth Garrett Anderson, Sophia Jex-Blake and other like-minded women in their struggle to gain access to medical training forms part of the story of women's fight for equality of education and opportunity, which is well documented and will be examined later.

It seems appropriate to end a chapter on birth, healing and death with a verse from Mrs Oliphant, who knew sorrow at first hand after losing her husband, her five children and the nephew raised with her own family: the author who had written so much over fifty years that she had worn a hole in her finger. On her deathbed she dictated the following poem, which opens:

> On the edge of the world I lie, I lie,
> Happy and dying and dazed and poor,
> Looking up from the vast great floor
> Of the finite world that rises above
> To God and to Faith and to Love, Love, Love!
> What words have I to that world to speak,
> Old and weary and dazed and weak,
> From the very low to the very high?
> Only this . . .[17]

CHAPTER ELEVEN

The Three Rs

In a speech delivered to a North Surrey District school on 13 February 1909 the President of the Local Government School Board said to the boys in his audience: 'I want you to be happy craftsmen, because you are trained to be healthy men.' To the girls he said: 'To keep house, cook, nurse and delight in making others happy is your mission, duty and livelihood.'[1] This makes it clear as to how the education of boys and girls differed: boys were educated to be themselves, to foster whatever talents they might have and to go into the world and earn their living; in contrast, generations of girls were educated to please men, because of society's emphasis on marriage as the sole 'career' open to women.

Since the Reformation and the closure of all but one religious foundation in the country, marriage had been considered as the only suitable way in which women could earn their daily bread. To be unmarried was regarded as unfortunate, to say the least, and rendered a woman legally dependent on either a father, brother or other male relative for the rest of her days. Marriage, therefore, being regarded as a necessity and a profession, a woman was educated according to her theoretical marriage partner, while success in the marriage market depended on the acquisition of skills pleasing or useful to the potential husband.

As long as the housewife's calling was acknowledged to be one of dignity and importance to the well-being of her household and as long as she continued to participate in the work and to direct her servants, then an education based on a range of domestic skills was no handicap to her anticipated lifestyle. Even so there were those who, like Hannah Woolley, were mindful of the upsets of the Civil War period and warned that a girl should always have some way in which she could maintain herself since marriage plans could not always be relied upon to work out as expected. By the first decades of the eighteenth century social attitudes were changing and by the end of the century the housewifely attributes of former years came to be considered very old fashioned indeed. Virtuous idleness being the hallmark of gentility, the likes of Florence Nightingale, Emily Davies, Dora Pattison and Beatrix Potter suffered for years from the aimlessness of the lives imposed upon them by their families; Marianne North and Mary Kingsley were devoted daughters, caring for their parents but it was only after their parents' deaths that they set off on their travels.

Nor was that all. The potential for every girl to find a marriage partner was diminishing and by the 1870s it was becoming obvious that a million or so women would not have the option of living in genteel idleness; these 'surplus women', even then, 'were engaging the attention of economists and philanthropists' along with some of their more articulate sisters. What were they to do with their lives? Their customary upbringing was proving inadequate for these middle-class women 'who are in want of bread, but who have perhaps only untrained minds and unskilled hands to bring into a market that is already overcrowded'.[2] Meanwhile, working-class women suffered equally but for different reasons, labouring long hours in appalling conditions for a mere pittance and generally to the detriment of their health.

Over the years many women had seen education as the route to improving not only their own lives but those of their husbands and sons and, by extension, of their daughters, too: 'If they could but see and feel as I do', said Mrs Jesser Reid, founder of Bedford College, 'that we shall never have better Men, till men have better Mothers, they would come flocking about us.'[3] The fact that a better education could also be interpreted as the route to emancipation from domestic thralldom and to financial independence certainly complicated the matter and stirred up considerable opposition from both sexes, thereby prolonging the struggle.

Women had always been involved in the upbringing of children, teaching them from infancy to say their prayers and learn their catechism, and inculcating habits of obedience, courtesy, respect for their elders and religious devotion. Girls learnt about domestic practices by watching and by helping; if mother or nurse had the ability then reading and writing were added, as well as enough in the way of arithmetic to keep track of the household expenses. The early lessons were given with the aid of a 'horn-book' consisting of a bat-shaped piece of wood covered with a paper on which the alphabet, some numbers and the Lord's Prayer were printed and the whole covered with a sheet of transparent horn to keep it clean from little fingers. If there were boys in the family a tutor might be employed and so girls were sometimes able to share in their brothers' lessons, but when the boys went off to school the tutor would depart and the girl be left to fend for herself; alternatively, she was submerged in household duties.

Some parents took a greater interest in their daughter's education. Anna Bradstreet's father was steward to the Earl of Lincoln and she was encouraged to make use of the earl's library. Lucy Apsley, later Hutchinson, could read fluently by the age of four and repeat the sermons she had heard. She was provided with a French nurse, so learnt French and English simultaneously and, by the age of seven, had tutors for languages, music, dancing, writing and needlework. She was quicker at Latin than her brothers and was the despair of her mother as she spent every spare moment with her head in a book. However, she was human after all since she admitted to skimping her music practice whenever she could and loathing needlework! Lady Mary Wortley Montagu (1689–1762), as befitted her rank, was taught French, Italian and drawing while a carving master came in three times a week to teach her the art of carving the meats set upon the dinner table – a necessary accomplishment in polite society until well into the nineteenth century. She also took advantage of her father's library to read widely and taught herself Latin with the aid of dictionaries and grammars. Elizabeth Carter (1717–1806) was taught Latin and Greek by her father but was so slow that he implored her to give up.

Mary Kingsley on the other hand was one whose schooling was neglected. Although £2,000 was spent on her younger brother's education at Cambridge, she was merely the recipient of some private German lessons in order that she might be more useful as her father's researcher and amanuensis. Along the way, though, she was able to make use of his library and listen to the conversation of his learned friends.

The majority of girls were taught along more traditional lines: Ann Fanshawe described her own upbringing with its customary lessons in French, singing to the lute, playing on the virginals and the art of needlework but she confessed how, despite being quick at learning, she had much preferred 'riding . . . running, and all active pastimes'.[4] In 1705 Lady Grisell Baillie wrote to her daughter's governess outlining a timetable of similar subjects for the youngster. The schooling of girls changed little during the century. Mary Fairfax (1780–1872), known to the world as Mary Somerville, attended school in Edinburgh for a year, which was largely devoted to deportment: 'I was enclosed in stiff stays with a steel busk in front, while, above my frock, bands drew my shoulders back till the shoulder-blades met. Then a steel rod, with a semi-circle which went under the chin, was clasped to the steel busk in my stays.'[5] Once home again she studied birds and learnt Latin in order to pass the time. She found mathematical puzzles in women's magazines but had no idea what the symbols meant until she borrowed books from her brother's tutor. Her parents were disturbed by her intellectual studies and denied her a candle in her room at night so, instead, she memorised the puzzles and worked them out in her head. Emily Davies (1830–1921), founder of Girton College, Cambridge, was so keen to learn and so frustrated by her domestic duties that she asked her father for help and he, schoolmaster and cleric though he was, reluctantly agreed to correct just one essay of hers a week.

Girls kept at home would be taught by a governess who was supposedly familiar with a wide range of subjects; sometimes her skills would be supplemented by those of itinerant tutors for the more specialised accomplishments – as, for example, the carving master who instructed Lady Mary. Many were the daughters of clerics, as were the three Brontë sisters, and earned some sort of a living in this way when they had no other skills to offer: during the 1840s over 100 governesses a day advertised their services in *The Times* and by 1851 over 21,000 women were registered as governesses.[6] A few found themselves welcomed into the family and treated kindly; the majority found themselves being neither family nor servant and isolated in the schoolroom with their charges. If these women had received little in the way of education themselves, they could pass on little more to their pupils; nor were they able, out of their meagre earnings and non-existent free time, to acquire the training to improve themselves.

As in every profession there were notable exceptions. The seventeenth-century author Hannah Woolley spent some years as a governess, during which time she came to act as her employer's 'woman', steward of her household and scribe or secretary. Elizabeth Elstob, nicknamed 'the Saxon Lady' (1683–1752) was largely self-taught and could read eight languages. She had already published an English Saxon homily prior to her Anglo-Saxon grammar, which appeared in 1715, the same year that her brother died. She was eventually persuaded to become governess to the young family of the Duchess of Portland who outlined her duties: 'To instruct her childen in the principles of religion and virtue, to teach them to speak, read and understand English well, to cultivate their minds as far as their capacity will allow, and to keep them company in the house, and when her strength and health will permit, to take the air with them.'[7] She adored her charges and it is nice to record that the little boy always acknowledged the debt he owed to his governess. Selina Trimmer (1765–1829) was welcomed into the household of the Duke and Duchess of Devonshire and brought some semblance of order into that unconventional set-up which included the Duke's mistress and their offspring, as well as one or two cousins. Throughout the two years of the Duchess's banishment Selina had sole charge of the children. After the Duchess died in 1806, she stayed on as chaperone to Lady Harriet and to protect her from her father's 'Lady Liz' even though she had been invited to take charge of the Princess Charlotte, heiress to George IV. Selina's mother, Mrs Sarah Trimmer (1741–1810) had long had an interest in educational matters, had taught her own numerous offspring and written innovative books for children, the most famous being the *Story of the Robins,* which remained in print until early in the twentieth century.

During the nineteenth century some governesses went abroad to pursue their careers: an English governess was considered to be on a par with the French lady's maid and the Scots gardener. Catherine Davies spent the years 1802–15 as governess to the family of Murat, King of Naples. The widowed Maria Graham travelled to Brazil in 1824 to care for the Emperor's daughter but was caught up in the many Court intrigues and returned to England within the year; the little girl became Queen of Portugal in her own right. Anna Bricknell went to the Tuileries in 1852, to the daughters of the Grand Master of the Empress Eugénie's household. Anna Leonowens was at the Royal Court of Siam for several years, teaching an assortment of children and wives, including the Crown Prince and it was during his reign that slavery was abolished and social reforms began. Emmeline Lott worked in Egypt, looking after the Viceroy of Egypt's five-year-old son and heir, His Highness the Grand Pasha Ibrahim. Edith Cavell was a governess in East Anglia and Brussels before she took up a career in nursing at the age of thirty, while Miss Eager was in charge of the daughters of Nicholas II in St Petersburg. Mary Fellows (b. 1868) had been a governess in India, in France and in Russia and left St Petersburg with her employers when the Revolution broke out. Her family back home had lost touch and believed her to be dead, but many years later Brigadier Sir Fitzroy Maclean discovered her living in Tiflis on the Caspian Sea and caring for the son of her original pupil. Searching for the English lady whom he understood was tending the British war graves in the local cemetery, the author described how he turned into the courtyard of a tumbledown house, where washing hung over the balconies, and heard an unmistakably English voice calling to the little Georgian child playing in the yard: 'Come here at once, Tommy, it's time you were in bed' and the child answering in perfect English: 'Coming, Miss Fellows.'[8]

Governesses, whether at home or abroad, were not for every household, even at the diminutive wages they were expected to survive on. Schools existed at many different levels: charity schools, dame schools, Sunday schools and similar institutions were set up by pious people to help those who otherwise would miss out on learning the three Rs. Poorer folk might send their children to the local dame school for a year or two; these were often, though not invariably, kept by a woman who could just about teach the children to read and write and earned a tiny income from the penny or so charged per week. The school was run in the teacher's house, with a minimum of books and equipment. Elizabeth Elstob kept a (superior) dame school in Evesham between leaving Oxford after her brother's death and becoming a governess. Elspeth Buchan opened a small school in which needlework and the rudiments of spelling were taught but parents were chary of her religious fanatism and the school closed. It was at a dame school in Lichfield that Samuel Johnson received his earliest lessons.

Charity schools that fed and clothed the children expected in return a full day's labour from the children in their charge: spinning, sewing or lacemaking from the girls and weaving or field work from the boys were common. Some were run by caring and considerate folk, others were scandalous in their treatment of children.

In towns and villages throughout the country schools were established by folk of good intent, in order to assist in educating those who would otherwise get nothing. The school at West Wittering in Sussex was doubtless typical of many up and down the country. In 1702 a bequest of property established a school for twelve boys in nearby Chichester as well as an annual payment to West Wittering parish for the teaching of six poor children. The first named teacher was 'Goody' (Goodwife) Light who received payment of £1 14s (£1.70) for her year's labour and 7s 11d (40p) for books. From 1721 to 1851 the trustees paid 'the School Dame' at the rate of 1s (5p) a week but from 1830 it seems they paid out a further £3 a year to teach reading and needlework to six poor girls; the schoolmistress from 1827–51 was a Mrs Jordan.⁹ In Ambleside the future Principal of Newnham College, Miss Clough, gave £2,000 to build a new school for the boys there, the existing one being dilapidated.

Prior to the 1870 Education Act and the beginnings of State education, villages without a benefactor or local patron could well have nothing in the way of a school or else rudimentary teaching might be supplied by the Society for the Promotion of Christian Knowledge, which was set up late in the seventeenth century. Here, a few basics would be taught – reading the Bible, learning the catchism and maybe a little writing or arithmetic. By 1740, over 2,000 schools had been founded by the SPCK and the Sunday schools by this time were also contributing to the campaign against ignorance. The children, though, rarely attended long enough, leaving to earn a penny or two towards the family income or to help with the chores around home or farm and, even when they had been taught to read and write, they were apt to lose the ability without the need for constant practice in their everyday lives.

The education provided for the fictional hamlet in *Lark Rise* was representative of the time shortly after the introduction of compulsory education for all between the ages of five and thirteen, with certain exemptions. The children walked to and from the National School in the neighbouring village 1½ miles away. Some forty-five children attended altogether, all taught in the same room by Miss Holmes who was assisted by two 'monitors', a grand title for the ex-scholars aged about twelve who were paid 1s (5p) a week for their services. Each day started with morning assembly and the singing of a hymn. 'Reading, writing and arithmetic were the principal subjects, with a Scripture lesson [taught by the rector] every morning, and needlework every afternoon for the girls.'¹⁰

Schools existed for girls of middle-class families, particularly in the environs of London and other large towns, but girls might only be sent to them for a year or so to acquire the necessary accomplishments – the 'finishing' touch. In *Emma* Jane Austen describes a decent, honest-to-goodness middle-class school where forty girls were treated with common sense and kindness:

> Mrs Goddard was the mistress of a school – not of a seminary, or an establishment, or anything which professed, in long sentences of refined nonsense, to combine liberal acquirements with elegant morality, upon new principles and new systems, – and where young ladies for enormous pay might be screwed out of health and into vanity, – but a real, honest, old-fashioned boarding-school, where a reasonable quantity of accomplishments were sold at a reasonable price, and where girls might be sent to be out of the way, and scramble themselves into a little education, without any danger of coming back prodigies.[11]

The educational system filtered down through the social hierarchy and affected the way rural labourers' children were taught, in a pale imitation of middle-class culture, and more than a little divorced from the realities of their own future lives. William Cobbett (1763–1835) bewailed the prevalence of the genteel parlour of farmers' families where the wife and daughters declined to participate in practical work around the farm. At the end of the century, too, others were pointing out that the prevailing influences did not always lead in the desired direction: middle-class habits of domesticity 'instead of setting cottage women on the road to middle-class culture of mind and body has side-tracked them – has made them charwomen and laundresses, so that other women may shirk these duties and be "cultivated"'.[12] There was also an economic factor in that the cottage women were taking on paid work in order to make up the decreased earnings of their husbands at a time of agricultural depression and were too pre-occupied to teach their daughters even the rudiments of domestic practice. To correct this situation Mrs Buckton and others, as noted in an earlier chapter, campaigned to have 'domestic economy' adopted into the elementary school syllabus, since the girls would be the mothers of the future and, for any progress to be made, it was they who needed to be educated.

For many women, though, it was precisely such domestic matters that they were trying to evade. Over the years many had been asking for the freedom to learn, to tackle a wider range of subjects and to be given similar educational latitude as their brothers. Those who functioned 'in education' often did so on several levels, simultaneously, and it is difficult to disentangle the various strands since one merges into the next, so it is not altogether surprising that efforts to improve the education of girls were frequently regarded as an attack on men's position in society. Women taught, either privately or in a school; they wrote school books, hymns and stories aimed specifically at children, put forward educational theories or campaigned for an improvement in the standards of teaching. The ladies of learning who enjoyed the acquisition of knowledge for its own sake and those who collected objects or catalogued information have been met with earlier.

Hannah Woolley was not only a writer on domestic matters but also had considerable practical experience of teaching. Her theories on education included pleas for the gentler treatment of children. She was vehement about the difference in the education lavished on sons and the general neglect of daughters' brains in favour of their social skills – thereby pre-dating by some 200 years the headmistresses who complained 'that they are called upon to "finish" what has never been begun'.[13] Bathsua Makin was formerly governess to Charles I's daughter Elizabeth but she then taught privately and, in 1673, opened a school at Tottenham High Cross; she, too, had distinct ideas on what was and what was not 'education', of which more later.

In the eighteenth century Lady Mary Wortley Montagu expounded her views on the education of girls in a series of letters to her daughter Lady Bute who found them rather too advanced for her liking. The granddaughter at whom they were directed was Lady Louisa Stewart (1757–1851), a writer herself and close friend of Sir Walter Scott; she was held in high regard for her powerful mind and qualities of friendship. Mrs Trimmer established schools for the poor and needy in the Brentford area as well as producing a plethora of books for teaching their pupils. In addition to her famous *Story of the Robins* she wrote *An Easy Introduction to the Knowledge of Nature*, introduced the concept of using pictures in the teaching of children and published various biblical studies. Mary Wollstonecraft earned her own living from an early age and she started out as companion to an old lady, then acted as governess and school teacher in Dublin and Bristol. She opened a school in 1784 and three years later published *Thoughts on the Education of Daughters*, the first of her many publications. Hannah More (1745–1835), instrumental in setting up Sunday schools in the Cheddar area, wrote pastoral plays for school children to act in, then the more serious *Sacred Dramas* as well as numerous religious and moral tracts suitable for schools. In 1799 her *Strictures on Female Education* were published which proved popular with governesses on both sides of the Atlantic. She wrote: 'It is a singular injustice which is often exercised towards women, first to give them a most defective Education, and then to expect from them the most

Plas Newydd, Llangollen, home to Lady Eleanor Butler and Sarah Ponsonby from 1780 until their deaths in 1829 and 1831 respectively. Originally a small cottage, it was enlarged on several occasions.

The tomb of Grace Darling, Bamburgh, who died in 1842. Her effigy lies full length, holding an oar, commemorating her part in rescuing four men and a woman from the Forfarshire, *wrecked off the Farne Islands in 1838.*

In 1915 Edith Cavell was shot by the Germans for assisting Allied soldiers to escape from Belgium. After the war her body was brought back to Britain with great ceremony and laid to rest outside Norwich Cathedral.

Currently called the United Elizabeth Garrett Anderson Hospital and Hospital for Women, Soho, this establishment is the direct successor of the small clinic opened in 1866 by Elizabeth Garrett Anderson for women and children.

Emily Davies by Rudolph Lehmann,
1880. She fought to establish the right of
women to a university education and her
college started initially at Hitchin, some
25 miles from Cambridge, prior to moving
to Girton. (By kind permission of
The Mistress and Fellows, Girton College,
Cambridge)

Girton College, the Tower. The college
Miss Davies established in Cambridge first
opened its doors in 1873 before the building
was properly completed. Since that time it has
expanded considerably.

Frontispiece to Jane Loudon's Gardening for Ladies, *1840. Although the care of a garden was considered to be one of the housewife's duties, few women wrote on the subject until the Victorian era.*

The start of a day's work for these women, leading out their teams of Clydesdales on an East Lothian farm during the Second World War. The headgear was to protect their faces from the weather. (By kind permission of The Scotsman Publications Ltd)

An Alderbourne Pekingese. Mrs Clarice Ashton Cross established the Alderbourne Kennels in 1904. Prior to that she had been involved in breeding Arab horses and bloodhounds. (Original drawing by Mary Stewart)

ALDERBOURNES

MISS ASHTON CROSS

THE WILDERNESS
ASCOT
BERKS

6, LANSDOWNE ROW
BERKELEY STREET
W.1

Name *Brunette of Alderbourne & Batman of Alderbourne*
Sex *Bitch & dog*
Breed *Pekingese*

Breeder *W. Webster*
Date of Birth *12.1.46*
Colour *Black, white markings*

PARENTS.	GRAND-PARENTS.	GREAT GRAND-PARENTS.	GREAT GREAT GRAND-PARENTS.
SIRE.			
Selkquae Minstrel Boy	*Singlewell Batling*	*Singlewell Batman*	*Singlewell Samurai* / *Black Monarch × Singlewell Brunette*
		Singlewell Brunette	*Chip o'Tai of Jerristov × Singlewell Silhouette*
	Princess of Anvigny	*Tansy Holmes Snowball*	*Toydom Cha Bee × Ming Queen*
		Fotelaws Sweetie Tu	*Tosca of Fotelaws × Fotelaws Red Beauty*
DAM.			
Tina Tree of Brookshire	*Minalghi Chonaskapan*	*Alderbourne Chinese Prince*	*Chinatown of Alderbourne × China Pakpa of Alderbourne*
		Cinderella of Minalghi	*Ch Welwise Hero × Coralie of Minalghi*
	Princess of Anvigny	*Tansy Holmes Snowball*	*Toydom Cha Bee × Ming Queen*
		Fotelaws Sweetie Tu	*Tosca of Fotelaws × Fotelaws Red Beauty*

Notes

A pedigree form of the Alderbourne Kennel detailing a puppy's parents, grandparents, great-grandparents and great-great-grandparents. The trademark logo shows a Peke leaping a tennis net.

The Marianne North Gallery, Kew Gardens, London, is filled with a collection of her botanical paintings and was set up by the author herself. After her parents died she travelled extensively, painting wherever she went.

Women gutting and packing herring into barrels of salt on the quayside in Aberdeen, 1903. Baskets for carrying fish and containers for the salt lie on the ground. Many followed the herring shoals south. (By kind permission of The Trustees of the National Museums of Scotland)

A silver medal awarded for walking all the way from Edinburgh to London on the Women's Suffrage March, October–November 1912. Similar marches arrived in the capital from other parts of the country. (By kind permission of The Trustees of the National Museums of Scotland)

Postwomen in Glenesk, Angus. During the First World War women filled many of the jobs vacated by the men and their labour was essential in maintaining services. (By kind permission of the Glenesk Museum, Angus)

A portrait by Emily Osborn of Barbara Bodichon, herself a gifted artist. She supported numerous women's causes but was especially involved with Emily Davies and her plans for a women's college at Cambridge. (By kind permission of The Mistress and Fellows, Girton College, Cambridge)

This roundel from a stained-glass window commemorates Elizabeth Fry's work with prisoners. The wording is from Proverbs Ch.31 v.6. Florence Nightingale with her lamp is depicted on a neighbouring pane.

undeviating purity of conduct; – to train them in such a manner as shall lay them open to the most dangerous faults, and then to censure them for not proving faultless.'[14] Maria Edgeworth (1767–1849) was a prolific writer in several genres but her first work *Letters to Literary Ladies* was a plea for women's education, while *Practical Education* was written with her father and became one of the best-known school books of the century. She also wrote lessons for and stories about children, as well as her regional and historical novels.

Harriet Martineau (1802–76) was celebrated for her writings on politics and economics although she had strong views on other topics, too, including the education of girls. Her books followed the format set earlier by Jane Marcet (1769–1858) who, though of Swiss birth, was married to a wealthy English merchant and refused to believe that ordinary folk could not understand 'science'. She wrote a series of handbooks on chemistry, natural philosophy, political economy and so on, a formula that proved extremely popular with teachers. P.B. Wakefield (1751–1832) specialised in books for children, alongside her numerous works on botany and related subjects. Maria Graham's experiences of teaching resulted in the writing of *Little Arthur's History of England* which was lavishly illustrated and went through many reprints. Arabella Buckley produced natural science books for the younger reader and edited one of Mary Somerville's works. More recently, Mary Holt wrote a play for Welsh schoolgirls, to interest them in their own history.

Until the eighteenth century, childrens' leisure reading had either been tales primarily written for adults, such as *Aesop's Fables* or *The Pilgrim's Progress*, or sternly moralistic stories but as education gradually became more humane so books designed to appeal to children began to appear, with women making many contributions – far too many to mention individually. Mrs Trimmer's works have already been noted. Ann and Jane Taylor published two books of children's verse early in the nineteenth century, including the lines of 'Twinkle, twinkle, little star', as well as other works for children.[15] Mrs C.F. Alexander (1818–95) wrote hymns for children, many of which are firm favourites to this day. A.L. Barbauld (1743–1824) ran a Non-conformist school in Suffolk and published several popular works for children, while Mrs Markham (1780–1837) wrote history for the young. Mrs Sherwood's *History of the Fairchild Family* appeared in three parts between 1818 and 1847 alongside her many other pieces for children and young adults. Mrs C.I. Johnstone's *Scenes of Industry* introduced beekeeping to children. Charlotte Yonge (1823–1901) was not only a writer of novels and family sagas but also of historical romances for children. Frances Hodgson Burnett (1849–1942) wrote *Little Lord Fauntleroy* and *The Secret Garden*. Mrs Molesworth's books of stories and fairy tales were celebrated in their day, whereas Anna Sewell's *Black Beauty* (1877) and Alison Uttley's animal stories of a later era have retained their popularity as, indeed, have E.E. Nesbit's tales. Kate Greenaway (1846–1901), Helen Bannerman, whose *Little Black Sambo* (1899) remains a firm favourite, and Beatrix Potter, famous for the much-loved 'Peter Rabbit' and other characters, illustrated their own books, although Kate Greenaway illustrated other people's work too.

It is interesting to find corroboration of children's reading habits in the story of *Lark Rise*. In the 1880s the hamlet children generally had little to practise their reading on, but Flora at the centre of the story not only had the customary *The Pilgrim's Progress* and the Bible but was fortunate in that her mother's former employers had provided several cast-offs for the family, including *Grimms' Fairy Tales*, *Gulliver's Travels*, Charlotte Yonge's *The Daisy Chain* and two of Mrs Molesworth's books, *Cuckoo Clock* and *Carrots*.

Books about children and their needs or books for children to read were not the only topics that women wrote about. The whole field of female education exercised many of them over the years and it is interesting to see how women, at a very early stage, were aware that the lack of education was a principal cause of so many of their problems; it is also significant that women's struggle to gain access to a sounder, more academic education should have become caught up in demands for the vote and financial independence.

Bathsua Makin, that former governess and school teacher able to teach her pupils Greek, Latin, Hebrew, French, Italian, Spanish and mathematics, was counted as 'the most learned Englishwoman of her time'.[16] In 1673 she put forward her proposals on female education, suggesting that the more academic subjects could be fitted in after the domestic matters and that the benefits would lie in producing better mothers: ignorance never could lead to piety. Poorer women did not have the opportunity of education, she said, it was designed for rich women – but only after they had acquired their usual accomplishments when there would be time enough for 'Arts, Tongues and Useful Knowledge'.[17] There was no intention of promoting a career for women outside their home in her proposals. Even Margaret, Duchess of Newcastle, in all her writings did not seek that: 'Man is made to govern Commonwealths,' she wrote, 'and Women their Private Families.'[18] However, occasions might well occur, and here Mrs Makin was recalling the troubled times of the Civil War, when education might be of use in itself as, for example, when wives might have to run an estate in the husband's absence or widows to support their families. She advertised this education as being available at her school at Tottenham High Cross (4 miles from London) where half the time was spent on domestic subjects (including writing and accounts) and half on Latin, French and so on, at a cost of £20 per year.

Mrs Makin's suggestion was followed some years later by Mary Astell's *Serious Proposals to the Ladies*. Her idea was to establish a religious 'retirement' in which women could prepare themselves for doing the maximum amount of good in the world. Although there would be daily services, no vows were involved. Married women, she said, would be fully taken up with their families but the unmarried had an even greater potential for improving the lot of others. Initial reaction was favourable and £10,000 was offered, probably by the future Queen Anne, to establish the college but the project foundered through fears of a Roman Catholic takeover. Instead, Mary Astell founded a school for the daughters of 'Chelsea Pensioners'. The struggle to obtain a sound education continued through the years: Lady Mary Wortley Montagu, Mary Wollstonecraft, Maria Edgeworth, Hannah More, Harriet Martineau and others all pleaded the cause of woman's education and, in general, their pleas fell on deaf ears. Any suggestion that women might withdraw from the world and enter an institution for whatever purpose, but especially for the purpose of learning, was regarded as a Catholic plot and condemned out of hand.

While the education provided for boys gradually advanced over the years, that for girls did not. Pockets of improvements could be found but little real progress was made overall and thus it was that the Royal Commission into Education in the 1860s – once it had actually been persuaded of the necessity of including girls' schools in its remit – could conclude that the education for girls was defective in almost every category. However, by that time things were beginning to change thanks to a campaign waged by a determined coterie of women and backed by a few men. Without assistance from these men, whether in the form of financial or administrative aid, in providing a toehold of opportunity, however slight, or in simply understanding what their women folk were about, the campaign to improve the education of girls would have taken even longer.

Despite the fact that for half a century or more authors of the calibre of Mrs Rundell, Mrs John Sandford and, indeed, Mrs Beeton had been emphasising the high ideals of the housewife's calling and insisting that her duty and greatest influence lay within the home circle, other concepts were slowly gaining ground. The first step towards improving standards in girls' education was taken when Queen's College, Harley Street, opened with the backing of the Governesses' Benevolent Instititution. In his inaugural address the Revd F.M. Maurice described how the GBI, in aiming to relieve distress among its members, which was itself linked to the inadequacies of their own education, intended to achieve this by providing instruction in a wide range of subjects to a much higher level, thereby raising their professional status. In 1853 the

College gained royal recognition with its Charter. For much of the century the organisation and teaching was directed by men, women holding only a subordinate position; women then assumed a greater share of the responsibilities – but it was 1931 before a woman principal took office.

Hard on the heels of Queen's College there followed Bedford College, founded by Mrs Elizabeth Jesser Reid in 1849 in order to give women a liberal education. The objective was to widen their cultural perspectives and enrich their whole lives rather than train them to be better governesses but the initial response to the project was disappointing. The two colleges were markedly different in character as women were involved in the running of Bedford right from the beginning, which engendered male hostility and harsh comments on the subject of women and of education in general. After a slow start the College flourished and in 1880 it became part of the University of London, just two years after women had been allowed to take that University's examinations.

The 1850s and '60s were a vigorous period with regard to education, with women pursuing different routes to advance their cause. Frances Buss (1827–94) was an early student at Queen's College. By the age of twenty-three she was running the North London Collegiate School which she and her mother had founded, and she remained as headmistress until her death in 1894. Dorothea Beale, with whom she is always linked,* was appointed Lady Principal of Cheltenham Ladies' College in 1858, having been previously in charge of a church school in Cumberland. Together they revolutionised the education given to girls of middle-class families as, indeed, did Emily Davies, founder of the first women's college in Cambridge. She was tied to her domestic duties until after her father's death but had already met with the feminists Barbara Bodichon and Millicent Fawcett and together they were laying their plans. A committee was set up that lobbied for the right of girls to sit the same examinations as the boys; Miss Davies wished to have nothing to do with separate exams for girls, something that many thought would be more suitable for them. To her 'different' meant 'lower' and she was resolute in pursuit of her objective. The campaign took its time but a college for women began life in Hitchin, some 25 miles from Cambridge, and well-disposed professors travelled there to teach the students, the lecture schedule being dependent on the timing of the trains. Land was bought outside Cambridge and in 1873 Girton College, far from complete though it was, opened its doors with Emily Davies as Mistress. Education to her was part

---

*   The following rhyme was chalked up on the blackboard one day: 'Miss Buss and Miss Beale, Cupid's darts do not feel. How unlike us, Miss Beale and Miss Buss.'

of a greater project – the admission of women to full equality – and for the rest of her days degrees for women, College finances and women's suffrage were foremost in her thoughts. Despite the intensity of her efforts it was not until 1948 that Cambridge saw fit to grant degrees to its women graduates.

Meanwhile, higher education for women was also being tackled from a different standpoint: 'Ladies' Lectures' had started in the north of England, largely through the efforts of Josephine Butler, Jemima Clough and others of the North of England Council and the idea had spread widely. Although lectures were given on a range of subjects and to a higher level than previously considered 'suitable', there was no systematic syllabus or depth of study involved; the exams set were unrelated to any public exams and were pitched at a lower level. Many women had no quarrel with this and were comfortable with the maxim that 'half a loaf was better than no bread'. The menfolk were less upset by this level of provision, whereas demands for equal educational opportunities aroused considerable ire. In time, accommodation was provided for those who wished to attend but could not live at home and Miss Clough, with her wide experience of teaching, was appointed to take charge of the residence in Cambridge. In 1872 Miss Clough's hostel became Newnham College with Miss Clough as Principal.

Something similar happened at Oxford where both Somerville College and Lady Margaret Hall began as hostels. During the 1860s some Ladies' Lectures were organised by Eleanor Smith, sister to the Savile Professor of Geometry who was accounted the most brilliant academic in Oxford, with one exception, his sister.[19] Later, John Ruskin's lectures on Italian art attracted large numbers of women and Louise Creighton formed a committee to promote further courses. One who attended was Elizabeth Wordsworth, whose brother John was tutor at Brasenose College and the first married Fellow. She was invited to be Lady Principal of the then Church Hall, later named for the mother of Henry VII, Lady Margaret Beaufort, 'a gentlewoman, a scholar and a saint and after being married three times she took a vow of celibacy'. Elizabeth Wordsworth wrote of her: 'What more could be expected of any woman?'[20] Miss Wordsworth went on to found St Hugh's as she was concerned that those of narrower means, such as the daughters of doctors, parsons or service officers and especially girls from larger families, would be excluded from spending three years at Oxford on the grounds of cost.

Many of the beneficiaries of higher education, such as Miss Buss and Miss Beale, went into teaching, thereby raising standards for later generations. Louisa Lumsden, a 'Girton Pioneer', taught classics at Girton itself and at Cheltenham Ladies' College, where the subject became so popular that another 'Pioneer' became her assistant.

Miss Lumsden spent eight years as head of St Leonard's School in St Andrews and five years as Warden of a Women's Hall at the University there. In 1882, her erstwhile assistant, Constance Maynard, became the first Mistress of Westfield College (which became part of London University) and remained in office until 1913. Jane Frances Dove, sometime head of St Leonard's, went on to found Wycombe Abbey School. Of the other early Girtonians one devoted herself to the cause of Owens College and the Victoria University of Manchester, one married John Lewis of the John Lewis Partnership, another taught mathematics at Manchester High School, one retired to Italy as a painter and one was a future Mistress of Girton. A final member, when speaking as a very old lady of her work for woman's suffrage, told her listeners: 'I will give you a useful hint, my dears,' she said, 'if you ever have to go to prison, remember two things; take a change of linen, so they will know you are a lady; and say you are a vegetarian, the food is better if you do.'[21]

Early students at Lady Margaret Hall included Gertrude Bell, prior to a career as explorer, archaeologist, author and diplomat; Janet Hogarth, a Civil Servant who turned journalist and author; and Eglantyne Jebb, the future founder of the Save the Children Fund. Gertrude Bell had previously attended classes at Queen's College, as did Frances Buss, the novelist Mrs Gaskell and Barbara Bodichon, whose name appears in a variety of feminist contexts. The influence of these women and their colleagues permeated in every direction. Their numerous personal and social relationships, as well as their differing or converging objectives, form a complex web that is difficult to disentangle: sitting alongside the struggle for higher educational standards was the campaign to gain entry to medical training and those involved in the one often proffered advice and support to the other. The campaign for 'votes for women' ran alongside both, as did efforts to achieve a modicum of independence for women within marriage, with numerous advocates advising or offering financial assistance to their like-minded sisters. For the first time women were united in their efforts rather than acting as individuals.

CHAPTER TWELVE

Over the Garden Gate

In March and in Aprill, from morning to night
In sowing and setting, good husewives delight:
To have in a garden, or other like plot,
To trim up their house, and to furnish their pot.
The nature of flowers, Dame Physicke doth show;
She teacheth them all, to be knowne to a few:
To set or to sowe, or else sowne to remove,
How that should be practiced, learne if ye love.[1]

Thomas Tusser's verse details the housewife's involvement in her garden.
It was not only the spring-time planting that concerned her: thereafter she
must tend her plot, gather the crops at the appropriate moment and know
how to process them for future use. Some sixty years later, the message was
reinforced by a little book on gardening aimed specifically at the country
housewife and William Lawson was in no doubt that the garden and its
produce should come under her charge. She should, he suggested, divide
the area into two gardens. One was to be the kitchen garden, for
'furnishing the pot', which loses its attractiveness once produce starts
being taken. The other is termed the summer garden which was for the
more permanent planting in the elaborate designs favoured at the time –
whether following the examples given of the 'fret', the 'lozenge', the
'flower de luce', the 'diamond' or any other convoluted format which the
housewife might devise for herself: 'Especially', as Lawson says, 'seeing to
set down many, had been but to fill much paper.' Roses are his first
choice, alongside 'Rosemary, Lavender, Bee-flowers, Isop, Sage, Time,
Cowslip, Pyony, Dasies, Clove-Gilliflowers, Pinckes, Sothernewood,
Lillies',[2] and he promises fuller details later on. He recommends that
some of these should also be planted in the kitchen garden as edgings to
the plots so that picking them in bulk, for lavender water, for example,
would not destroy the symmetry of the summer garden.

Despite this insistence on the housewife's duties, Scotland's first book
on gardening, published in 1683 specifically for the Scottish climate,
makes no mention in its pages of who should or should not be doing the
work. From these and other books of the period the actual horticultural
practices would seem, in many instances, to be remarkably similar to
those of today.

A garden was expected to supply not only fruit, vegetables and herbs for the kitchen but also material for decorative, medicinal and cosmetic purposes. Many plants, or parts of plants, were credited with remedial properties and the seventeenth-century housewife was expected to have ready to hand a store of nostrums that might be needed at any moment, all the more so if she lived in a remote area or was unable to afford the services of a doctor. At the optimum moment for each individual item, be it root, stalk, leaves, flowers or seed heads, she must harvest the material and spend long hours putting together her potions and mixtures.

Information would be handed down from mother to daughter, from housewife to housewife, but herbals and other sources of knowledge were available to those who could read and had the money to buy them. Works by Gerard, Parkinson, Culpeper and others remained popular for many years and instructed the housewife how to grow the plants, when to gather them, which parts to use and about their 'vertues' or what they were good for. Elizabeth Blackwell compiled *The Curious Herbal* in 1737 and this two-volume work contained 'Five Hundred Cuts of the most useful plants which are now used in the practice of Physick . . . to which is added a short description of yᵉ plants and their common uses in Physick'. Each illustration is signed 'Eliz: Blackwell delin.sculp.et Pinx.'

Cookery books also provided information since the making up of the lotions and cures was akin to cookery and were placed under such chapter headings as 'Cookery for the Sick' or 'Various Receipts',[3] whereas in earlier days the latter were unequivocally entitled 'Beautifying Waters, Oils, Ointments, and Powders, to adorn and add Loveliness to the Face and Body.'[4] The dividing line between remedy and cosmetic was frequently slim as, for example, in mixtures intended 'To take away Sunburn' or 'To make the hair grow thick'. No such ambiguity existed in the directions for 'A sweet scented Bath for Ladies' which required a cornucopia of ingredients: 'Take of Roses, Citron-peel, sweet Flowers, Orange-flowers, Jessamy, Bayes, Rosemary, Lavender, Mint, Penny-royal, of each a sufficient quantity, boil them together gently, and make a Bath; to which add Oil of Spike [*Lavendula spica*] six Drops, Musk five Grains, Amber-greese three Grains, sweet Afa one Ounce'. It must have been a bath for a special occasion, seeing as it would take quite some time to put so many ingredients together, always supposing they were all simultaneously available when required. The recipe ends with the words 'Let her go into the Bath for three Hours.'[5]

The emphasis on this branch of a housewife's skills has a long history as has the link between herbs and health. The common stock of knowledge was largely forgotten during the nineteenth century, but not completely. During the First World War women were exhorted to grow herbs on a large scale, to replace those formerly imported from Austria and Germany. In the 1920s Hilda Leyel became fascinated with the subject and made a detailed study of the old herbals. She came into contact with Mrs Grieve who at that time was running a herb farm and school and the two collaborated on *A Modern Herbal* which gave details of American herbs too. The first Culpeper shop opened soon afterwards, to be followed by others throughout the country, as the idea proved popular, not only for the creams and lotions but also for the medicinal herbs and Mrs Leyel was surprised to find that many of her customers retained memories of, or even a specialised knowledge of, herbal cures. In 1926 her friend Dorothy Hewer started up The Herb Farm at Seal, in Kent, and having originally trained as a teacher took in a few students who learnt about the practical aspects of herb growing while providing the labour force for the farm. Several of them went on to run similar concerns of their own.

At much the same time E.S. Rohde was writing on herbs and herb gardens, although she wrote on most aspects of the garden and contributed innumerable articles to the periodicals of the era. She recalled the delights of the well-filled store room with loving descriptions of home-made confectionery: 'And I remember also the bunches of white and red currants candied whole . . . as though they were made of glass', alongside the candied petals from roses and carnations, and syrups flavoured with elder, clove carnation, mint, quince and saffron.[6] As well as her writing she ran a herb nursery and during the Second World War, as before, herb growing for medicinal purposes was at a premium.

It all seems, from the viewpoint of the early twenty-first century, to be a perfectly normal occupation for women to be engaged in but it is, in reality, of fairly recent origin. Prior to this the fact that women, often designated as 'widow women' or 'weeding women' in household accounts, were able to earn themselves a few pence by doing unskilled gardening jobs would suggest they were of humble means and lowly status. However, this may be a questionable assumption. One of the places visited by Celia Fiennes on her travels late in the seventeenth century was 'Ouborn' (Woburn) where she found much to admire in the extensive grounds, including the 'great quantety of ye Red Coralina goosbery', which she ate. She describes how she went 'under an arch into a Cherry garden, in the midst of wch stands a figure of stone resembling an old weeder woman used in the garden, and my Lord would have her Effigie wch is done so like and her Clothes so well that at first I tooke it to be a Real Living body',[7] but the motive for having a permanent reminder of a lowly garden labourer in a prominent site is hard to fathom at this distance in time. Scottish records certainly indicate that widows continued to run their late husband's gardening concerns and in one instance, in 1670, the two 'gardeners at Holyroodhouse', named specifically as John Broun and Grisell Bruce, were paid a weekly sum for supplying the kitchens with a varied assortment of garden produce and herbs.[8]

It is harder to estimate how many middle-class women worked in their own gardens. Picking a few flowers to bring indoors was one thing but replanting the rose beds and trundlng 'muck' around the place was probably going too far – the concepts of ladylike behaviour must have kept many from an enjoyable occupation, even though there were numerous complaints about the stubborness and ineptitude of the average jobbing gardener. It was during the Victorian era that gardening was promoted as a suitable ploy for ladies and since then many have taken up the spade and the hoe with great enthusiasm and admirable results but, before that, there is little firm evidence of their involvement. That some women were unconcerned by the conventions is known, Hannah More, philanthropist and author, being one: 'I am growing a prodigious gardener,' she wrote to a friend, 'and make up by my industry for my want of science. I work at it for two or three hours every day, and by the hour of visiting arrives I am vastly glad of a pretence for sitting down.'[9] Jane Austen's mother was another and at Chawton, as a widow in her seventies, she handed over the household duties to her daughters and chose to work in the garden herself, clad in a green smock. Marianne North, while confined to being housekeeper and assistant to her father, had three greenhouses in the garden at Hastings, one for orchids, one for temperate plants and one for vines and cuttings and dreamt of the day she herself would see these and other exotic specimens in their own landscapes. Later in the century that great garden designer Gertrude Jekyll (1843–1932) did indeed labour in the garden herself, as there is not only her portrait by William Nicholson, which is considered to be a striking likeness, but there is also a 'portrait' of her gardening boots. A team of gardeners worked at Munstead Wood, it is true, but it should be remembered that for almost 40 years she was running a nursery business that supplied the majority of plants needed for the 350 gardens she designed during that period.

In the twentieth century Vita Sackville West and her husband created the world-famous gardens at Sissinghurst in the 1930s, while at the other end of Britain Marie Sawyer carried on the work at Inverewe begun by her father, Sir Osgood Mackenzie, on a rugged, windswept, peaty ridge many years earlier.

Even if the housewife did not personally dig and delve she would surely have had her say as to what should be grown: only in the grandest households would she be removed from such matters, though her preference for certain flowers might be catered for. Even here there were exceptions: Mary Capel, Duchess of Beaufort, and friend of Sir Hans

Sloane was celebrated for the gardens she developed at Badminton and her enthusiasm for botanical pursuits. Decades later the widow of the 4th Earl of Hopetoun, who spent much of her time in East Lothian and died in 1836, took a personal interest in the gardens of Ormiston Hall and established 500 herbaceous plants and 270 varieties of roses. One of her husband's great-aunts, a hundred years earlier, had had ambitions too large to be contained within a mere garden. Helen Hope, sister to the 1st Earl of Hopetoun and by marriage Countess of Haddington, was a planter of trees on a grand scale. In recalling how it had come about, her husband gave her full credit for her achievements and for introducing him to the potential benefits. She began by planting on a small scale and then turned her attention to a sizeable area of rough moorland and, despite everyone's advice to the contrary, gained her husband's permission to go ahead. When the two of them failed to agree on a focal point for the design they called in three friends to arbitrate on the matter and ended up with three focal points! Her initiative was later commemorated in verse:

Thus can good wives, when wise, in every station,
On man work miracles of reformation,
And were such wives more common, their husbands would endure it,
However great the malady, a loving wife can cure it,
And much their aid is wanted, we hope they use it fairish,
While barren ground, where wood should be, appears in every parish.[10]

Despite the fact that gardening was considered to be a very feminine interest and an activity within the housewife's remit, despite the fact that the growing of things in a garden is creative and therapeutic in the same way as embroidery or painting, and despite the fact that many women derived great pleasure from their gardens, it is curious how few women wrote on the subject until well into the nineteenth century, even though they were not shy of appearing in print on so many other topics.

Of the female authors Jane Loudon (1807–58) is generally credited with being the first and, as it happens, gardening was not her original career. When a young woman she wrote a novel called *The Mummy*, which nowadays would be termed 'science fiction'; in it she portrayed an England of the future with labour-saving devices such as milking machines and air conditioning, a well-organised welfare state and a form of space travel by balloon. John Claudius Loudon enjoyed the book, reviewed it in *The Gardener's Magazine* and never even considered the possibility that the author of such a scientific work was anything other than a man. They met and were married just seven months later: 'When I married Mr Loudon, it is scarcely possible to imagine any person more completely ignorant than I was, of every thing relating to plants and gardening; . . . My husband, of course, was quite as anxious to teach me as I was to learn', she wrote in her *Instructions in Gardening for Ladies* and she dedicated the book to him 'to whom the author of the following pages owes all the knowledge of the subject she possesses'.[11] She regarded her previous ignorance as one of her chief qualifications as she felt that the professionals were unable to write simply enough. Chapters cover soil, manuring, sowing and transplanting, modes of propagation, pruning and training, the kitchen garden and and so on in a thorough, but pleasant, manner. She produced many other books on gardening and related topics, including one for younger folk, and continued writing when widowed. Later in life she was the first editor of *The Ladies Companion at Home and Abroad*, a magazine for the 'new woman' of Victorian England.

While Mrs Loudon was promoting gardening as a suitable occupation not only for married women but even for mothers, Louisa Johnson was seeing the matter in a different light: in her opinion gardening might be a way for a spinster to lose herself 'as a distraction from the disappointments of life'.[12]

Despite the claim made on behalf of Jane Loudon, names can be found that pre-date hers by a number of years. Henrietta Moriarty's *Viridarium: Coloured Plates of Greenhouse Plants*, with its modicum of growing instructions, came out in 1806. A decade later saw Maria Jackson's *Florist's Manual or Hints for the Construction of a Gay Flower Garden – with Observations on the best methods of preventing the depredations of insects.* This examined the use of herbaceous plants and annuals to provide colour in the garden from February to August, though hopefully they would last through to October. The author's advice on the subject of insects is to pick them off manually – 'the simple and laborious mode'. The book is dedicated to her 'highly esteemed friend Lady Broughton, as a tribute to the taste and ingenuity which she has displayed in the formation and arrangement of her peculiarly beautiful flower garden'. Almost twenty years earlier she had published *Botanical Dialogues . . . designed for the use of schools* and another book aimed at children, although its title *Sketches of the Physiology of Vegetable Life* was unlikely to see them rushing to the bookshelf. *The Florist's Manual* went through several editions and was succeeded in 1840 by *The Pictorial Flora or British Botany Delineated*, for which she engraved 1,500 lithographs.

As a subject botany was a more popular theme for women than horticulture. In 1769 Mrs Delany translated Hudson's *Flora Anglica* (1762), which she sub-titled *An English Translation of the Linnaean Names of all the British Plants*.[13] Lady Charlotte Murray's *British Garden* was published in 1799 and again in 1806. P.B. Wakefield (1761–1832) specialised in books for children and her *Introduction to Botany* went through eleven editions by 1841. Katherine Baily was the author of *Irish Flora* (1833) and the first woman admitted to the Botanical Society of Edinburgh shortly after its founding in 1836. The Kirby sisters co-operated in compiling the county *Flora of Leicestershire* (1850), while Anne Pratt (1806–93), author and illustrator, published some fifteen botanical works on the wild flowers, ferns and flowering plants of Great Britain and included some folklore and information on potential usage.

Entomology also attracted them. Mary Capel, Duchess of Beaufort, was a notable breeder of insects, as well as a collector of rare plants. Anna Blackburne (1726–93) corresponded with many famous names of the day, including Linnaeus, built up her museum at Orford Hall in Lancashire and had several species named after her, including a North American bird, a beetle and a plant from 'New Holland'. P.B. Wakefield wrote not only on botany but also on insects and animal instincts. Both Margaret Stovin and Margaretta Riley were in the forefront of studies on ferns and in 1840 the latter read a paper to the Botanical Society of London. Another contributor to scientific journals was A.W. Russell (1807–76) who compiled catalogues of flowering plants in the Bristol and Newbury areas and made a study of bats; she also worked as a botanical artist and made over 700 drawings of fungi.

Others with artistic talents who found inspiration from the plant world have already been mentioned. The Duchess of Beaufort's sister Elizabeth, Countess of Carnavon, was a celebrated exponent of flower painting. Mary Moser was another and a founder member of the Royal Academy of Arts where her work was frequently exhibited over a span of thirty years. A.C. Bartholomew (d. 1862) exhibited flower and fruit pieces in watercolour. Marianne North grew her own exotic plants and honed her artistic skills in her father's garden in Hastings; she travelled round Europe with her father, painting and sketching local scenes, but after his death she travelled the world and the resulting collection of her botanical drawings is housed in its own gallery in Kew Gardens. Her sister Catherine was similarly talented. Anne Nasmyth was another who took a keen interest in growing the flowers she wished to paint or embroider and had considerable talent in both arts.

During much of the nineteenth century botanical publications were illustrated by women. They were artists of the calibre of Miss Drake (fl. 1818–47); Mrs Withers (fl. 1827–64), who was also a noted teacher and 'Flower Painter in Ordinary to Queen Adelaide' (wife of William IV); and Elizabeth Twining (1805–89), who supplied her own drawings for her *Illustrations of Natural Orders* (1849–55) and later botanical works. C.L. Brightwell (1811–75) drew and lithographed figures to accompany her father's (unpublished) book on the fauna of east Norfolk.

From using flowers and foliage as the inspiration to their art it was but a step to creating artical flowers in a variety of materials. In describing her early married life, Hannah Robertson, a granddaughter (illegitimate) of Charles II, doubtless represented the relationship of many women to their gardens. She wrote: 'I studied nature with a view to imitate her most elegant productions. A new creation rose between my hands. I formed flowers of art, I painted, and I embroidered. So, like Penelope of old, I charmed away with works of fancy the tedious hours, during the absence of my lord.'[14] Presumably these were the creations she was later to advise her readers how to make. Few could have achieved as much in copying nature than Mrs Delany with her 'paper mosaics' which eventually filled ten volumes of botanically accurate illustrations along with forty-seven pages of text. Unfortunately, not all the creative processes were undertaken in such a leisurely fashion and it should be remembered that many occupations employing women, such as the making of artificial flowers for the millinery trade, for example, or painting botanical motifs on china were carried out in poor conditions, often using materials injurious to the workers, over very long hours and with minimal pay. It took time and persistence to track down and curtail the worst abuses and the part played by the Woman's Inspectorate of Factories and Workshops from its beginnings in 1893 will be considered later.

Setting aside the realities of botanical works carried out in the name of art or of fashion, the academic side of horticulture flourished with many women writing on different facets of plants and gardening. Mary Pirie wrote on *Flowers, Grasses and Shrubs* which she hoped would encourage a study of botany and a love of flowers – wild flowers in particular. Agnes Catlow had already produced *Popular Field Botany* before writing her *Popular Greenhouse Botany*, 'containing a familiar and technical description of a selection of the Exotic Plants Introduced into the Greenhouse', illustrated with twenty hand-coloured plates.[15] 'Charlotte Elizabeth' wrote about plants from a different viewpoint as she says she is not writing a botanical treatise but 'a floral biography' since so many of her past and present friends have become associated with a particular flower and 'my garden bears a nomenclature which no eye but mine can decipher'.[16] Despite the personal element it went through many editions. Miss F.J. Hope (d. 1880) ran a large garden north of Edinburgh and contributed many articles to the gardening press including an influential series on flower arranging in the 1870s. Some of her associations of plants or combinations of colours must have seemed bizarre at the time although a hundred years later they are common practice. She bred hellebores and rescued several forms which have since been lost to cultivation. Her planting schemes came to the attention of William Robinson who was sufficiently impressed to list no less than eighteen of them in his authoritative work on *The English Flower Garden*, seemingly oblivious to the fact that she was Scots born and bred.

At much the same time Gertrude Jekyll (1843–1932), having turned to gardening later in life, was also attracting Robinson's attention. Aged seventeen she had enrolled at the Kensington School of Art and become skilled in working with brass and silver, in woodwork and embroidery; later she added a proficiency in carving and gilding. It was not until after her father's death in 1876 that she designed a garden for her mother's new house, which met with the approval of several eminent men of the horticultural world. In 1881 she was asked to judge at the Botanical Show in Regent's Park, a forerunner of the Chelsea Flower Show, and started to contribute gardening articles for the periodical published by William Robinson. In 1891 her eyesight began to cause concern and she was advised to give up her embroidery and other close work. At this point she made the acquaintance of a young architect just setting out on his career, Edwin Lutyens. She introduced him to wealthy or well-connected patrons; he built a new house for her on land that she had already laid out as her garden; she designed the garden for his own house. The combination of Lutyens house and a Jekyll garden became the height of fashion and they collaborated on over a hundred, though she carried out many more commissions on her own. In 1899 Miss Jekyll published the first of a dozen or more books on gardens and gardening, all illustrated with photographs taken and processed by herself. They included her book on *Flower Decoration for the Home*, then largely an unknown subject and one taken up at a later date by Constance Spry with enormous success, and *Children and Gardens*, in which she gave recipes for cooking the fruits and vegetables they might grow. Meanwhile, she was collecting material on the rural way of life for her book *Old West Surrey*, again illustrated with her own photographs. She continued working, planning and writing throughout her long life and, afterwards, it was Edwin Lutyens who designed her memorial, describing her as 'Artist. Gardener. Craftswoman.'

The later Victorian era produced other 'gardening women'. Theresa Earle was a contemporary of Gertrude Jekyll's, a passionate gardener, an early promoter of herbs and a believer in a vegetarian diet. She was into her sixties before she wrote the first of her books, *Pot Pourri from a Surrey Garden*, a mixture of gardening hints, reminiscences, recipes, extracts from other authors and so on which proved a popular format. Ellen Willmott was equally passionate about her garden, even though she employed a considerable number of gardeners to maintain Warley Place, and she was the first woman to be elected Fellow of the Linnaean Society. She produced a book on her garden, with her own photographs, and another, *The Genus Rosa*, to which she contributed the historical and cultural notes while others supplied the text and the illustrations. She supported plant-hunting expeditions, commissioned botanical artists and numerous plants were named after her or her garden. After the First World War her income dwindled and she was unable to maintain the gardens; after her death in 1934 the house itself was demolished.

A happier story was that of Frances Wolseley and the Glynde School (later College) for Lady Gardeners, which she opened at the beginning of the twentieth century. For two years the students were trained in her parents' garden which she had planted but the school then moved to land nearby where a new teaching garden was laid out. Her objective was to make gardening into an acceptable career for women but she realised that they would first have to prove their ability. The students received a practical training in the basics of gardening, elements of design and lay-out, and in management techniques for private gardens; they were expected to remain becoming and feminine in their dress and a working uniform was devised comprising short skirts over breeches, with gaiters and boots. This was an improvement on the outfits of the girls taken on at Kew in 1895 where the matter of their dress had led to endless discussion:

> The girls were instructed to wear clothing similar to that of the ordinary gardeners. They adopted thick brown bloomers and woollen stockings, tailored jackets and peaked caps. The Director ordered them to wear long macintoshes on their way to work, so disguising the bloomers. Londoners found that they were visible at work inside the gardens, and this was recorded in a daily newspaper.

> > 'They gardened in bloomers, the newspapers said,
> > So to Kew without waiting all Londoners sped;
> > From the tops of the buses they had a fine view,
> > Of the ladies in bloomers who gardened at Kew.'[17]

The Women's Farm and Garden Union (later Association) was contemporary with Glynde and shared similar aims – to promote agriculture and horticulture as suitable careers for women – and it set up an employment bureau to assist them in finding work. Swanley College in Kent admitted girls in 1900 and two years later restricted its intake to women only; it closed in the 1960s. Studley, in Warwickshire, was another horticultural college established in 1910 for women students. Others followed suit including one in Edinburgh that same year and, later, Beatrix Havergal's Pusey School, which developed into the Waterperry Horticultural School and also closed in the 1960s.

The timing of these training schemes proved fortuitous: at the outbreak of war in 1914 so many men were called up for military duties that gardens would have been left untended at precisely the time when it was necessary to maximise the home production of foodstuffs. As it was, competent women with horticultural experience were ready to take over and train up others at the same time. Help with harvesting was provided from the newly established Land Service Corps, formed in 1914 under the auspices of the WFGA and set up by Louisa Jebb, the first woman to read for an agricultural degree at Cambridge. The service was later taken over by the government and renamed the Women's Land Army. The women tackled many farm jobs, such as milking and ploughing, and proved themselves invaluable; their services were required again during the years of the Second World War. Meantime, training schools had been set up to help women capitalise on the skills they had learnt during the war years and to encourage them to find employment in horticulture and agriculture.

Allied with gardens and food production generally were the skills associated with beekeeping and poultry rearing, all of which provided new opportunities for women. Beekeeping was encouraged primarily for the production of honey to replace imported sugar, but also for the vitally important pollination services of the bees as they foraged, which encouraged the much-needed crops of fruit. The part played by women in both beekeeping and poultry rearing has been mentioned earlier. To set alongside the 'many volumes on Poultry, Pigeons and Cage Birds' the Hon. Rose Hubbard wrote on *Ornamental Water Fowl: A Practical Manual on the Acclimatisation of the Swimming Birds*. She listed over 200 birds, covered a wide range of topics and indexed both the English and the Latin names of the birds; under the pseudonym of 'Henwife' she had earlier produced *Table Poultry &c.*

It was song birds that William Lawson enjoyed seeing around the garden: 'One chief grace that adorns an Orchard, I cannot let slip: a brood of Nightingales . . . who with severall notes and tunes . . .', he asserts, 'will beare you company night and day' while ridding the trees of caterpillars, worms and flies. He also liked to see the robin red-breast, the wren, the blackbird and the throstle (song thrush).[18] For Lady Luxborough (1699–1756), banished by her husband for alleged infidelities, it was an aviary that provided solace, along with the garden she had created on the derelict estate, and she proposed making a fountain for her birds 'and a grotto to sit in and hear them sing in, contiguous to it'.[19] Beatrix Potter's writing career was enhanced by nature studies undertaken during childhood holidays near Dunkeld and by visits to the British Museum's Natural History Department. Edith Holden recorded her observations of flora and fauna for the twelve months of 1906, accompanied by meticulous paintings and some favourite poems and personal thoughts; as *The Country Diary of an Edwardian Lady* it achieved fame some seventy years after it was written.

On the whole the gardener welcomes birds, bees, butterflies and small mammals but woe betide the one that takes advantage – the bird that pulls out the seedlings, the mouse that eats the pea seeds or the wasps that attack the bee hives. Old-time accounts often mention the necessary remedial measures: mouse traps, netting, black soap, tobacco, powder and shot, sulphur and rat poison. Garden accounts of the larger establishments also include items of harness, fodder or medical treatments 'for the pony'; this animal drew the carts of manure or stones, shifted unwanted soil or garden rubbish, transported the tools from place to place and was useful in many other ways. By the 1830s the pony was pulling the new lawnmowers and needed leather 'boots' so its hooves would not cut into the lawns.

When it came to domestic animals it was not a pony but a cow, an Alderney cow, that was the delight of an old lady in the fictitious community of *Cranford* and also the subject of a small drama. Miss Betsy Barker looked upon this animal as a daughter and when it fell into a lime pit one day and lost all its hair there was sympathy all round and much advice as to what to do next. One suggestion was 'Get her a flannel waistcoat and drawers, ma'am' and so, 'she set to work, and by and by all the town turned out to see the Alderney meekly going to her pasture, clad in dark grey flannel'.[20] Fiction aside, Beatrix Potter after her marriage took up farming in the Lake District, became a highly respected breeder of Herdwick sheep and judged at agricultural shows. A hundred years or so before her, Jane, Duchess of Gordon, had not only been a patroness of Scottish music and dancing but had established a 'farming society' at Badenoch for her tenants and a woollen manufactory for the employment of Highland spinsters. By all accounts Lady Loudon (d. 1777) had been actively engaged in agricultural improvements in Ayrshire since the 1720s, having started with her own garden and orchard where she carefully superintended the work: years later it was noted 'Many of the fruit and forest trees were actually planted and pruned with her own hands, and still remain stately and pleasing monuments of her laudable industry.'[21] From there she went on to improve her agricultural land and others followed her example.

In the home itself pet animals were often to be found and, just as a woman's portrait might well display flowers in some way, so the portraits of children or families included their cats, dogs, monkeys or horses. Formerly, a symbolic significance had been attached to animals in portraiture but, latterly, they take on the appearance of family pets. Jane Loudon's literary output included *Domestic Pets, their Habits and Management with illustrative Anecdotes*, in which dogs, cats, white mice and gold fish are discussed, as might be expected, with, in addition, squirrels, ravens and other British and foreign talking birds.

Dogs had been used for hunting and sporting purposes since time immemorial and the 'lady's lap dog' goes back a long way, too: after Mary Queen of Scots was beheaded her pet dog, probably a little spaniel, was found beneath her petticoats. Elizabeth Barrett Browning's dog was a spaniel, a gift from authoress Miss Mitford, and she wrote a lengthy poem entitled 'To Flush, My Dog'. Catherine Hutton's feelings are all too recognisable, even at this distance of time: 'My poor little pug is gone the way of all canine flesh; I wept as I saw him stretched motionless on the floor, and when I saw him laid on the ground; but his loss was less to be regretted as he was asthmatic, paralytic, half-blind, three-quarters deaf, and nearly thirteen years old.'[22]

With the enormous increase in the numbers of town dwellers during the eighteenth century, coupled with the reduction in the size of their dwellings, it was the smaller types of dog that grew in popularity. Breeders responded to the demand and new breeds were also imported, such as the Maltese terriers given as a gift to Queen Victoria in 1841. Some twenty years later she was presented with something even rarer, a Peking Palace dog (a Pekingese) named 'Lootie', rescued after the Summer Palace had been sacked and burned. In all, five of these Imperial dogs survived the journey back to England. Various stories are told of their rescue, one of which runs as follows: as French and British troops advanced towards Peking the Imperial household, some 10 miles away at the Summer Palace, fled north to Jehol. Such was the haste of their flight that there was no time to pack their belongings on to carts and so many of their possessions were thrown down the Palace wells. When the allies reached the Palace it was the French who rescued the concubines while the English rescued the dogs.

One little dog was presented to the Queen, although it lived out its days in the Royal kennels. Lord John Hay kept one himself but he presented a bitch to his sister, the Duchess of Wellington, who established the breed at Stratfield Saye; two others brought back were given to the Duchess of Richmond and Gordon who founded the famous 'Goodwood' strain, the basis of several bloodlines, and her work was continued by Lady Algernon Gordon-Lennox. In 1904 the Alderbourne kennel was founded, the best-known Pekingese kennel, some would say, in the world. It all started when Mrs Clarice Ashton Cross was crossing Piccadilly one day and was intrigued by a strange little dog being carrried in its owner's arms. At the time she was already breeding Arab horses and had a kennel of bloodhounds but the little dogs soon predominated and almost immediately she was successfully breeding them to the highest standard. All four of the Misses Ashton Cross, her daughters, were involved with the dogs and two became judges of international repute but it was Miss Cynthia who was the acknowledged expert and her dogs were exported all over the world.

Arab horses were also a passion with Lady Anne Blunt (1839–1917), the daughter of Ada Lovelace, and she was an intrepid rider, traveller, Arabic scholar, musician and writer. She travelled widely with her diplomat husband and latterly alone through North Africa, searching for the horses to implement their celebrated stud at Crabbet Park, the house they built in Sussex. Horse racing itself continued to be a masculine preserve for many a long year but shortly before she died in 1714 Queen Anne established racing at Ascot where 'Ladies Day' is still very much a fixture in the social calendar. Lillie Langtry (1852–1929), the Jersey-born actress and favourite of Edward VII, was the first woman to own a racing stable, although she had to adopt the *nom de plume* of 'Mr Jersey' to do so.

Throughout the century animals and their welfare were becoming a matter of increasing concern to a large number of people. Even earlier, Hannah More had involved herself in a campaign to stop bull-baiting. In 1824 the Society for the Prevention of Cruelty to Animals was founded and it gained the prefix 'Royal' in 1840. In 1835 the first Act to prevent cruelty to animals was passed, the first successful prosecution for cruelty to dogs took place and bull-baiting with dogs and dog fighting were banned, though they continued clandestinely. From 1840 the use of dogs to draw carts, carriages, trucks or barrows was prohibited in the London area; and in the 1850s further provisions extended the prohibition throughout the UK.

By the 1870s the subject of animals and their treatment was much to the fore, due in part to the increased interest in public health and hygiene and allied to the serious problem of food adulteration. Mrs Buckton, promoter of lessons in domestic economy for all schoolchildren, included in them 'the Treatment of Animals'. She said: 'During the course of my lectures I determined to plead the cause of dumb animals as well as of little children . . . I was pleased to observe the strong expressions of disapproval . . . when instances were given of the cruel and ignorant way in which they were often treated'.[23] Her friend Mrs Loftie, a regular contributor to the *Saturday Review*, thought rather that it was for the local parson to exert his influence by which 'he could do much to check that cruelty to animals which arises more from ignorance and thoughtlessness than from an actual desire to inflict pain'. The parson should be able to stop the unnecessary killing of animals 'for crimes they had not done and were not convicted of' and instead make the children aware of the beauties of living organisms and their mechanisms.[24]

In the 1890s the treatment of domestic pets was still unsatisfactory and the catalogue of potential cruelties delineated does not make for happy reading. 'The mistress of a house in which animals are unkindly treated',

Frances Power Cobbe thunders, 'is guilty of *a very great sin*; and till she has taken care that the dog has his daily exercise and water, and that the cat and the fowl, and every sentient creature under her roof, is well and kindly treated, she may as well, for shame's sake, give up thinking she is fulfilling her duties.'[25] Other women had similar objectives. Anna Sewell wrote her classic story *Black Beauty* as a protest against the ill-treatment of horses. Louisa Lumsden, an original student at Girton College, recalled how she had been a lifetime supporter of the Anti-Vivisection cause and had edited the Scottish Society's magazine for eleven years. Angela Burdett Coutts not only organised drinking troughs for equines but shelters for donkeys, too, among her wide-ranging activities. Others founded charities for animal welfare, such as Miss Ivory's Scottish Society for the Prevention of Vivisection of the 1890s or the International League for the Protection of Horses founded in 1927 by Ada Cole.

It was a long time before women were accepted for veterinary training as it was genuinely thought that women would not have the physical strength to cope with the demands of a rural practice. Not until after the First World War and a change in the law did the Royal College of Veterinary Surgeons finally accept women into the profession. The first to gain her professional qualification was Aleen Cust, late in 1922, although she had entered Edinburgh's New Veterinary College in 1895* and had been in practice in Ireland since the turn of the century. The RCVS had refused to allow her to sit her exams at that time as it was contrary to all established precedent. In 1923 Miss Knight passed her final examination in Liverpool, to become the second British woman vet. However, it was 1928 before the first major intake of women students took place, with 3 in January, 12 in October, and 1 the previous year. Since then the College has seen women members of Council and, more recently, has elected its first woman President.

---

* Later this College moved to Liverpool University.

CHAPTER THIRTEEN

Here and There

When women were involved in so many activities outside the home it surely comes as no surprise to learn that they were often away from their homes altogether. Travelling was not as rare as it might be thought. Women have always travelled, maybe not as often as their menfolk and maybe not in such numbers but, as a group, they were far from being the stay-at-homes so often portrayed. A number have already been met with in previous chapters and in different contexts.

What reasons did women have for leaving their homes? Over the years, the incentives changed little. Women not only went as companions to husbands or other relations in a variety of situations – domestic, family, political, social, health and so on – but also set off in pursuit of their own ventures, which were similarly wide-ranging in motivation.

That is the short answer to the 'why' of women's travel, of which more later, but what about the 'how'? During the course of the period the means of transport improved greatly. In the early days it was often slow, uncomfortable, dangerous and expensive. Horses could only go so fast; seaborne transport was governed by tides and weather; and inland waterways were relatively slow and primarily designed for shifting heavy loads. Ballooning had potential, but without a means of controlling the direction of travel or the accuracy of landing it was hardly a commercial proposition. It was steampower that revolutionised the movement of people and goods during the nineteenth century, both on land and at sea; latterly, the bicycle contributed greatly to personal mobility and freedom, while the impact of 'the horseless carriage' is still making itself felt a hundred years after its introduction. Later again came powered flight in which women were involved surprisingly early.

There was also, of course, the personalised form of locomotion known as 'Shank's pony'. Generally speaking, women were accustomed to walking, whether for pleasure or while going about their everyday labours. Fetching water from a well might involve several trips a day, of maybe half a mile or so each way and frequently further in times of drought. It was often easier to take the washing to the river bank and deal with it there rather than transporting all the water needed to do it at home. Going to and from the local market might mean several miles there and back: the story of the Yorkshire woman who walked the 3 miles to her local market, sold her goods and then walked back again, knitting all the while, has already been told.[1] In South Wales it was observed how the roads on market day were thronged from an early hour, the majority of folk on foot though some were in carts. The women walked with large, weighty baskets on their heads and carried their high-crowned, broad-brimmed hats in their hand or tied to an arm or an apron, so as to be able to wear them on arrival. However, another report said that the Vale women were energetic walkers whereas the hill women were not 'and therefore are by no means lissom. As a rule they are heavily built, short and stout'.[2] In Scotland women also walked. Elizabeth Grant of Rothiemurchus describes how she and her sister would wander far afield when in the Highlands. In Edinburgh, too, walking the 4 miles or more to friends at Craigcrook Castle was a frequent occurrence: 'In the mornings,' she wrote, 'we made walking parties, and one day we went to Rosslyn and Lasswade, a merry company.'[3] (A good distance, too, Lasswade being some 6 miles and Roslin about 8 from the city centre.)

For short distances within towns an alternative mode of transport was the sedan chair which was carried on poles between two 'chairmen'; some women had their own chairs and chairmen, others were available for hire like a modern taxi – in general, prices charged were based on the distance and time involved. One had been central to the plan to rescue a husband imprisoned in Edinburgh Castle while a generation or so later one of the sights of the city was to see the Countess of Eglintoune and her seven daughters arriving in a train of sedan chairs at the Assembly Rooms off the High Street. A century or so later a more modest sighting took place in *Cranford*. Rumours were rife about a gang of thieves terrorising the quiet neighbourhood at just the time when Miss Matty and her friends were bidden to take tea at an address in the ominously named 'Darkness Lane'. While Miss Matty was quite glad to be shut into the hired sedan chair, she was also fearful that, should the robbers attack the little party, the chairmen might drop their burden and leave her to her fate. To the great relief of the ladies, nothing untoward happened on either journey.

A horse-litter resembled a sedan chair slung between two horses and these were for the sick or the elderly – Lady Anne Clifford, for example, travelled in one towards the end of her life. They were supplanted by variations of the cart and the carriage but, as long as roads resembled rutted tracks, wheeled vehicles were of little use. There were those who rode pillion behind husband or man servant and are portrayed holding on to his coat with one hand while carrying the marketing basket with the other. This method was also used for long-distance travel such as that undertaken by Dorothy Forster when she set off from Bamburgh in the middle of winter to rescue her brother from London's Newgate Gaol, where he was held after the 1715 Jacobite Rising. Women also managed their own horses, riding side-saddle, a habit reputedly introduced by Anne of Bohemia, wife of Richard II.

Sea travel along the coast was a viable alternative and avoided the problems associated with horse-drawn transport and badly maintained roads. Goods of every description regularly went by this method, as did household servants, and people travelled this way even after the railways had been developed. In 1862 the four-year-old Elizabeth Cadbury went with her family by boat from London to the Yorkshire coast to visit relations in Redcar. But sea travel was not without its hazards: almost 200 years earlier, John Hope of Hopetoun was drowned in a shipwreck while en route to Holyroodhouse in the entourage of James, Duke of York. Margaret Hamilton, his widow, was left to bring up two small children and in due course signed the contract for the building of Hopetoun House. In marked contrast Sarah Churchill's husband survived the very same shipwreck, thanks to the Duke of York himself. Had he not been saved, history might have taken a very different turn. Even steamships when introduced were not immune to the effects of wind and weather as witnessed by the exploits of the young Grace Darling and her father when the *Forfarshire* was wrecked off the Farne Islands.

Whatever mode of travel was used, women moved in the earlier days with husbands and households from one residence to another according to the seasons, a peripatetic existence dictated as much by the produce available from the estates and the social opportunities of the locality as by the imperative to move on when the smells arising from the lack of drains became overpowering. No matter whether it was the Lady Anne Clifford who, as head of her own household, decreed when and where she would go within her northern properties or whether, 300 years later, it was the interior decorator Elsie de Wolfe (Lady Mendl) of New York City whose summers were spent close to Versailles, at the villa which she had re-decorated in sumptuous style and used for entertaining on the grand scale.

Between these two were innumerable women who moved around the country or went abroad for primarily domestic and personal reasons. They travelled as the wives of diplomats, which was why Ann Fanshawe, Lady Mary Wortley Montagu, Emma Hamilton and others besides came to be in foreign parts. Isabel Arundell waited several years to marry the Victorian explorer Richard Burton, meantime preparing for life as an explorer's wife by learning to fence, shoot, set up a tent and ride astride. Although she was not allowed to follow him to West Africa, she accompanied him on his diplomatic postings to Brazil and then to Damascus: 'Pay, pack and follow' he ordered his wife when dismissed as British Consul there[4] and she played the part of the devoted wife until the day she died. Others were abroad because husbands or fathers were there for business or professional purposes. Aphra Behn went to Surinam with her parents. Anne Grant (1755–1838) spent ten years of her childhood in New York, learnt Dutch and later incorporated her experiences into her *Memoirs of an American Lady*. Frances Brooke (1724–89), on the other hand, married the chaplain appointed to the garrison at Quebec and used the scenario as the setting for one of her novels, though she also wrote a tragedy, a successful musical entertainment and several works of history and translation.

Dorothy Wordsworth accompanied her brother William and their friend Coleridge on a tour of Scotland in 1803 and her journal of those six weeks, kept mainly to entertain the family circle, was only published afterwards. Similarly, the diaries of Elizabeth Grant of Rothiemurchus were written primarily for the sake of her children: after a childhood mostly spent in Edinburgh and the Highlands the family sailed to India in 1827 after her father was appointed to a judgeship in Bombay. It was there that she met and married Colonel Henry Smith who inherited the estate of Baltiboys, south of Dublin, where the couple resided thereafter. In 1843 they left Ireland to live in France for a couple of years as an economy measure, so that the money saved could be ploughed back into further improvements to the estate. One year was spent at Pau, near the Pyrenees, and the second at Avranches, in Normandy.

Mary Moffat, by contrast, spent much of her life abroad. The daughter of a missionary to Africa, she became, in 1844, the wife of another, David Livingstone. Accompanying him on his travels was far from easy; she was constantly pregnant, exhausted by caring for the young family and trekking in unknown and often inhospitable country. Livingstone found travel *en famille* an encumbrance, so wife and children were sent back to England and it was four years before he rejoined them. In 1862 Mary returned to Africa with him and, aged forty, succumbed to fever and was buried under a baobab tree. On the other hand, Jane Moir left her little daughter at home with relatives in Scotland when she journeyed into Central Africa with her husband as a result of several motivations: trade, missionary work and anti-slavery ideals. Her letters home were subsequently published and vividly portray her experiences. William and Lucy Johnson, missionaries in Madagascar, also left their children in England, although their youngest daughter remained with them. In 1896, during a local uprising against the French the three were barbarously murdered and the mission station looted and burnt; the rebels were routed and a favourable reaction resulted.

On a happier note there were those who travelled for pleasure. Authoress and society leader Mrs Montagu visited Paris during the peace of 1763, where the literati were dazzled by the brilliance of both her learning and the entertainments she hosted. In the company of Mrs Carter, another 'literary lady', and Lord Bath, Mr and Mrs Montagu toured Germany in the same year, while they went to Scotland in 1766. Half a century later, after the lengthy period of war against France, ended by the Battle of Waterloo and Napoleon's exile on St Helena, the British flocked to the Continent once more. The Countess of Blessington (1789–1849), a society hostess of the 1820s whose salons were legendary, travelled abroad in considerable style with her third husband, meeting up with various celebrities along the way. She turned to writing to augment her income and contributed to the *Daily News* but was declared bankrupt in 1849, fled the country and died shortly afterwards. Her house was later demolished and the Royal Albert Hall built on the site.

Emigration took the poet Anna Bradstreet with her husband and family away to a new life, in the way that innumerable women set sail with mingled hope, fear and sadness to virtually every quarter of the globe. Political exile took the Verneys to France in the 1640s and that was where Margaret Lucas met and married the Duke of Newcastle; following the sequestration of the husbands' properties it was the wives who returned to England to plead in person before the authorities for the restitution of their due 'portions'. The situation in Scotland during the 1680s sent the whole Hume family, including Grisell the eldest daughter, to Utrecht for several years where she came to know her husband-to-be George Baillie and wrote some of her songs. Personal rancour as much as political expediency took Sarah Churchill and her husband out of the country until Queen Anne's death; they returned the following day.

Family prestige was another reason why women left their homes. From time to time it would be expedient for country dwellers to put in an appearance at Court or in the appropriate political circles and, although the man of the family could do this on his own, there were occasions when his lady would add lustre to the proceedings. Anne, Duchess of Hamilton, rarely accompanied the Duke to London but she did travel south if occasion demanded. Both in London and in Edinburgh their public entertainments were on a grand scale, with a view not only to impressing their guests but, in so doing, upholding their social and political prestige. With a number of sons and daughters to plan for the Hamiltons were no different from other parents: the future of the family was an important consideration to many, especially where marriage partners from outwith the immediate domestic locality needed to be found. Thus efforts were made to enter a wider social circle, either in London or some other centre such as Bath or Edinburgh. In due course mothers might wish to be with a daughter about to give birth, while they might also rush to the bedside of a family member who was ill. Death was ever present. Ann Fanshawe and Lucy Hutchinson sank their grief in writing biographies of their husbands; Anna Bradstreet turned to verse when mourning the loss of her little granddaughters; Elizabeth Fry concentrated on her prison visiting following the death of a beloved daughter; and Mrs Gaskell's husband advised her to write something lengthy to assuage her grief at losing her son – the result being *Mary Barton*, the first of her novels.

The search for improved health was a major motive for women whether for themselves or some other family member. Whereas the religious elements of a pilgrimage to some holy place (as portrayed, for example, in Chaucer's *Canterbury Tales*) was curtailed after the Reformation, its sister activity of a visit to a source of water to bathe an afflicted part of the body was actively pursued throughout the seventeenth century, as Celia Fiennes so often observed during her travels. These healing waters became the spas of the eighteenth century, where people went to drink the waters, and the seaside resorts of the next, for sea air and bathing. Spas such as Bath, Harrogate, Moffat, Llandrindod Wells (where a Mrs Jenkins is said to have rediscovered the sulphur and saline springs in 1736) and so many more became recognised as centres of social life, seeing that wherever folk with money and leisure gathered together there followed in their wake the tailors and dressmakers, barbers and hairdressers, milliners, booksellers, confectioners, musicians, the keepers of milch-goats, lodging houses and livery stables and all the other suppliers of adjuncts considered necessary to the well-to-do lifestyle. Tunbridge Wells gained in popularity and prestige after Queen Henrietta Maria visited the place, which proved its efficacy when she gave birth to the future Charles II and, in due course, Charles' wife Catherine of Braganza would also try the waters but without the desired results. Later again Queen Anne visited not only Tunbridge but also Bath with its hot springs, thereby setting the town on its way to becoming one of the most popular social centres outside London and giving writers such as Fanny Burney and Jane Austen a backdrop for some of their novels.

Lady Grisell Baillie's accounts reveal an expedition to Bath in 1696, the first of many such visits; the following year they went to Prestonpans, a few miles east of Edinburgh, and in 1701 the venue was Scarborough. However, in 1731 it was to Italy that Lady Grisell Baillie and her family went, in the hope of improving the health of her son-in-law and after a six-month journey they set up house in Naples where Lady Grisell learnt Italian in no time and directed domestic affairs, just as she had done in Utrecht long before on behalf of her invalid mother. The party were away from home for well over two years but, despite the change of climate, Lord Binning died in Naples.

Mariana Starke was another who spent some years in Italy looking after a consumptive relative and this led her to write her two-volume *Letters from Italy*, in effect a comprehensive guide book for tourists. She looked at the history of the country and pointed out the works of art in various cities: 'Also specifying the expense incurred by residing in various Parts of Italy, France &c., so that persons who visit the Continent from economical motives may select the most eligible Places for permanent Residence. With instructions for Invalids, relative to the Island of Madeira; and for the use of Invalids & Families who may wish to avoid the Expense attendant upon travelling with a Courier. By Mariana Starke, Author of . . .'[5] and it lists her published works. The second edition of 1815 was 'Revised, corrected and considerably enlarged by an itinerary of Chamouni, and all the most frequented passes of the Alps, Germany, Portugal, Spain, France, Holland, Denmark, Norway, Sweden, Russia and Poland.' Also given were hints on tipping ostlers and porters, indications regarding the state of the roads, the preferred routes and what to look for on the way. Later editions were augmented, the author claimed, by her own lengthy wanderings around Europe.

That prolific author Mrs Jameson travelled around Italy while gathering material for her four-volume work on sacred and legendary art: *Legends of the Saints* (1848), *Legends of the Monastic Orders* (1850), *Legends of the Madonna* (1852) and *The History of Our Lord*, which was incomplete at her death. These books, illustrated most beautifully with numerous engravings and etchings, were regarded as essential reading for those intending to visit Italy. Over and above these labours Mrs Jameson wrote vigorously on many other themes and wielded her pen to campaign for an amelioration of conditions for the women of England, while giving support to others working in related fields. The subject of Italian art also attracted 'Leader Scott', the pen name of Lucy Baxter (1837–1902), who moved to Florence following her marriage and lived there for the rest of her days. *The Cathedral Builders* was probably her most popular work.

Italy was the destination for Elizabeth Barrett and Robert Browning after their elopement and marriage in 1846 and Florence their main home thereafter, where their only son was born in 1849. A social exile of another sort was forced upon some women, banished on account of real or imagined misdemeanours. Lady Luxborough (1699–1756) was packed off to her husband's dilapidated estate in the Birmingham area where she kept herself busy by putting things in order, creating a garden, tending her aviary and making friends with the locals. Lady Sarah Bunbury, one of the four redoubtable Lennox sisters, left her husband in 1769 to live with her lover and their child; in the ensuing scandal and eventual divorce, it was her sisters who demanded she should leave the lover, live in retirement and show due penitence for her untoward behaviour. They deemed it to be a lengthy process as she was kept out of the public eye for a number of years but in 1781 Sarah took matters into her own hands and married again, rapidly becoming the mother of eight children. Society itself took to banishing many women prisoners to the new colony in Botany Bay, forcing them to travel whether they would or no. The conditions they endured both on the way out and the treatment they met with on arrival beggars description. Elizabeth Fry was one who exerted herself to assist these unfortunates; she accompanied them to their port of embarkation and demanded that the authorities provided a reputable female to oversee their welfare during the voyage.

These are just a few examples of women whose travelling was primarily undertaken in company with others or carried out on someone else's behalf or at someone else's instigation. Each situation mentioned can be echoed by women acting independently or travelling in pursuit of their own objectives – for business, for social expediency, for pleasure, or in search of health or adventure.

In the first place, it is only necessary to think of the innumerable women who met the unceasing demand for domestic servants in the larger towns, many of whom travelled a considerable distance from their homes. The days when they were all the daughters of a landowner's tenants were long gone, if, indeed, they had ever existed. Registry offices, like the one started by Elizabeth Raffald in Manchester, were designed to overcome the shortfall in locally available female domestics. In this instance, the travel was incidental to the main occupation and many similar examples can be cited: the women who followed the shoals of herring along the east coast, gutting, salting and packing the fish into barrels; governesses setting off for far-flung posts or artists going to Rome or Paris for further study or to gain commissions from well-to-do visitors. Catherine Read, the Scots-born artist, went even further afield: late in life she set off for India where there was a promising clientele among both Indian potentates and British nabobs.

Writing rather than painting was the outcome of Aphra Behn's travels. She accompanied her parents to Surinam, South America, where she married a Dutchman but, widowed shortly afterwards, in 1666 she was sent as a spy to Antwerp on behalf of Charles II. Thrown into prison for debt, she started writing for the stage to free herself; meantime, her novel, *Oroonoko*, about the noble savage of that name alerted her readers to the realities of slavery. The female spy and the secret agent belong to a genre with a long history and Aphra Behn is just one of that ilk. Women of all nationalities have played a part in times of war, whether operating behind the lines or engaging in resistance work and their bravery should not go unremarked. During the First World War Edith Cavell, matron of a Red Cross hospital in Brussels, was shot by the Germans for harbouring Allies and in turn Mata Hari, the beautiful 'exotic dancer', was executed by the French for passing information to the Germans.

Meanwhile, whenever or whatever the war, women played their part, especially in their traditional role as carers. From the days when

'Parliament Joan' was nursing sailors in Portsmouth and Harwich and petitioning Cromwell for funds as she had even sold her bed to raise money to support her work, through the struggles of Florence Nightingale in the Crimea and on to the First World War and beyond when the name of Elsie Inglis (1864–1917) was revered for the field hospitals she established, women were very much involved. In 1914 Elsie Inglis raised £25,000 within a month and on offering her Scottish Women's Hospitals to the War Office the answer was: 'Go and sit quietly at home, dear lady.'[6] Her services proved more than acceptable to the French and she took two units across the Channel and another to Serbia; latterly she went to Odessa to care for the Serbs who by then were part of the Russian Army.

Not so much a war but a revolution inspired Mary Wollstonecraft to set off for Paris in 1792 and it was her published account of those times on which Thomas Carlyle based his masterpiece on the French Revolution several decades later. Mary was later sent to Sweden by the publisher Gilbert Imlay, the father of her child born in Paris. Her *Letters Written in Sweden* were the result – or, at least, one result. For William Godwin said that it was those *Letters* that had caused him to fall in love with her; they married just before their daughter was born in 1797 and Mary died a few days later.

In an earlier era some women had themselves engaged in warlike activities. Mary Read was a pirate. An illegitimate child dressed in boy's clothes, she led a tomboy existence. Eventually she ran away to join a regiment of horse in Flanders but fell in love with and married a young Flemish soldier. Widowed soon afterwards, she reverted to her boy's clothing and joined the crew of a Dutch merchant vessel which in turn was raided by the notorious pirate 'Calico Jack'. She signed on as a crew member, whereupon complications ensued. She fell in love with one of the sailors, while another sailor seemingly fell in love with her. Mary revealed herself as a woman to this other sailor who, it turned out, was also a woman and none other than the captain's common-law wife, Anne Bonny. A second female pirate! Anne had a similarly colourful background, including a disastrous marriage that had taken her to the Bahamas and a meeting with 'Calico Jack'. She joined him for a life at sea, sailing the Caribbean in search of booty, although they did put into Cuba at one stage where she gave birth to their child. Both Mary and Anne won fearsome reputations for themselves but the end came when the pirate ship was captured in 1720. The two women were recognised from an earlier episode of piracy and thrown into jail; both pleaded pregnancy, whereupon the death penalty was lifted but Mary died while still in prison. 'Calico Jack' was hanged, having given in to the authorities, which Anne considered an unnecessary ending: 'Had he fought like a man,' she is reputed to have said, 'he need not have died like a dog.'[7]

Other women were to be found at sea, even though women only officially entered the regular Navy in 1917, as 'Wrens' from the Women's Royal Naval Service, intended as an auxiliary force to release men from shore duty. There was Mary Lacy, for instance, alias William Chandler, who served as seaman and shipwright for twelve years and published her autobiography in 1773. Although women were supposedly absent from ships at sea, a few could be found on board assisting the surgeons in tending the sick and wounded after a battle. Sometimes, though, the noise and vibrations from the guns precipitated matters, as several births occurred while a ship was in action: one such babe, born on board during the Glorious First of June, carried the name Daniel *Tremendous* McKenzie in recognition of the place and date of his birth. In 1847 it was decreed that all the survivors of the major sea battles of the previous fifty years would be awarded the Naval General Service Medal and three women applied – two had been present at the Battle of the Nile in 1798 and one had been at Trafalgar in 1805. Although initial reaction to the women's claim was favourable, it was decided that they should not be awarded their medals, even though that same baby born on board during the battle got his.

Mary Read had initially run away to become a soldier and other women had also signed up to the military life. Christian Davies (1677–1732) was an Irish girl who disguised herself in order to follow her husband, forced into the Army; she found him eventually but was wounded more than once during her active service. Afterwards, she ran a hostelry and then retired to London where she ended her days in the Royal Hospital, Chelsea, itself established through Nell Gwyn's efforts to persuade Charles II to make provision for retired soldiers. Hannah Snell (1723–92) was another who knew the Hospital: the daughter of a hosier in Worcester and orphaned at seventeen she joined up as 'James Grey' and saw action at Culloden. She left the Army in 1750 and was granted a King's Pension in recognition of her service in India. Meanwhile, Phoebe Hassall (b. 1713) saw active service in Europe with the Fifth Foot (Royal Northumberland Fusiliers) and claimed to have been wounded in Flanders. Her gravestone says she was 108 years old at her death.

Even stranger than these women who managed to deceive the authorities and their own colleagues was the case of James Miranda Barry (1799–1865), who rose through the ranks to be Inspector General of the Army Medical Department at a time when medical training was denied to women. She saw many years service in Malta and the Cape of Good Hope and it was only after her death that the truth emerged. Apparently, there had been an earlier episode when the two doctors attending James Barry during a severe bout of illness had been sworn to secrecy. The motive for such singular conduct was supposedly love for an Army surgeon.

Medical training for women in its early days necessitated travel as so few institutions would accept them; those that did promptly closed the loophole thereafter. Dr Elizabeth Blackwell, British born but the first woman to be registered as a doctor in the USA, had to go to Paris for her midwifery qualification, which was also where Elizabeth Garret Anderson, the first female doctor in Britain, took her final exams. Sophia Jex-Blake and others of that circle qualified in Berne or Dublin. An article of 1876 regarding medicine as a career for women warned that difficulties might still be encountered in finding acceptance but listed three institutions in Britain where women might go: the London School of Medicine for Women, itself set up by Dr Sophia Jex-Blake, the Royal Infirmary of Edinburgh and the Edinburgh Extra-Mural School (with certain restrictions). Elsewhere the École de Médecine in Paris, the University of Zurich in Switzerland and the University of Michigan, USA, accepted female students.[8] Dr Elizabeth Blackwell was friendly with Florence Nightingale but the 'Lady of the Lamp' had to defy her family and, having studied on her own, set off for Germany to gain some experience prior to her public career in nursing.

Outwith the arena of wars and their aftermath the search for improved health affected women from all walks of life, as noted earlier. In the later seventeenth century Celia Fiennes made a series of journeys throughout England and is credited with being, as are Queen Elizabeth and Lady Godiva, the original figure in the nursery rhyme that runs:

> Ride a cock-horse to Banbury Cross,
> To see a fine lady ride on a white horse;
> With rings on her fingers and bells on her toes,
> She shall have music wherever she goes.

Celia Fiennes maintained that she undertook her journeys 'to regain my health by variety and change of aire and exercise' and she kept a record of her observations as a means of occupying her mind while she did so, a method she heartily recommended to others.[9] Her journal was not published until 1888, under the title of *Through England on a Side Saddle*, and was edited by Mrs Griffiths, herself a descendant of Celia's grandfather.

Sarah Murray travelled extensively throughout Scotland in order to provide tourists with a reliable guidebook and this was published a year before Mariana Starke's on Italy. She was a widow and a sister-in-law to the 3rd Earl of Dunmore; she was, seemingly, in vigorous health as her travels involved not only carriages, carts, walking and riding but also sailing, rowing boats and the Oban excise cutter. 'I write because I think my Guide will be really useful to travellers', she tells her readers, 'by informing them of these objects which are worthy of notice and at the same time acquainting them where, and by what means, they can get at them in the safest and most comfortable manner. A plan, I believe, never attended to . . . by any of my predecessors in Tour writing.' Scotland at this time was still suffering from the aftermath of the 1745 Jacobite Rebellion, the country being considered as rugged and wild as its people. Mrs Murray's advice starts with fitting up the carriage and the spare parts to take along (linch-pins, four shackles, a turn-screw for fastening the shackle-nuts, a hammer and leather straps). She deals briskly with how to set up the internal arrangements to maximum effect, how the man servant should sit behind the carriage rather than on his own horse and advises on the extra articles that might be handy either en route or at overnight stops (mainly bed linen and a stock of food and drink). This is followed with many an anecdote and observation along the way with details of the route that she herself had taken when 'with my maid by my side, and my man on the seat behind the carriage, I set off, May the 28th, 1796'.[10] Not long afterwards Elizabeth Spence followed a similar route when producing her two-volume account of the manners, customs and scenery of Scotland.

In the 1840s, it was a three-volume guide to Ireland that co-authors Mr and Mrs Hall published, which they followed with what they called a companion-guide to South Wales, stating that 'it is, however, that which is by far the most interesting, including nearly all the leading and most popular towns, and the districts wealthiest in mines that yield coal and iron – the true jewels of the British Crown; where there are vales and hills, rivers and sea-coasts, abundantly rich in the picturesque'.[11] The Halls allowed themselves frequent diversions and found much to say about the people and their way of life. In 1894 Marie Trevelyan was writing in a similar vein, with the author claiming that her objective was 'to awaken English interest in the land and life of the Cymru' seeing that, beyond the main towns and tourist resorts, the remoter districts remained unknown.[12] It was, in fact, a way of life that was fast vanishing and these authors managed to record much detail that would otherwise have been lost. It was that aspect in particular that caused Gertrude Jekyll, the garden designer, to collect together as much information as she could about domestic life in her own corner of West Surrey and other women to collect old-fashioned artefacts from around the home or farm that are now the greatly prized collections of domestic bygones such as those found in Glamis (Angus), Kingussie (Highland) or Hawes (North Yorkshire).

Maybe as a result of such 'Companion-Guides' four schoolmistresses, university educated, set off for Wales one day to take advantage of the summer holidays that were 'fast becoming a national institution'. They walked for twenty-one days, enjoying the scenery and commenting on where they had been, the people they met and the accommodation they stayed in, mostly cottages. They remarked on a kindly hostess here, an unfortunate choice of lodgings there, the almost 'inevitable' suppers of ham and eggs and the problems of a wardrobe-bed which 'was most attractive to sleep in while it remained a bed, but apparently liable to become a wardrobe again at a moment's notice'.[13] Their belongings were sometimes sent ahead 'in the coach', while parcels from home containing 'tea, chocolate and other necessities' were collected from various post offices, designated in advance.

Women, of course, were not confined to depicting their own countryside or journeys in their own homeland but took to writing of their experiences in foreign parts too. They described the places and the people, they spoke of their travels whether by camel or caravan, steamship or cycle, they published their academic researches, commented (favourably or otherwise) on local customs and social activities and conjured up exotic scenery and characters in their novels and other literary output. Some travelled 'alone' by which they meant they had no associate of their own education or upbringing; others travelled with, or in the wake of, husbands, fathers or sons. Mary Gaunt sang the praises of her small-scale companion called 'James Buchanan', a black and white k'ang dog 'who . . . thought everything I did was pefect and declared he was willing to go with me to the ends of the earth'.[14]

Isabella Bird (Bishop) (1831–1904) suffered constant ill health and depression while in her father's parsonage, although she was lively and energetic during summer holidays spent in the Highlands. In 1854 her doctor suggested a long sea voyage and, quite extraordinarily given the prevailing attitudes of the time and her own upbringing, her father gave her £100 and told her to stay away for as long as it lasted. She went to the USA and successfully wrote of her experiences there (*The Englishwoman in America*, 1856). She was an indefatigable traveller to the end, preferring the lesser-known quarters of the globe such as Japan, Tibet, Persia and Korea and publishing accounts of her wanderings but, in the interludes at home, she relapsed into ill-health and depression and spent her time on a day bed, writing moralistic tracts and sewing clothes for the poor.

Lady Anne Blunt (1837–1917) was renowned not only for being a granddaughter of the poet Lord Byron but for being the first Englishwoman to write about the Arabian peninsula, which she explored with her husband Wilfred Blunt. She dressed in tweeds but wore an Arab headdress and as a result of her travels wrote several books. She lived in Egypt for the last ten years of her life. Egypt had previously attracted the attention of Amelia Edwards (1831–92), one of the first British women to explore the country, and she published accounts of her journeys, promoted Egyptology as an academic subject and co-founded the Egypt Exploration Fund. She bequeathed her vast library to London University and funds to set up a Chair of Egyptology. Another woman who travelled throughout the Middle East was Gertrude Bell (1868–1926), a fluent speaker of several languages and an archaeologist. In 1915 she was employed by the Arab Bureau in Cairo, the following year she was sent to India by the British government and, after the war, was appointed to Baghdad as Oriental Secretary, in which position she had considerable influence in the region.

Lady Anne Blunt, Isabel Burton, Emily Beaufort and many others visited Damascus in the course of their travels and met up with Madame Digby el Mezrab and her Bedouin sheikh. During the twenty years of their marriage she spent many months at a time in the desert with her husband and his people, despite building a house complete with an enchanting garden and splendid stables; she was a celebrated horsewoman and Anne Blunt acknowledged how much she had learnt from her friend. It was not the first time that a woman had withdrawn from Society because of her personal life: Lady Hester Stanhope, as already noted, had left England and settled in the Lebanon, where she died, alone and in poverty.

Others travelled for a limited time for reasons of expediency. The Duke of Devonshire's 'Lady Liz' retreated abroad until her child should be born, meantime expressing an interest in looking at Italian antiquities with her brother. A few years later it was the Duchess who set off for France in the company of her mother and her sister, supposedly on behalf of the sister's health but in reality to disguise the fact that the Duchess was pregnant with her lover's child and she stayed abroad for two years. France was also the venue of an unexplained episode in the life of cookery writer and poet Eliza Acton, and those months spent in the south of France and a subsequent but brief engagement to a French Army officer have interested researchers ever since. Eliza lived thereafter with a married sister and her family, among whom was a girl who is said to have fondly kissed the portrait of 'Aunt Eliza' every night.

There were those that made the journey in reverse, arriving in Britain and staying here thereafter. The Italian singer Adelina Patti eventually settled in Wales; astronomer Caroline Herschel came from Hanover; Theresa Cornelys the 'Sultana of Soho' came from Austria, Marie Rambert of the Ballet Rambert from Poland, and Adeline Génee from Denmark. From the USA came Dr Elizabeth Blackwell, Jennie Jerome, who married Lord Randolph Churchill, and Nancy, Lady Astor. Elsie Inglis was born in India and lived in Tasmania before her family settled in Scotland. From Australia came Mary Gaunt, author and traveller, (Dame) Adelaide Anderson, Principal Lady Inspector of Factories, and Marion Phillips (1881–1932), Labour councillor, Secretary to the Women's Labour League and the Labour Party's chief woman officer.

There were also women who were involved in the actual means of transport. Many were notable horsewomen or celebrated for their skills in driving carriages and such like. It was said that Irish-born Daisy Bates (1860–1951) was able to ride or drive any horse. She certainly rode thousands of miles side-saddle in the Australian outback and covered as many more driving herself in horse or camel buggies during the forty years she spent with the Aborigines, who adopted her as their magical grandmother 'Kabbarli', an ancestor of their people's dreamtime.

When the bicycle became popular it gave women a freedom that few had previously experienced, though the long skirts, tightly belted at the waist, had to be carefully managed to avoid either catching in the wheels or causing the cyclist to show too much leg. The answer lay in Mrs Amelia Bloomer's pantaloons which became increasingly acceptable wear for cycling.

Ballooning, though, had already offered women freedom of another sort. Within a year of the first flight in 1783 a woman had ascended into the skies; by 1810 Madame Blanchard in France had become a notable exponent of the art and organised displays for the public. By the 1850s Britain had its own balloonist, Mrs Graham, a mother of seven who thrilled the public with her ascents in a gaily decorated, be-ribboned basket, often accompanied by a bevy of pretty girls. Edwardian crowds were entertained by Bill Cody's parachute team which included the young Dolly Shepherd who parachuted gracefully back to earth in a variety of ways.

Powered flight was different again and women were involved surprisingly early. Amy Johnson won fame by being the first woman to fly solo from England to Australia in 1930, a journey which took her 19½ days. Two years earlier Sophie Pierce (later Lady Heath) had been the first woman to fly solo from Cape Town to Cairo; meantime, Lady Mary Baillie, a mother of five, was creating her own record for the first solo round trip between England and South Africa. Women were also building their own planes. The 'Bland Mayflower' was the handiwork of Lilian Bland, granddaughter of the Dean of Belfast: 'Constructed of steamed ash, piano wire, bicycle pedals and treated calico, the Bland Mayfly sold for £250 – or £350 with an engine.'[15]

Apart from the record breakers there were others, such as Mary, Duchess of Bedford ('The Flying Duchess'), who took up flying at the age of sixty-one as a means of getting around instead of using a car or a train. These pioneers talked gaily about the problems they faced; they generally serviced their own machines, survived crash landings in desert or jungle, coped with violent rainstorms, sandstorms and the glare from sea, sand or snow, were either frozen or suffered sunburn in the open cockpit but, generally, managed to retain their femininity.

CHAPTER FOURTEEN

Women on the March

From the preceding chapters it must now be apparent that the generally perceived sterotype regarding women in past times is, in many respects, quite wrong. It is not to say that all women were active beyond the home but a much greater number were so engaged than is often credited, while their enterprises reached far beyond those usually considered 'ladylike' or even 'suitable'. Their activities should be set against the considerable disadvantages under which they operated until the middle years of the nineteenth century when it was recognised, by the women themselves if not by men, that the current laws relating to them were outdated and outgrown.

Woman's perceived role encompassed her husband and home, her children and servants where present and, by dint of Christian precept, her neighbours and any of the poor and needy that might cross her path. Many were happy to accept a future where the sole options were marriage and motherhood and to submerse themselves in their household responsibilities. Within these domestic parameters hers was a multi-faceted life and she was expected to be conversant with each branch of knowledge associated with housewifery, especially in the earlier part of the period. An education of greater academic content was considered unnecessary for the majority of girls and so access to university or training for the professions – the Church, law, administration, diplomacy, medicine and so on – was thereby denied them. Thus, when these women left their homes and ventured into the wider world it was their training as housewives and mothers that tended to be basis for their extra-mural activities.

At the same time, innumerable lower-class girls became wage-earners at a very early age, many of them being absorbed into domestic service or into factory work, and they contributed a few pence to the family income or saved up a small nest-egg against their own eventual, but anticipated, marriage. At that point, they too were likely to leave their paid employment for a life of domesticity but might return to being wage-earners later in life or if driven by necessity.

The message that girls were destined to be wives and (hopefully) mothers and that married women stayed at home to care for husband, household and family was reiterated by countless authors throughout the nineteenth century and well through the twentieth. However, the world outside the home was changing rapidly. Society was changing. Census statistics for the mid-nineteenth century reveal an imbalance in the very composition of the population, with an awkward 1 million or more 'surplus females', for whom there would be no husbands. Above all, the concept of the housewife herself was changing from that of pivotal person to figurehead, accompanied by the viewpoint that since domestic work was a matter for servants, domestic work was of lowly status and demeaning, therefore, to anyone with a modicum of education or social worth. This meant that the middle-class housewife and her daughters were left with many empty hours, to be filled with little except self-made schemes for reading, music or handicrafts and the agonies of genteel idleness were suffered by Florence Nightingale, Emily Davies and Beatrix Potter, among others. In addition, women were expected to undertake work on behalf of those less fortunate than themselves, for which innumerable opportunities existed.

This the housewife had already been doing for many years and limitless examples of women as 'ameliorators' and 'improvers' have already been given, whether by way of direct hands-on help to the poor and unfortunate or by women in 'educational mode'. Where the former, assistance could be given in many formats whether that meant teaching in a Sunday school, giving money to rebuild a parish church or village hall, tending the sick who passed the door, providing cooking depots to feed the hungry or drinking fountains for the cab driver and his horse. If the latter, the preceding chapters include a multiplicity of women who, via their written works, offered an improved method of carrying on some activity – whether cookery, religious observation, childcare, moral guidance or a new method of making gloves – and all were designed to improve lifestyle or to increase a skill or sphere of knowledge.

However, charity *per se* is an open-ended concept and it was but one further step for the housewife to become the campaigner, fighting to improve the level of care provided for the disadvantaged. In this area women increasingly found a voice and a determination to do what their conscience told them was right, even if it meant making themselves unpopular, if not notorious, by taking on the powers that be and asking for changes in the laws of the land. The work of Elizabeth Fry (1782–1845) in connection with female prisoners and those sentenced to transportation is generally well known; Louisa Twining's (1820–1911) career is perhaps less so. She fought to improve workhouses for the destitute and hospitals for the dying, campaigning in the newspapers with a series of letters protesting vehemently about existing conditions in these institutions; although facing considerable opposition against such external interference, she set up a Workhouse Visiting Society. Thereafter her life was committed to improving conditions in the workhouses, separating the sick from the healthy and recognising the need for specially trained nurses for this type of care.

The name of Caroline Norton (1808–77) in connection with the cause of children working in factories is, again, relatively unknown though Lord Shaftsbury's is celebrated. Her narrative poem *A Voice from the Factories* (1836) makes an impassioned plea for children to be allowed a childhood. She delineates the unutterable weariness of a child labouring long hours in such a workplace, falling asleep and being brutally awoken, too tired to eat when at home, too tired to sleep and dreading the start of the next day's toil. Although all men are not born equal, she said, Christians in a Christian land must show mercy and follow Christ's injunction 'To suffer the little children to come unto Me.' And she asks: 'And shall we His bequest treat carelessly?'[1] The theme was taken up some years later by Elizabeth Barrett Browning in *The Cry of the Children*.

One of the earliest campaigns for social reform in British history related to the abolition of slavery and although William Wilberforce's name is ineradicably connected with the cause, his is not the only one to be considered. Hannah More (1745–1833), teacher and writer, met Wilberforce in 1787 and found they had much in common. She used ingenious ways to promote their cause, urging friends to boycott West Indian sugar and pulling out a plan of an African slave ship to show to fellow guests at dinner. Even though she had abandoned her career as playright, she advocated the production of a play on slavery (itself based on Aphra Behn's novel *Oroonoko*) because, as she pointed out, far more people go to the theatre than to church. Her poem on slavery was intended to maximise publicity prior to Wilberforce presenting his resolutions to Parliament and their crusade started off promisingly, although it took a further twenty years of campaigning before the bill for abolition received the royal assent in 1807.

Frances Wright (1794–1852) was born in Scotland but, having witnessed harrowing scenes of Highlanders being evicted from their lands under the Clearances and emigrating to the New World she, too, set sail in 1818. There she was horrified to see negroes chained together and she bought 2,000 acres of land on which to establish a community of freed slaves but the experiment did not succeed. However, she continued to uphold their cause and became a sparkling public speaker, taking up with other campaigns such as female education and the reform of the laws relating to inheritance and to divorce. After her marriage she continued to air her views in the *Free Inquirer*, the journal she founded with Robert Dale Owen, the son of Robert Owen, socialist, philanthropist and owner of the New Lanark Mills.

In the USA, and elsewhere, the crusade to abolish slavery continued for very much longer. The world's first Anti-Slavery Convention was held in London in 1840, where debate spilled over into the area of human rights in general. American woman delegate Lucretia Mott and the newly married Elizabeth Cady Stanton were outraged that they were prohibited from sitting in the hall itself and had to listen, in silence, from behind a screen. The two women became firm friends and vowed to organise a convention, once home, to tackle the subject of women's rights. Several years intervened when the latter was engaged with motherhood and housekeeping but an encounter with her former friend led to the calling of the Seneca Falls Convention in July 1848, where a Declaration of Sentiments was promulgated along the lines of the eighteen grievances of the Declaration of Independence. It was at this meeting that, for the first time, women gathered to debate the inequality and exploitation inherent in their lives and to put forward a demand for universal suffrage, which is considered to have heralded the start of the feminist movement and united assorted campaigns under one banner.

Meanwhile, there were those who had already begun to fight for the rights of women. Mary Wollstonecraft was an early exponent with her famous publication *A Vindication of the Rights of Women* (1792) in which she queried the very roots of contemporary society with its male dominance. Having investigated the numerous situations in which women were subjugated to men and debated the principles underlying such a situation, she declared: 'Would men but snap our chains, and be content with rational fellowship instead of slavish obedience, they would find us more observant daughters, more affectionate sisters, more faithful wives, more reasonable mothers – in a word, better citizens.'[2]

Caroline Norton, poet, authoress and social campaigner, took up the fight on behalf of married women. She was one of the three beautiful granddaughters of Richard Brinsley Sheridan who, in 1772, had eloped with Elizabeth Linley, the celebrated soprano; history was to repeat itself in that Caroline's marriage was equally unsuccessful. Nine years and three children later she left her husband and discovered the reality of the law as it stood: children were the property of their father and that her former husband was legally entitled to anything she earned by her writing or inherited from her mother. Single-mindedly, she dedicated herself thereafter in fighting not only to gain access to her own children, one of whom died aged eight without her having seen him again, but to gain rights of access on behalf of other mothers too. In 1839 the first Infant Custody Act was passed but despite further alterations over the years it was not until the 1973 Guardianship Act – almost a century and a half later – that a mother gained equal legal authority over her child with the father and she was, at the same time, deemed to be equally responsible for its support.

The second branch of her campaign regarding the financial situation facing women estranged from their husbands kept her name in the public eye for rather longer. When her own personal situation was aired in court both she and her husband wrote letters to the press vindicating their position and Caroline wrote more than one pamphlet outlining the inequalities facing women and ridiculing the idea that the law was fixed and unchangeable. By this time other women were contributing to the campaign, including Barbara Leigh-Smith, later Bodichon, who compiled a *Brief Summary of the Laws of England concerning Women* and organised a petition calling for a proposed Married Women's Property Bill which attracted 24,000 signatures: among the first signatories were the novelist Mrs Gaskell and authoress A.B. Jameson, whose long-estranged husband claimed the earnings from her writing. After several promises to reform the marriage laws and as many postponements, Caroline Norton outlined her case again in *A Letter to the Queen*, repeating why the laws stood in need of reform and refuting the idea that such changes were too difficult to incorporate in law. A Bill on The Reform of the Marriage and Divorce Laws was drawn up and became law in 1857 which brought in some of the changes demanded but it was a relatively modest advance. Further changes were introduced in 1867; finally, The Married Woman's Property Act, 1882, enshrined in law the principle that married women should have the same rights as unmarried women. By which time Caroline Norton herself was dead and other campaigns were engaging the public's attention.

It was in the 1860s that Josephine Butler (1828–1906) took up the cause of the prostitute, an area where misery and degradation were rife and a subject of which no 'lady' was supposed to have any knowledge. Indeed, to know about such matters was to reveal oneself no lady and so to champion their cause took courage of heroic proportions. Attitudes to prostitution fluctuated throughout the nineteenth century. Women became prostitutes because they frequently had no option – starvation being the only alternative particularly for those without some skill to offer or a reference from a former employer. The Quaker authoress Amelia Opie, for example, found herself in a predicament when she discovered her maidservant was dishonest. She could not keep the girl on, could not give her a reference and could not recommend her to anyone else; the girl herself was pleading for 'a character'. As Mrs Opie said: 'A young maid-servant turned out, without the chance of a character, is in so exposed and desperate a situation that I shudder to think of the consequences, and, as my too great confidence and my carelessness <u>may</u> have laid temptation in her way, I feel a degree of responsibility for her faults, which distresses me exceedingly.'[3] Few felt as she did and many servant girls were turned out of the house for alleged misdemeanours without any thought being given to their future.

What is not in doubt is that the sexual double standard was commonplace throughout the period and that middle-class married men made widespread use of prostitutes. There was no such leeway for their wives who were expected to lead lives of the utmost purity both before and after marriage. The reasons here were not entirely moral but had to do with matters of inheritance and a natural wish for any property to go to a man's rightful heir. However, a flagrant gap frequently existed between male and female behaviour. By the 1850s and '60s prostitution was rife and rich men's mistresses were highly visible in Society, 'the pretty horse-breakers' having taken to riding in London's Hyde Park for all the world to admire. Mothers were complaining that their well-brought-up, expensively educated daughters were at a disadvantage in these circumstances. The counter-claim was that as long as girls were ignorant, frivolous and vapid and so often anything but a desirable partner for a man who wanted a woman rather than a wax doll, so the situation was unlikely to change. Official thinking was that since prostitution was inevitable it should be regulated by the state, with licensed brothels and a morals police as in certain continental countries. This, it was hoped, would help curtail the problem of venereal disease, which had reached epidemic proportions and was being used as a scapegoat for military failures. The three Contagious Diseases Acts of 1864, '66 and '69 were intended to achieve the regulation of prostitutes in naval and garrison towns and secure disease-free women for other ranks.

The Acts stirred up a ferocious protest against the idea of women being subjected to draconian regulation in such personal matters while their clients went free. Harriet Martineau complained about the way the legislation was rushed through with no proper debate in either House; Florence Nightingale was also involved, as were many other well-known names, and women from various strands of the feminist cause combined under the formidable leadership of Josephine Butler. To her it was not only the working-class women in the specified towns who were debased by the Acts but women of all classes; women were being declared by law to exist for the gratification of male lust and, she argued, prostitution was another form of male persecution. Within ten years, a forceful pressure group of women had formed which, in turn, met with massive resistance.

The tide turned when the question of 'white slavery' (i.e., the forcible detention of British women in European brothels) was revealed, alongside the crusading efforts of the editor of the *Pall Mall Gazette*, W.T. Stead, who caused uproar with a series of articles entitled 'The Maiden Tribute to Modern Babylon' in which he disclosed how he had bought a girl of thirteen for £5. There was also a major investigation organised by the Salvation Army, protest meetings throughout the country and a petition in favour of reforming the law which collected some 393,000 signatures; such was the strength of support that the government bowed to the inevitable and pushed through the necessary measures in a few short weeks. The problems over attitudes to prostitution continued. Demand for sexual services was driven underground when brothels were closed down and the poorest prostitutes were forced on to the darker streets and back alleys, which made it all the easier for Jack the Ripper and others. After Josephine Butler retired from the fray, her place was ably taken by Christabel Pankhurst, whose pamphlet *The Great Scourge and how to end it* (1913) brought the subject of the sexual exploitation of women into the arena of public discussion.

Meantime, going back to the 1850s and '60s, the recognition by women themselves that they were disadvantaged by their lack of education and rendered unfit for anything other than domestic life was the focus of Chapter Eleven, as was their struggle to gain access to a higher level of education to enable girls to be responsible wives and mothers. For many the intention had been to widen the horizons of middle-class girls to facilitate entry thereafter to the universities and professions, currently closed to them through lack of qualifications. Others took 'education' in a different format to working-class women. The necessity for having courses on housewifery and related topics in the State school curriculum has already been noted. Mrs Alice Acland (1849–1935) was instrumental in promoting the Women's League for the Spread of Cooperation (later called the Women's Cooperative Guild) and between 1883 and 1886 was editor of its newspaper's section for women. At that point the women's role was as the buyer of provisions; she suggested locally organised 'working meetings' for members where their hands would continue to work while they listened to speakers or discussed matters of the day: 'Men are going forward,' she wrote, 'let us go forward, too. Bravely and hopefully, not going out of our province, but working in it, making each household a truly co-operative establishment.'[4] There was an immediate response and, increasingly, women came to play a part in the running of both branch and district organisations and attended classes for intending officials held by the Central Committee; they also offered themselves for election to such bodies as the Poor Law Guardians. The Guild soon produced leaders of the calibre of Mary Lawrenson, General Secretary from 1885 to 1889; Catherine Webb, founder and secretary of the Battersea Branch, who chaired the first national Conference in 1886 and wrote on industrial cooperation and the movement's history; and Miss Reddish, Guild organiser from 1893 to 1895, who had left school to start work as a silk-winder, aged eleven, and worked her way up to become forewoman of a cotton mill.

Margaret Llewelyn Davies, a former Girtonian and niece to Emily Davies, became Secretary in 1889 and ran the Guild from Kirkby Lonsdale; from 1893 she was assisted by Lilian Harris. Under their guidance the nature of the Guild changed, with divorce-law reform, votes for women and the temperance movement becoming matters of general debate. Maternity benefits were the focal point of their campaign after the 1911 National Insurance Act failed to include married women in its proposals but, after massive lobbying and considerable male opposition, their suggestions were incorporated in the amendments although a further battle took place over the 1917 National Insurance Amendment Bill. The Guild became an international organisation involving twenty-seven countries, including Soviet Russia. The movement had enormous influence on the lives of women who were too old to benefit from the changes in education at school level and proved, also, that working-class women could partake fully in public life.

The Cooperative Guild predated women's participation in the Labour Party by some years and, by then, they had already been involved with trade unionism. One estimate suggested that, by 1900, some 4 million women over the age of 15, a third of the female population, were in paid employment and of those about half needed to be self-supporting; the rest were contributing to the family income.[5] Domestic service swallowed up large numbers but by this time had a rather tarnished image, while conditions in the 'sweated industries' were appalling. Both sets of workers were too scattered to do much towards improving their lot. Factory workers were different: although they worked extremely long hours and in frequently disgraceful conditions, they were in contact with their fellow workers and aware of what was going on around them. Women faced problems not only *vis-à-vis* their employers but also with the attitudes of their own menfolk, who were apt to believe that 'a woman's place was in HIS home'[6] and that women took jobs away from the men which led, in turn, to lower wages all round.

The Women's Trade Union League was founded in 1874 initially as a protective organisation to promote the cause of trade unionism among women and it gathered together several infant organisations, though many proved short-lived. The prime mover was Mrs Emma Paterson, a bookbinder by trade. One of the first successful actions taken by women workers was the celebrated Match Girls' Strike of 1888. It was led by Annie Besant who at that point was much involved with social and political reform and had founded a newspaper with a regular feature exposing faults in the working environment. The strike was not only about pay and working conditions but drew attention to the menace of 'phossy jaw', a form of cancer associated with phosphorus used in the industrial process. The struggling local unions were formed into the National Federation of Women Workers and in 1903 Mary MacArthur became the Secretary; eventually it merged into the Women's Department of the Trades Union Council. The part played in the trade union movement by Margaret Bondfield, whose working life started in a drapery business in Brighton, has already been described and she went on to become the first woman member of the Privy Council, a minister and member of the Cabinet.

Women were supporting the general principles of the Labour movement for some twenty years before the party was born which meant that by 1900 there were a number of experienced women activists – Katherine St John Conway (later Mrs Bruce Glasier), Carolyn Martin (founder of Socialist Sunday Schools) and Enid Stacey, a high-school mistress who lost her job after police took her name at a prohibition rally. In 1905 the Railway Women's Guild requested the formation of a National Women's Committee; the following year saw the inaugural meeting of the Women's Labour League under the presidency of Margaret MacDonald, wife to the future Prime Minister Ramsay MacDonald, and with Mary Macpherson as Secretary; and in 1909 the Women's Labour League affiliated to the Labour Party.

Another name from the era is that of Marion Phillips (1881–1932). Australian born and educated, she was an early student at the London School of Economics, established in 1895 by the social reformers Sidney and Beatrice Webb, who together founded the left-wing weekly journal the *New Statesman* some years later. She worked for the Webbs and then became a research assistant with the Royal Commission on the Poor Laws, looking into matters relating to public health, poor-law medical relief and the treatment of destitute children. In 1912 she was elected Labour councillor for the London Borough of Kensington and campaigned for the public provision of baby clinics, school meals, improved council housing, employment schemes and the prohibition of sweated labour. During the First World War she was Secretary to the Women's Labour League, a member of the Consumers' Council of the Ministry of Food and on the Central Committee of Women's Training and Employment. In 1918 she became the Labour Party's Chief Woman Officer, with an exceptional knowledge of and interest in campaigning for community centres for housing estates which would incorporate nurseries, restaurants, libraries, concert halls and home-help services – all of which she regarded as essential to the emancipation of working-class housewives. At the same time she was also a member of the advisory committee of the London magistrates and the Editor of the *Labour Woman*. In 1929 she was elected MP for Sunderland.

A fellow Australian and a former student at Queens' College and Girton was (Dame) Adelaide Anderson (1863–1936) and it was through lecturing on philosophy and politics to the Women's Cooperative Guild that brought home to her the realities of working-women's lives. In 1891 she was appointed clerk to the staff of the Royal Commission on Labour;

in 1894 she was appointed as a 'lady factory inspector' at the Home Office; and in 1897 she became Principal Lady Inspector and headed the newly formed Women's Branch, a position she held until her retirement in 1921. The Branch investigated working practices in factories and other workplaces where women were employed, checking on whether legal requirements relating to safety and other such matters were being followed. To begin with they faced much hostility and had to use considerable guile to gain access to the premises or to hear what the workforce had to say. Under Dame Adelaide's leadership the workload of the Woman's Branch expanded greatly, although it was constantly understaffed and the work involved excessive travelling. During the First World War they were covering for the men's Inspectorate too and, paradoxically, this led to the demise of the separate Woman's Branch in 1922 when the two branches merged.

With so many women involved in movements connected to the Labour Party it became increasingly obvious and logical that women should be given the right to vote, whether property owners or not; but this continued to be denied them. In James VI and I's time the question of women's right to vote had been raised and judicial decree ruled that, for an unmarried woman or a widow, a freehold did carry voting rights; in general, though, their rights had been abrogated due to their 'original sin'. Rights or no, returning officers consistently ignored these women or disallowed their vote and when the 1832 Reform Act substituted the word 'male person' it deprived female property owners of their constitutional rights. In 1867 a Mrs Maxwell, a shopkeeper in Manchester, discovered her name on the Parliamentary Register and set off to vote, accompanied by some friends. A loud cheer followed the casting of her vote and the successful candidate said: 'This woman is a hard-working, honest person, who pays her rates as you do – who contributes to the burdens of the State as you do, – and, therefore, if any woman should possess a vote, it is precisely such a one as she.' The following year some 10,000 women across the country claimed their rights, but they were mostly rejected 'as long usage was against the women's claims'.[7]

It was not until the turn of the century that the suffrage question really gathered momentum, since women were waiting patiently in the expectation that the Liberal Party would honour their much-repeated declarations of support. Some women preferred to follow a passive line, such as the Girton don who refused to pay her rates as she held fast to the long-established principle of no taxation without representation 'and had sometimes to be rescued from the consequences of this stand'.[8] Other women joined with their more militant sisters in the Women's Social and Political Union, founded by the Pankhursts in 1903. Members were ready to face up to prison, hunger strikes and force feeding to achieve their objective and over the next 10 years some 1,800 women were sent to prison for political reasons, as a result of campaigns waged by the WSPU; their activities included parliamentary lobbying, torchlight processions, rallies that attracted vast crowds (on both sides of the argument), heckling, demonstrating, brick-throwing and the disruption of sporting events. One such was the Derby of 1913 when Emily Davison threw herself in front of the King's horse and was killed, her funeral attracting a vast concourse of mourners and much publicity for the cause. The Suffragettes called a halt to their more strident activities on the outbreak of the First World War, although they kept themselves in the public eye by other means. Women of all classes turned instead to filling the jobs in industry, agriculture and the professions* vacated by menfolk joining the services and won high praise for their exemplary behaviour and whole-hearted efforts in carrying out their duties.

After much discussion and further lobbying a compromise was effected: a government bill became law in February 1918 by which the franchise was granted to all adult males and to certain categories of women over thirty years of age. That same October a further bill enabled women to be elected to and to sit and vote as a Member of the House of Commons. Constance Markiewiecz, the Irish Nationalist leader, was elected to Parliament in 1918 by a Dublin constituency while serving a lengthy prison sentence but she refused on principle to take her seat; Nancy, Lady Astor, despite being American by birth, was the first woman to sit in the Commons, as Conservative MP for the Sutton division, Plymouth, and held the seat from 1919 to 1945.

Following the granting of limited voting rights for women further advances were made: they became eligible for jury service and the magistracy; they could aspire to the upper echelons of the Civil Service; as wage-earners they became eligible for national insurance benefits; nursing was for the first time recognised as a full profession, on the setting up of the State Registration Scheme; and it is from this date that the first female veterinary surgeons, barristers, solicitors and architects can be found as discrimination to the professions on the grounds of sex was made illegal. At this stage, though, this was more of a legality rather than a reality; further legislation proved necessary in due course. In 1928 the right to vote was given to all adult women.

The First World War hastened the acknowledgment that the old social order would never be the same again. The mould had been broken and

* 'As a result of public need, in 1916 women were admitted to medical examinations, the first concession given since 1881.' M. Bradbrook, *That Infidel Place*, p. 66.

new ways must be devised for the future. In 1915 one Member of Parliament commented: 'But not only has the War provided an incentive to women's work on a scale never dreamt of in times of peace, it has caused women, more particularly those engaged in new occupations, to realise, as they have never done before, their own capacity.' Looking into the future and the longed-for peace, he continued: 'Be that as it may, women workers, both in skilled and unskilled occupations, have come to stay, and the sooner this cardinal fact is recognised by all concerned the sooner will the situation right itself . . . The whole economic position of labour will be changed after the War, and for that change both employers and employees should prepare themselves without delay.'[9]

Although there was a general recognition that the war would bring immense changes in its wake the 'working woman' was no novelty. She had been around for many years. In the 1890s it had been pointed out that, whereas the only job enumerated for women in the 1831 census was domestic service, by 1881 women were involved in no less than 330 different types of employment and there were only 70 described in the census in which they did not participate: 'The tale is plain enough. . . . With this new condition of affairs, new duties and new views must be accepted.' However, a cautionary note is sounded thereafter: 'Whether or not the change which has taken place is advantageous or otherwise is a matter of opinion. That it has been accomplished, however, is an undoubted fact'.[10]

Other authors were taking a similar stand. In the 1870s 'L.M.H.' (Louisa Mary Hubbard) was able to produce an annual *Handbook of Women's Work* in which she proffered advice not only on what was entailed in the careers themselves but on where best to go for training and so on. Some of the careers suggested were potential rather than actual but the general picture was encouraging: 'I trust,' she wrote, 'it may soon be considered as honourable for a woman to earn her own bread as to eat it unearned, or more so',[11] and she pities those women whose ideas of gentility prevent them from increasing their income. The work carried the dedication: 'To the Men of England . . . in full reliance upon their chivalry as men and their justice as Englishmen'.

That mention of chivalry is significant, since it was one of the two principles upon which the position of women had been based for so long, the other being biblical precept enforced through ecclesiastical authority. A decade before 'L.M.H.' and her *Handbook* Charles Kingsley had given a series of lectures in which he outlined the historical background to women's subordinate position. He described how, over the centuries, a concept had grown up whereby a woman was under the guardianship of father, brother, husband or other male relation and by this means became his legal responsibility. This, in turn, had called forth the concept of male chivalry by which it was his duty and an honour to protect the physically weaker sex; woman meanwhile considered her influence to be not so much physical and legal but moral and spiritual and therefore resting on a ground nobler and deeper than the man's. Modern experiments for emancipating women from their current position and making them physically and legally equal with men, he said, '. . . may be right, and may be ultimately successful. We must not hastily prejudge them. But of this we may be almost certain; that, if they succeed, they will cause a wide-spread revolution in society, of which the patent danger will be, the destruction of the feeling of chivalry, and the consequent brutalization of the male sex.'[12] After such dire warnings he hoped that man would learn to adjust to the new attitudes demanded of him.

Meantime, increasingly strident remarks were being aimed not only against the contemporary position of women within marriage but against marriage as the sole profession for women. Not that comments have been lacking at any time within the 300 years reviewed here: the debate both for and against woman's 'traditional' place within marriage has been aired at frequent intervals. In 1673 the scholar and teacher Bathsua Makin, accounted the most learned Englishwoman of her time, argued:

> God intended Woman as a help-meet to Man, in his constant conversation, and in the concerns of his Family and Estate, when he should most need, in sickness, weakness, absence, death &c. Whilst we neglect to fit them for these things he hath appointed Women for, we renounce God's Blessing, are ungrateful to him, cruel to them, and injurious to ourselves . . . Seeing Nature produces Woman of such excellent Parts, that they do often equalize, some-times excel man, in what ever they attempt; what reason can be given why they should not be improv'd?[13]

Her contemporary Hannah Woolley, who promoted the importance of domestic virtues and of educating daughters for a career should the looked-for marriage not materialise, had protested: 'Vain man is apt to think we were meerly intended for the World's propagation, and to keep its humane inhabitants sweet and clean; but, . . . had we the same Literature, they would find our brains as fruitful as our bodies. Hence I am induced to believe, we are debarred from the knowledge of humane learning, lest our pregnant Wits should rival the towering conceits of our insulting Lords and Masters.'[14] Across the years many took up the refrain. Mary Wollstonecraft again: 'Man, taking her body, the mind is left to rust; so that while physical love enervates man, as being his favourite recreation, he will endeavour to enslave women – and who can tell, how many generations may be necessary to give vigour to the virtue and talents of the freed posterity of abject slaves?'[15]

Florence Nightingale in her turn, was scathing about women's subjection. She demanded: 'Why have women passion, intellect, moral activity . . . and a place in society where no one of the three can be exercised?'. She also asked why a women's time was accounted of less value than a man's: 'Why is she not Murillo? From a material difficulty, not a mental. If she has a knife and fork in her hands for three hours a day she cannot have a pencil and brush. Dinner is the great sacred ceremony of this day, the great sacrament . . .' she protested and she complained vociferously of the way women allowed themselves to be at everyone's beck and call, as if their activities were of little importance. It was no wonder, she wrote, that one married woman was heard to wish that she could break a limb that she might have a little time to herself.[16] Florence Nightingale had first written down her bitter and impassioned thoughts when she was thirty-two but she re-wrote them in 1859, after her return from the Crimea, and had the work printed privately but she was advised by her friends not to publish it.

This was the time when women were about to see the first fruits of their campaigns to improve their own lot. For so long they had been content to care for others, to help, sustain and educate in so many diferent ways; they had proved themselves to be more than competent in wide-ranging activities relating to art, literature, music and drama; and there were those whose intellectual achievements amazed their contemporaries. Women were now uniting, for the first time, in taking action to improve the position of the generality of women in various spheres. Caroline Norton's lengthy struggles to free herself from her violent husband led, in due course, to improvements relating to the custody of children and to economic independence for married women. Education was another area in which results were noticeable. Girls' schools were showing a marked improvement; Queen's College, Harley Street, had been founded to raise the standards of governesses; Mrs Jesser Reid's Bedford College opened the following year to provide an education of a higher standard than was generally available to girls; Emily Davies and a university education for women were just a decade or so away. The medical profession was on the verge of opening its doors to women, thanks to the pioneering spirit of Drs Elizabeth Blackwell, Elizabeth Garrett Anderson, Sophia Jex-Blake and their colleagues. Nursing was becoming a recognised profession for women. Josephine Butler was only a few years away from the start of her crusade against the (official) viewpoint that a class of women existed for the gratification of male lust. Extending the franchise to women was a question raised in the past, but the 1860s saw more concerted demands being made. In general terms various work-related opportunities were opening up to women. In 1859 the Society for Promoting the Employment of Women was founded and there was also Emily Faithfull's Industrial Bureau. Just around the corner were new types of work to which women gained access, as telegraphists, post mistresses and counter staff, and as office clerks, shorthand writers and, in time, typists and telephonists.

In the 1890s Georgiana Hill was able to paint a most optimistic picture of the progress made by women in their search for social and economic equality and she outlined with confidence a future they would share equally with the menfolk. The educational revolution of recent years especially in regard to the middle classes she considered:

> has enabled them to enter with perfect freedom into the world of letters, to follow professional and business careers – in a word, to carve out for themselves an independent course. A new conception has arisen of what is woman's place in society. She now bears an active part in all the great movements – political, religious, philanthropic; her co-operation is sought in public work, and her presence welcomed, rather than resented in all new social enterprises . . . Never were such advantages placed within the reach of women; never were so many opportunities – social, literary, educational, commercial – open to them. But these advantages and opportunities would have been useless if women had not been ready, and shown their fitness for the new trusts. They have themselves largely created the public sentiment which now so strongly impels them towards wider action, and imposes on them greater responsibilities.[17]

Her confidence was, perhaps, too great. The story of women's struggle to find acceptance in the workplace was far from told and has taken most of the twentieth century to come to fruition. Since her day ever more women have chosen to work outside the home; the wisdom of what they are doing has been queried on many counts.

The fact of their being in paid employment is nothing new; women have been working 'beyond the home' for many years and have been found in many spheres, exercising a wide range of talents. The predecessors of today's working women had few of the advantages of education, training and encouragement that have become available over the last hundred years or so. Instead, it was for them a question of using what skills they had, which were predominantly domestic skills honed in the home, or those that were considered to be 'natural' to a woman. 'But of every one of them it may be said that they did worthy work in the world.'[18]

Notes

Place of publication is London, unless otherwise stated.

PREFACE

1. E. Abbott, *Women in Industry* (New York and London, D. Appleton & Co., 1910), pp. viii–ix.

CHAPTER ONE

1. *Dictionary of National Biography* (*DNB*), eds L. Stephen and S. Lee (22 vols, Smith, Elder & Co., 1908), Vol. 1, p. vi.
2. *DNB, Missing Persons*, ed. C.S. Nicholls (OUP, 1993), p. vii.
3. G. Ballard, *Memoirs of Several Ladies of Great Britain* (Oxford, W. Jackson, 1752), p. vi.
4. D.M. Stuart, *The English Abigail* (Macmillan & Co., 1946), p. 23.
5. G. Markham, *The English Housewife*, fifth edn (John Harrison, 1637), p. 4.
6. Ibid., p. 2.
7. Mrs I. Beeton, *Book of Household Management* (Ward, Lock & Tyler, n.d. '140th thousand'), p. 1.
8. C. Hutton, *Reminiscences of a Gentlewoman of the Last Century*, ed. Mrs C.H. Beale (Birmingham, Cornish Bros, 1891), p. 57.
9. S. Whatman, *Housekeeping Book*, ed. T. Balston (Geoffrey Bles, 1956), p. 40.
10. By A Lady, *New System of Domestic Cookery*, 'new' edn (John Murray, 1818), p. xxvi.
11. H. More, *Strictures on the Modern System of Female Education* (2 vols, T. Cadell junior & W. Davies, 1799), Vol. 1, pp. 97–8.
12. *Cassell's Book of the Household*, special edn (4 vols, Cassell & Co., *c.* 1893), Vol. 4, p. 220.
13. Ibid., p. 291.

CHAPTER TWO

1. H. Glasse, *The Art of Cookery Made Plain & Easy*, fifth edn (printed and sold at Mrs Ashburn's china shop, 1755), p. 6.
2. M. Hamlyn, *The Recipes of Hannah Woolley* (Heinemann Kingswood, 1988), pp. 10–16.
3. Markham, *Housewife*, title page.

4. S. and S. Adams, *The Complete Servant* (Knight & Lacey, 1825), p. 369.
5. *Oxford Dictionary of Quotations*, third edn (Book Club Associates, 1979), p. 413.
6. *Lady Grisell Baillie's Household Book 1692–1733*, ed. R. Scott Moncreiff (Edinburgh, T. & A. Constable, 1911), pp. li–liii.
7. *DNB, '1951–60'*, p. 629.
8. M. Harrison, *Rosa* (Peter Davies, 1962), p. 133.
9. Mrs Frazer, *The Practice of Cookery, Pastry, &c.* (Edinburgh, P. Hill & T. Cadell, 1791), title page.
10. G. Bourne (Sturt), *Change in the Village* (Duckworth & Co., 1912), p. 235.
11. C. Buckton, *Our Dwellings, Healthy & Unhealthy* (Longmans, Green & Co., 1885), pp. vii, 137.
12. M.J. Loftie, *XLvj Social Twitters* (Macmillan & Co., 1879), pp. 270–1.
13. D. Stone, *The National*, second edn (Robert Hale & Co., 1976), pp. 16, 48.
14. *Elinor Fettiplace's Receipt Book*, ed. H. Spurling (Viking Salamander, 1986), pp. 17–18, 98, 187.
15. *Lady Castlehill's Receipt Book*, ed. H. Whyte (Glasgow, The Molendinar Press, 1976), pp. 1, 12, 18, 35, 50, 59, 71.
16. *The Compleat Cook by Rebecca Price*, ed. M. Masson (Routledge & Kegan Paul, 1974), pp. 3, 126, 127, 184, 231.
17. J. Boswell, *Life of Samuel Johnson* (2 vols, George Newnes Ltd, n.d.), Vol. 2, p. 249.
18. E. Cleland, *A New & Easy Method of Cookery*, second edn (Edinburgh, C. Wright & Co., 1759), title page.
19. E. Hewlett, *Cottage Comforts*, fourth edn (Simpkin & Marshall, 1827), 'advertisement'.
20. M. Dods, *The Cook & Housewife's Manual*, third edn (Edinburgh, Oliver & Boyd et al., 1828), pp. 8, 354–73.
21. F.M. McNeill, *The Scot's Kitchen* (London and Glasgow, Blackie & Son, 1929), Preface, p. vii.

22. *Early Diary of Frances Burney*, ed. A.R. Ellis (2 vols, George Bell & Sons, 1889), Vol. 1, p. 83.
23. *The London Encyclopaedia*, eds B. Weintreb and C. Hibbert (Macmillan, 1983), p. 532.
24. R. Chambers, *Traditions of Edinburgh* (W. and R. Chambers Ltd, 1912), p. 163.
25. Markham, *Housewife*, title page.

CHAPTER THREE

1. W. Davies, *General View of the Agriculture & Domestic Economy of North Wales* (Sherwood, Neely & Jones, 1813), p. 356.
2. F. Thompson, *Lark Rise to Candleford, A Trilogy* (OUP, 1945), p. 14.
3. W. Lawson, *A New Orchard & Garden – with The Countrie Housewife's Garden* (John Harrison, 1637), p. 97.
4. Ibid., p. 98.
5. Thompson, *Lark Rise*, p. 77.
6. *British Beekeepers Journal* (1877–8), Vol. 5, pp. 82, 97.
7. Mrs Dalgairns, *The Practice of Cookery*, second edn (Edinburgh, Cadell & Co., 1829), pp. 449–56, 457–72, 508–18.
8. A.B. Flower, *Beekeeping Up to Date*, fourth edn (Cassell & Co., 1936), p. ix.
9. M. Gaunt ('Mrs H. Lindsay Millar'), *Kirkham's Find* (Methuen & Co., 1897).
10. W. Harley, *Harleian Dairy System* (James Ridgeway, 1829), pp. 85, 94.
11. Ibid., p. 161.
12. Lord H. Cockburn, *Memorials of His Time* (Edinburgh, A. & C. Black, 1856), p. 435.
13. Mr and Mrs Hall, *Book of South Wales, the Wye & the Coast* (Arthur Hall, Virtue & Co., 1861), p. 299.
14. Cockburn, *Memorials*, p. 435.
15. J. Middleton, *View of the Agriculture of Middlesex* (R. Macmillan & Co., 1798), p. 382.
16. Sir J. Sinclair, *Statistical Account of Scotland*, a reissue (Wakefield, EP Publishing, 1975), Vol. 2, pp. 294–6.
17. J.H. Jamieson, 'Edinburgh Street Traders and their Cries', in *The Book of the Old Edinburgh Club*, original series (35 vols, T. & A. Constable, 1909), Vol. 2, p. 202.
18. *Laws Grocer's Manual*, ed. W.G. Copsey, fourth edn (Wm Clowes & Sons Ltd, 1950), p. 304.

19. R. May, *Accomplish't Cook* (R. Wood, 1665), p. 156.
20. Mrs Gaskell, *Cranford*, a reissue (London and Glasgow, Collins Library of Classics, n.d.), p. 118.
21. *Gentleman's Magazine* (1798), Vol. 68, Part 2, pp. 931–2.
22. L. Mason and C. Brown, *Traditional Foods in Britain* (Totnes, Prospect Books, 1999), pp. 275, 278, 305.
23. McNeill, *Scot's Kitchen*, p. 227.
24. Mason and Brown, *Traditional Foods*, pp. 303, 308.

CHAPTER FOUR

1. Adams, *Complete Servant*, p. 17.
2. J. Burnett, *Useful Toil* (Harmondsworth, Pelican Books, 1977), p. 140.
3. T. McBride, *The Domestic Revolution* (Croom Helm, 1976), p. 20.
4. Baillie, *Household Book*, p. 280.
5. *Purefroy Letters*, ed. G. Eland (2 vols, Sidgwick & Jackson, 1931), Vol. 1, p. 153.
6. Gaskell, *Cranford*, pp. 244, 251.
7. *The Highland Lady in Ireland*, eds P. Pelly and A. Tod (Edinburgh, Canongate Classics, 1991), p. 76.
8. *Munby, Man of Two Worlds*, ed. D. Hudson (John Murray, 1972), p. 40.
9. A.J. Munby, *Faithful Servants* (Reeves & Turner, 1891), pp. 74, 105, 189, 209.
10. Adams, *Complete Servant*, title page, iv.
11. Ibid., p. 8.
12. P.E. Malcolmson, *English Laundresses* (Chicago, University of Illinois Press, 1986), p. 7.
13. J. Woodforde, *Diary of a Country Parson*, ed. J. Beresford (5 vols, Humphrey Milford, 1924), Vol. 5, p. 198. Baillie, *Household Book*, pp. 278–80.
14. E.M. Parker, *The Rose of Avondale* (Robert John Bush, 1872).
15. *Eighteenth-Century Women Poets*, ed. R. Lonsdale (OUP, 1990), p. 207.
16. *Gentleman's Magazine* (J. Nicols, 1797), Vol. 67, Part 1, p. 223.

CHAPTER FIVE

1. H. Martineau, *Household Education* (Edward Moxon, 1849), p. 311.

2. Mrs Warren and Mrs Pullen, *Treasures in Needlework* (Ward & Lock, 1855), p. 1.
3. *Purefroy Letters*, Vol. 1, p. 147.
4. Markham, *Housewife*, title page.
5. Baillie, *Household Book*, p. 163: 'half a crown' = 2*s* 6*d* = 12.5p decimal; £1 12*s* 3*d* = £1.61 decimal; amounts paid in £ sterling, not Scots.
6. Adams, *Complete Servant*, pp. 236–7.
7. Ibid., p. 236.
8. *Memoirs of the Verney Family in the Civil War*, ed. F.P. and M. Verney (4 vols, Longmans, Green & Co., 1892–9), Vol. IV, pp. 451–2.
9. Adams, *Complete Servant*, p. 238.
10. H. Glasse, *Servants' Directory* (for the Author, 1760), pp. 16, 19.
11. Stuart, *Abigail*, pp. 47–8.
12. *Verney Memoirs*, Vol. 2, p. 227.
13. *Memoirs of Lady Fanshawe*, ed. B. Marshall (John Lane, The Bodley Head, 1905), p. 54.
14. R.M. Bradley, *The English Housewife* (Edward Arnold, 1912), pp. 39–40.
15. Adams, *Complete Servant*, p. 236.
16. C. Fiennes, *Through England on a Side Saddle*, ed. E. Griffiths (Field & Tuer, 1888), p. 305.
17. W. Dugdale, *Baronage of England* (2 vols, Thos. Newcomb, 1676), Vol. 2, pp. 251–4.
18. Thompson, *Lark Rise*, p. 19.
19. M. Trevelyan, *Glimpses of Welsh Life & Character* (John Hogg, 1894), p. 156.
20. *Costume of Yorkshire in 1814*, ed. E. Hailstone, facsimile edn (Leeds, R. Jackson, 1885), pp. 95–6.
21. Hewlett, *Cottage Comforts*, pp. 41–2.
22. *Cassell's*, Vol. 4, pp. 287–8.
23. Sinclair, *Statistical Account*, Vol. 6, p. 42; Vol. 7, p. 394.
24. Mrs Meredith, *The Lacemakers: Sketches of Irish Character* (Jackson, Walford & Hodder, 1865), p. 17.
25. Stone, *The National*, pp. 76–8.
26. E. Rosevear, *Textbook of Needlework, Knitting & Cutting Out*, revised edn (Macmillan & Co., 1907), title page.
27. Warren and Pullen, *Needlework*, pp. xiii–xiv.
28. A. Adburgham, *Shops & Shopping 1800–1914*, second edn (George Allen & Unwin, 1981), p. 30.
29. Ibid., p. 26.
30. A. Adburgham, *Women in Print* (George Allen & Unwin, 1972), p. 210.
31. Loftie, *Twitters*, pp. 130–6.

CHAPTER SIX

1. Cockburn, *Memorials*, pp. 33–4.
2. Ibid., pp. 40–1.
3. Lord E. Hamilton, *Old Days and New* (Hodder & Stoughton, 1924), p. 69.
4. *Book of the Home*, ed. Mrs C.E. Humphry ('Madge' of *Truth*) new edn (6 vols, The Gresham Publishing Co., 1909), Vol. 5, pp. 1–43.
5. E. Holt, *Encyclopaedia of Etiquette* (New York and London, McClure, Phillips & Co., 1901). E. Holt, *The Secrets of Popularity* (Methuen & Co., 1905), p. 3.
6. H. Graham, *Group of Scottish Women* (Methuen & Co., 1908), pp. 60, 76.
7. Chambers, *Traditions*, p. 276.
8. Graham, *Scottish Women*, p. 246.
9. W. Holmes, *Seven Adventurous Women* (G. Bell & Sons, 1953), p. 44.
10. Trevelyan, *Welsh Life*, p. 105.
11. Hudson, *Munby*, p. 96: Angelina Bosio (1830–59), a great favourite with London audiences, had died suddenly in St Petersburg.
12. A. Reid, *Lady Carolina Nairne and her Songs* (Bayley & Ferguson, n.d.), p. 5.
13. Mrs E. Smith (née Grant), *Memoirs of a Highland Lady*, Albemarle Library (John Murray, 1967), p. 125.
14. H.W. and Lady Pollock, *Amateur Theatricals* (Macmillan & Co., 1879), p. 1.
15. Humphry, *Home*, Vol. 5, p. 212.
16. *DNB*, Vol. XVIII, p. 198.
17. M. Reynolds, *The Learned Lady in England 1650–1760* (Boston and New York, Houghton Mufflin Co., 1920), p. 82.
18. Ibid., p. 81.
19. S. Pepys, *Diary & Correspondence of Samuel Pepys*, ed. R. Braybrooke (4 vols, Henry Colburn, 1854), Vol. 1, p. 138.
20. Hudson, *Munby*, p. 113.
21. Chambers, *Traditions*, p. 346.
22. Graham, *Scottish Women*, p. 245.
23. *DNB*, Vol. XVIII, p. 994.
24. *Quotations*, p. 8, no. 23.

CHAPTER SEVEN

1. H. Robertson, *The Young Ladies School of Arts*, second edn (Edinburgh, Wal. Ruddiman Junior, 1767).

2. M. Delany, 'Hortus Siccus', 10 vols. See R. Hayden, *Mrs Delany and her Flower Collages*, revised edn (British Museum Press, 1992), pp. 172–87.

3. G. Hill, *Women in English Life* (2 vols, Richard Bentley & Son, 1896), Vol. 1, p. 294.

4. Reynolds, *Learned Lady*, p. 85.

5. M.C. Borer, *Women who Made History* (Frederick Warne & Co. Ltd, 1963), p. 44.

6. Hudson, *Munby*, p. 33.

7. M. Girouard, *Life in the English Country House* (New Haven and London, Yale University Press, 1978), p. 204.

8. *Cassell's*, Vol. 4, p. 144.

9. F.J. Yerbury, *Architectural Students Handbook* (Technical Journals Ltd, 1922), p. 7. *Year Book of the Society of Architects 1924–25* (Society of Architects, 1924), pp. 35, 50.

10. *Scots Magazine* (Dundee, November 1986), p. 162. The visitor was Frau Schopenhaeuer.

11. E. de Wolfe (Lady Mendl), *The House in Good Taste* (Sir Isaac Pitman & Sons, 1914), p. 5.

12. Buckton, *Our Dwellings*, p. xii.

13. L. Orrinsmith, *The Drawing Room* (Macmillan & Co., 1877), p. 129.

14. M.A. Barker, *Bedroom & Boudoir* (Macmillan & Co., 1878), p. 19.

15. E. Wharton and O. Codman, *The Decoration of Houses* (Batsford, 1898), p. 160.

16. Barker, *Bedroom & Boudoir*, p. 20.

17. *Cassell's*, Vol. 4, p. 233.

18. Orrinsmith, *Drawing Room*, pp. 71–2.

19. T. Bewick, *A Memoir of himself* (Longman, Green, Longman & Roberts, 1862), p. 78.

20. S. Smiles, *Josiah Wedgwood F.R.S.* (John Murray, 1894), p. 257.

Chapter Eight

1. K.C. Ashburton, *Lady Grisell Baillie, A Sketch of her Life*, fourth edn (Edinburgh, R. & R. Clark, 1893), p. xxx.

2. *DNB*, Vol. III, p. 850.

3. Ashburton, *Baillie*, p. xxx.

4. Ibid., dedication.

5. L. Hutchinson, *Memoirs of the Life of Colonel Hutchinson*, ed. J. Hutchinson (Longman, Hurst, Rees & Orme, 1806), pp. 1, 428.

6. Marshall, *Fanshawe Memoirs*, p. 107.

7. A. Hughes, *Diary of a Farmer's Wife 1796–97* (Allen Lane, 1980), epigraph, p. 162.

8. Smith (E. Grant), *Memoirs*, Preface.

9. E. Sillar, *Edinburgh's Child* (Oliver & Boyd, 1961), Foreword.

10. Sir A. Heal, *The English Writing Masters 1570–1800* (Cambridge, 1931), p. 65.

11. D. Spender, *Mothers of the Novel* (London and New York, Pandora, 1986).

12. *The Complete Peerage*, eds H.A. Doubleday and Lord Howard de Walden (14 vols, St Catherine Press, 1936), Vol. IX, p. 526.

13. *Pepys' Diary*, Vol. 3, p. 404.

14. *Dictionary of British & American Writers 1660–1800*, ed. J. Todd (Methuen & Co., 1987), pp. 231–2.

15. *The Oxford Book of Short Poems*, eds P.J. Kavanagh and J. Michie (OUP, 1985), p. 92.

16. *The Oxford Book of Marriage*, ed. H. Rubinstein (OUP, 1990), p. 369.

17. Lonsdale, *Women Poets*, p. 44.

18. B.R. Parkes, *Vignettes* (Alex Strachan, 1866), p. 443.

19. *Letters from Dorothy Osborne to Sir William Temple, 1652–54*, ed. E.A. Parry, Wayfarers Library (J.M. Dent & Sons, n.d.), pp. 81, 100.

20. V. Woolf, *A Room of One's Own*, twelfth impression (Hogarth Press, 1954), p. 74.

21. *Oxford Short Poems*, p. 92.

22. *Oxford Companion to English Literature*, eds M. Drabble and J. Stringer, special edn (OUP, 1993), p. 378.

23. *Life of Samuel Johnson*, ed. J.W. Croker, new edn (6 vols, John Murray, 1831), Vol. 5, p. 229.

24. Cockburn, *Memorials*, p. 268.

25. M. Alic, *Hypatia's Heritage* (The Women's Press, 1986), pp. 188–9.

26. *Memoir & Correspondence of Caroline Herschel*, ed. Mrs John Herschel (John Murray, 1876), p. 142.

27. *DNB, Missing Persons*, pp. 688–9.

Chapter Nine

1. J.D. Young, *Women & Popular Struggles* (Edinburgh, Mainstream Publishing, 1985), p. 27.

2. E.G. Murray, *Scottish Women in Bygone Days* (Glasgow, Gowans & Gray, 1930), pp. 110–11.

3. Ibid., pp. 96–7.

4. R. Marshall, *The Days of Duchess Anne* (Collins, 1973), p. 85.

5. Graham, *Scottish Women*, pp. 80–1.
6. Murray, *Scottish Women*, p. 102.
7. Graham, *Scottish Women*, p. 81.
8. A. Fea, *After Worcester Fight* (J. Lane Bodley Head, 1904), p. 184.
9. J. Hutchins, *History & Antiquities of Dorset* (W. Bowyer and J. Nichols, 1774), Vol. I, p. 181.
10. *Letters of Lady Brilliana Harley*, ed. T.T. Lewis (Camden Society No. LVIII, 1854), p. xxxv.
11. I. Ross, *Margaret Fell Mother of Quakerism* (Longmans Green & Co., 1949), p. 53.
12. *Bishop Burnet's History of His Own Time* (2 vols, Thomas Ward, 1724), Vol. I, p. 609.
13. T. Fisher, *Prostitution and the Victorians* (Stroud, Sutton Publishing Ltd, 1997), p. 55.
14. J. Ellice Hopkins, *The Power of Womanhood* (Wells, Gardner, Darton & Co., 1899), p. 24.
15. *Quotations*, p. 568 (10).
16. Holmes, *Adventurous Women*, p. 43.
17. C.M. Yonge, *Hannah More* (W.H. Allen & Co., 1888), p. 83.
18. Graham, *Scottish Women*, p. 224.
19. *DNB*, Vol. XVII, p. 339.
20. R. Chambers, *Biographical Dictionary of Eminent Scots* (3 vols, Blackie & Sons, 1875), Vol. 2, p. 434.
21. Ross, *Margaret Fell*, p. 60.
22. Chambers, *Traditions*, p. 316.
23. *Salvation Army Year Book 1908*, p. 93.

CHAPTER TEN

1. C. Morsley, *News from the English Countryside* (Harrap, 1979), pp. 98, 183.
2. Humphry, *Home*, Vol. 5, p. 148.
3. Thompson, *Lark Rise*, p. 21.
4. *Fanshawe Memoirs*, p. 46.
5. E.W. White, *Anne Bradstreet, The Tenth Muse* (New York, OUP, 1971), p. 350.
6. Ibid., p. 353.
7. *Journal of Sir Walter Scott*, ed. D. Douglas (2 vols, New York, Harper & Brothers, 1890), Vol. 1, p. 28.
8. I.C. Clarke, *Six Portraits* (Hutchinson & Co., 1935), p. 226.
9. Ibid., *c.* pp. 203–6.
10. Ibid., p. 225.
11. Humphry, *Home*, Vol. 5, pp. 158–60.
12. J.H. Aveling, *English Midwives*, reprint of 1872 edn (Hugh K. Elliott Ltd, 1967), p. 55.
13. *London Encyclopaedia*, p. 628.
14. Markham, *Housewife*, title page.
15. Alic, *Heritage*, pp. 200–1.
16. The *Daily Telegraph*, 13/10/86, p. 21.
17. Clarke, *Portraits*, p. 229.

CHAPTER ELEVEN

1. C. Hamilton, *Marriage as a Trade* (Chapman & Hall, 1909), p. 51.
2. *Edinburgh Review* (Longmans, Green, Reader & Dyer), Vol. CXLIX (January–April 1879), pp. 102–3.
3. M. Tuke, *History of Bedford College for Women 1849–1937* (OUP, 1939), p. 20.
4. *Fanshawe Memoirs*, p. 54.
5. M. Somerville (ed.), *Personal Recollections & Correspondence of Mary Somerville* (John Murray, 1873), p. 22.
6. B. Howe, *A Galaxy of Governesses* (Derek Verschoyle Ltd, 1954), pp. 115–16.
7. C. Collett, 'Movement for Intellectual Training' in *Some Aspects of the Woman's Movement*, ed. Z. Fairfield (Student Christian Movement, 1915).
8. F. Maclean, *Eastern Approaches* (Jonathan Cape, 1949), p. 49.
9. R. Harris (ed.), *Weald & Downland Open Air Museum Guidebook* (1987), p. 9.
10. Thompson, *Lark Rise*, p. 172.
11. J. Austen, *Emma* (Simms & M'Intyre, 1849), p. 16.
12. Bourne, *Change*, p. 239.
13. E. Davies, *Higher Education of Women*, reprint of 1866 edn (London and Ronceverte, USA, Hambledon, 1988), p. 35.
14. H. More, *Strictures on the Modern System of Female Education* (2 vols, T. Cadell junior and W. Davies, 1799), p. ix.
15. A. and J. Taylor, *Rhymes for the Nursery*, twentieth edn (Harvey & Darton, 1828), p. 10.
16. *DNB*, Vol. XII, p. 835.
17. B. Makin, *Essay to Revive the Antient Education of Gentlewomen*, reprint 1980 (Los Angeles, William Andrews Clark Memorial Library publication No. 22, 1980), p. 22.
18. Ibid., p. ix.
19. Tuke, *Bedford College*, p. 108.
20. G. Battiscombe, *Reluctant Pioneer* (Constable, 1978), p. 75.
21. M.C. Bradbrook, *That Infidel Place* (Chatto & Windus, 1969), p. 48.

CHAPTER TWELVE

1. T. Tusser, *Five Hundreth Pointes of Good Husbandrie* (William Seres, 1590), p. 79.
2. Lawson, *Countrie Housewife*, pp. 79, 87.
3. By A Lady, *Domestic Cookery*, pp. xix, xx.
4. H. Howard, *England's Newest Way*, third edn (Chr. Coningsby, 1710), p. 180.
5. Ibid., p. 189, 'sweet afa' is difficult to identify.
6. E.S. Rohde, *The Scented Garden* (Medici Society, 1931), p. 186.
7. Fiennes, *Through England*, pp. 97–8.
8. Marshall, *Duchess Anne*, p. 52.
9. M.G. Jones, *Hannah More* (Cambridge, CUP, 1952), p. 125.
10. Sir W. Fraser, *Memorials of the Earls of Haddington* (2 vols, privately printed, 1889), Vol. 1, pp. 244–5.
11. J. Loudon, *Instructions in Gardening for Ladies* (John Murray, 1840), Introduction.
12. D. MacLeod, *Down-to-Earth Women* (Edinburgh, William Blackwood, 1982).
13. Hayden, *Mrs Delany*, p. 188.
14. H. Robertson, *Young Ladies School of Arts*, tenth edn (Edinburgh, James Tod, 1806), p. 41.
15. A. Catlow, *Popular Greenhouse Botany* (Lovell Reeve, 1857), title page.
16. 'Charlotte Elizabeth', *Chapters on Flowers*, ninth edn (Seeley, Jackson & Halliday, 1860), p. 2.
17. MacLeod, *Down to Earth*, p. 143.
18. Lawson, *Orchard & Garden*, p. 73.
19. M. Hadfield, *Gardening in Britain* (Hutchinson, 1960), p. 204.
20. Gaskell, *Cranford*, p. 9.
21. Sinclair, *Statistical Account*, Vol. 6, pp. 549–50.
22. Hutton, *Reminiscences*, p. 192.
23. Mrs Buckton, *Health in the House*, third edn (Longmans, Green & Co., 1875), pp. ix–x.
24. Loftie, *Twitters*, p. 188–92.
25. *Cassell's*, Vol. 1, p. 101.

CHAPTER THIRTEEN

1. Hailstone, *Costume*, pp. 95–6.
2. Trevelyan, *Welsh Life*, pp. 129, 157.
3. Smith (E. Grant), *Memoirs*, p. 329.
4. M. Russell, *The Blessings of a Good Thick Skirt* (Collins, 1988), p. 169.
5. M. Starke, *Letters from Italy*, second edn (2 vols, G. & S. Robinson, 1815), title page.

6. S. Raven and A. Weir, *Women in History* (Weidenfeld & Nicolson, 1981), p. 228.
7. Russell, *Blessings*, p. 80.
8. 'L.M.H.' (ed.), *Handbook of Women's Work* (Hatchards, 1876), pp. 91–2.
9. Fiennes, *Through England*, p. ix.
10. S. Murray, *The Beauties of Scotland* (Hawick, Byway Books, 1982), pp. 11–12.
11. Hall, *South Wales*, p. vi.
12. Trevelyan, *Welsh Life*, Preface.
13. Four Schoolmistresses, *Through North Wales with a Knapsack* (Kegan Paul, Trench, Trubner & Co., 1890), pp. 28, 38.
14. M. Gaunt, *A Broken Journey* (T. Werner Laurie Ltd, 1919), p. 8.
15. Russell, *Blessings*, p. 57.

CHAPTER FOURTEEN

1. C. Norton, *A Voice from the Factories* (John Murray, 1836), p. 40.
2. M. Wollstonecraft, *A Vindication of the Rights of Women 1792*, reprint (Everyman's Library, David Campbell Publishers Ltd, 1992), p. 162.
3. C.L. Brightwell, *Memorials of the Life of Amelia Opie*, second edn (Norwich, Fletcher & Alexander, 1854), pp. 93–4.
4. J. Gaffin, 'Women and Cooperation', in L. Middleton (ed.), *Women in the Labour Movement* (Croom Helm, 1977), pp. 113–14.
5. S. Lochhead, Introduction, in Middleton (ed.), *Women*, pp. 15–16.
6. Ibid., p. 19.
7. Hill, *Women*, Vol. 2, pp. 335–6.
8. Bradbrook, *Infidel Place*, p. 67.
9. Sir C. Kinloch Cooke, 'Women and the Reconstruction of Industry', in *The Nineteenth Century and After* (December, 1915), pp. 1405, 1416.
10. *Cassell's*, Vol. 4, p. 220.
11. 'L.M.H.', *Women's Work*, p. 12.
12. C. Kingsley, *The Roman & the Teuton*, new edn (Macmillan & Co., 1875), pp. 254–5.
13. Makin, *Essay*, p. 23.
14. Hamlyn, *Hannah Woolley*, p. 23.
15. Wollstonecraft, *Vindication*, p. 82.
16. R. Strachey, *The Cause* (G. Bell & Sons, 1928), pp. 396–402.
17. Hill, *Women*, Vol. 1, p. xii.
18. Parkes, *Vignettes*, Introduction.

Further Reading

Where London is the place of publication, this has been omitted.

Beddoes, D. *Discovering Women's History*, Pandora Press, 1983

Bennett, D. *Emily Davies and the Liberation of Women*, Andre Deutsch, 1990

Clark, A. *Working Life of Women in the Seventeenth Century*, Routledge & Kegan Paul, 1982

Davies, D. *A History of Shopping*, Book Club edn, Parnell Book Services Ltd (n.d.)

Davis, E. *The Higher Education of Women (1866)*, ed. and introd. by J. Howarth, Hambledon Press, 1988

Fairfield, Z. (ed.). *Some Aspects of the Woman's Movement*, Student Christian Movement, 1915

Fisher, T. *Prostitution and the Victorians*, Stroud, Sutton Publishing Ltd, 1997

Forster, M. *Significant Sisters*, Martin Secker & Warburg, 1984

Fraser, A. *The Weaker Vessel*, George Weidenfeld & Nicholson Ltd, 1984

Gaffin, J. and Thomas, D. *Caring & Sharing*, Manchester, Cooperative Union, 1983

Holmes, W. *Seven Adventurous Women*, G. Bell & Sons, 1953

Howe, B. *A Galaxy of Governesses*, Derek Verschoyle, 1954

Llewelyn Davies, M. *Life as We Have Known It*, Hogarth Press, 1931

MacLeod, D. *Down-to-Earth Women*, Edinburgh, William Blackwood, 1982

Marshall, R. *Virgins & Viragos*, William Collins & Co. Ltd, 1983

Middleton, L. (ed.). *Women in the Labour Movement*, Croom Helm, 1977

Murray, J.H. *Strong-minded Women*, Penguin Books Ltd, 1984

Peterson, K. and Wilson, J.J. *Women Artists*, The Women's Press, 1978

Quayle, E. *Old Cook Books*, Cassell Ltd, 1978

Robertson, U.A. *The Illustrated History of the Housewife*, Stroud, Sutton Publishing Ltd, 1997

Russell, M. *The Blessings of a Good Thick Skirt – Women Travellers and their World*, William Collins Sons & Co., Ltd, 1986

Spender, D. *Women of Ideas*, Ark Paperbacks, 1982

Stuart, D.M. *The English Abigail*, Macmillan & Co., 1946

Wollstonecraft, M. *A Vindication of the Rights of Women (1792)*, reprint, Everyman's Library, David Campbell Publishers Ltd, 1992

Woolf, V. *A Room of One's Own*, Hogarth Press, 1954

Index

Index